Fractured Fifties

Fractured Fifties

The Cinematic Periodization and Evolution of a Decade

CHRISTINE SPRENGLER

OXFORD
UNIVERSITY PRESS

Oxford University Press is a department of the University of Oxford. It furthers
the University's objective of excellence in research, scholarship, and education
by publishing worldwide. Oxford is a registered trade mark of Oxford University
Press in the UK and certain other countries.

Published in the United States of America by Oxford University Press
198 Madison Avenue, New York, NY 10016, United States of America.

© Oxford University Press 2023

All rights reserved. No part of this publication may be reproduced, stored in
a retrieval system, or transmitted, in any form or by any means, without the
prior permission in writing of Oxford University Press, or as expressly permitted
by law, by license, or under terms agreed with the appropriate reproduction
rights organization. Inquiries concerning reproduction outside the scope of the
above should be sent to the Rights Department, Oxford University Press, at the
address above.

You must not circulate this work in any other form
and you must impose this same condition on any acquirer.

CIP data is on file at the Library of Congress

ISBN 978–0–19–006735–9 (pbk.)
ISBN 978–0–19–006734–2 (hbk.)

DOI: 10.1093/oso/9780190067342.001.0001

For Jackson and Evelyn

Contents

List of Illustrations   ix
Acknowledgments   xi
Permissions   xv

Introduction   1

PART I. THEORY AND HISTORY (OF A PAST FUTURE)

1. Periodization, Cinema, and the Decade   27
2. The Futuristic Fifties   50

PART II. FOUNDATIONAL FRACTURES

3. The Leave It to Beaver Fifties   69
4. The Jukebox Fifties   100
5. The Cold War Fifties   127

PART III. LIMINAL FRACTURES

6. The Retromediated Fifties: Film and Photography   161
7. The Fifties Reframed: Borders and Boundaries   187

Conclusion   219

Works Cited   225
Index   239

List of Illustrations

2.1	Fencing in front of an automated orchestra, *High Treason* (1929)	51
2.2	Giant "televisor" broadcasting to the city, *The Tunnel* (1935)	60
3.1	Country kitchen in *Revolutionary Road* (2008)	76
3.2	Frank (Leonardo DiCaprio) approaching his car in *Revolutionary Road* (2008)	77
3.3	Mrs. Mayers's (Karimah Westbrook) "stoic non-reaction" in *Suburbicon* (2017)	83
3.4	Gracie (Melody Hurd) and Livia "Lucky" Emory (Deborah Ayorinde) in *Them* (2021)	92
4.1	The "Frosty Palace" diner in *Grease* (1978)	111
4.2	Danny (John Travolta), Sandy (Olivia Newton-John), and a Jukebox in *Grease* (1978)	112
4.3	Wink (Ian McClaren), Benny (Benjamin Barrett), and Georgie (Rene Rosado) in *Badsville* (2017)	116
4.4	Jennifer Greenburg, *The K-Wals*, Itasca, Illinois, 2004	120
5.1	Hal King's (Tyrik Ballard) performance at Madame Quickly's club in *Hal King* (2021)	136
5.2	Kat French (Sharae Moultrie) in *Hal King* (2021)	138
5.3	Nurses lined up for execution in "Meet Me in Daegu," *Lovecraft Country* (2020)	141
5.4	Joseph McCarthy and Edward R. Murrow (David Strathairn) in *Good Night, and Good Luck* (2005)	144
5.5	Dorothy Vaughn (Octavia Spencer), Mary Jackson (Janelle Monáe), and Katherine Johnson (Taraji P. Henson) in *Hidden Figures* (2016)	151
6.1	"Hail Caesar: A Tale of the Christ" movie in *Hail, Caesar!* (2016)	163
6.2	Mia (Emma Stone) and Sebastian (Ryan Gosling) in *La La Land* (2016)	165
6.3	Sylvie (Tessa Thompson) in *Sylvie's Love* (2020)	168
6.4	Carol (Cate Blanchett) standing in a doorway in *Carol* (2015)	174
6.5	Carol (Cate Blanchett) and Abby (Sarah Paulson) in *Carol* (2015)	177
7.1	The Boatwrights in *Bastard Out of Carolina* (1996)	190

7.2 The Cadillac El Dorado in *The Reflecting Skin* (1990)   193
7.3 Church basement dance in *Brooklyn* (2015)   200
7.4 Dinner at the boarding house in *Brooklyn* (2015)   201
7.5 The clouds part for the Maxsons in *Fences* (2016)   205
7.6 The Maxson home and backyard in *Fences* (2016)   211

Acknowledgments

I suspect that what follows here will, at times, read as a somewhat unconventional set of acknowledgments, though perhaps fittingly so, given the challenging circumstances of the last few years. This book did begin life in a fairly typical fashion, which is to say far too long ago and piecemeal as part of various essays and conference presentations, ones that tested several possible ways into the material at hand. However, as I note in the introduction, I kept getting distracted by other possible trajectories, finding it hard to commit to the project that I had truly wanted to pursue now more than twenty years ago. In some respects, I'm happy it took this long, for the potential case studies kept coming in droves, becoming ever richer and more interesting. The initial research phase also followed an expected course, with test runs at conferences and I thank the panel and session participants at SCMS and Film and History over the years. Some of those papers evolved into essays mined here and I deeply appreciate the advice of the editors of various collections in which they appeared: Oliver Gruner, Peter Krämer, and Matthew Leggatt. Their insightful and expert feedback was of tremendous help, and I am sincerely grateful to them.

I also want to mention, at the very outset, what an incredible privilege and honor it has been to work with Norman Hirschy at Oxford University Press. I have received nothing short of the strongest possible support and genuine encouragement for the duration of this process. From astute and incisive comments at the proposal stage to reassurance and understanding throughout the pandemic, this project would not have been completed without Norm's committed attention and kindness. I am beyond lucky to have benefited from this collaboration; it has been a true delight to work with Norm every step of the way. Norm also lined up two of the most generous and brilliant anonymous reviewers for this manuscript, and I cannot begin to thank them enough for the time and care they devoted to providing enormously detailed comments and for reining in my tendency toward flippant disregard for academic seriousness. (Yes, I knew I would have to take out that "squirrel" bit!)

Much support also came from my institution in the form of financial awards, research assistance from my phenomenal graduate students, and the steadfast moral support of magnificent colleagues. The Faculty of Arts and Humanities J.B. Smallman Fund as well as the Graham and Gale Wright Distinguished Scholar award provided both a grant and, in the case of the latter, a course release that enabled me to complete this manuscript. The expert research skills of Ira Kazi, Masha Kouznetsova, Katie Oates, Anahi Gonzalez Teran, and Zsofia Agoston Villalba unearthed new case studies and compelling research for me and I am exceptionally appreciative of their always enthusiastic aid. I have the pleasure to work with some incredible colleagues and good friends and want to note their continued support and role in sustaining an amazingly congenial and hard-working department. Thanks especially to Kirsty Robertson, Sarah Bassnett, and Kelly Wood for sporadic escapes into the social world, Cody Barteet, Linda Meloche, and Meghan Edmiston for always hilarious exchanges, and all my other wonderful colleagues: Soheila Esfahani, Sky Glabush, John Hatch, Joy James, Tricia Johnson, Patrick Mahon, David Merritt, Christof Migone, Alena Robin, and Daniela Sneppova.

Because this project was so long in the making, I need to acknowledge those who shaped my earliest thoughts on the topic and who guided me through its initial stages and trajectories, mentors who have now become dear friends: Laura Mulvey, Bridget Elliott, and Tony Purdy. Indeed, given the circumstances under which this was written I owe my friends, both old and new, my deepest gratitude for truly sustaining support, sometimes in the form of a hike or walk, a phone call or beer over zoom, a socially distanced visit, or a canoe camping excursion deep into the backcountry: Pippette Eibel, Debra Nousek, Donna Sasges, Sandy Smeltzer, Daniel Morgan, Connie Mackenzie, Sharon Wei, Susanna Pearl, and Laura Melnyk Gribble. A special thanks to Clint, Larry, Fred, Tim, Tony, Bob, Adam, and Ash—the logging crew of Dagger Lake Access Road—for stopping to chat on their way to work every morning, often before dawn, while I walked my dogs as far into the forest as I could manage, hikes that were absolutely essential to the completion of this project. I talked to them more than anyone else "in person" over these last few pandemic years and always appreciated their bear sighting reports, something else that I'm quite certain made it possible for me to finish this book.

Writing a book during a pandemic with young children at home and an elderly mother under my care was certainly a challenge. But their unwavering support is also the reason it is now finally finished. My mother has always wondered why on earth I do this (though her language, even at ninety years of age, is far more colorful than I'm likely permitted to print here), but nevertheless understands my love of research and writing. My partner, Devin Henry, knowing full well himself what is necessary to finish a book, helpfully aided and abetted my periodic escapes to our cabin deep in the woods to write. My amazing children, Evelyn and Jackson, are my inspiration and very reason for being. Their curiosity, creativity, energy, and confidence when it comes to loving what they do (wolves and mice, respectively) are the best sustenance. In the acknowledgments for my Master's thesis (arguably the first iteration of this project), I thanked the companionship of my pet rodents, so it only seems fitting I continue the tradition, though this time my gratitude must extend to companions slightly higher up the food chain, my dogs Thea, Echo, and Sparrow. In short, my family, both two- and four-legged, deserve my most heartfelt gratitude.

Permissions

Parts of Chapter 4, "The Jukebox Fifties" have appeared in "*Grease*, the Jukebox Fifties and Time's Percolations," in *"Grease Is the Word": Exploring a Cultural Phenomenon*, ed. Oliver Gruner, Peter Krämer, and C. Sprengler (Anthem Press, 2020), 113–130.

Parts of Chapter 5, "The Cold War Fifties" and Chapter 6, "The Retromediated Fifties" have appeared in "Midcentury Metamodern: Returning Home in the 21st Century Nostalgia Film," in *Was It Yesterday? Nostalgia in Contemporary Film and Television*, ed. Matthew Leggatt (SUNY Press, 2021).

Introduction

There is an unusual centenary on the horizon—one that I'm sure will go unheeded. Not that it deserves an official commemoration. Nevertheless, it is perhaps surprising and even novel enough to warrant mention. In a few years we might feel the inclination to turn up the hi-fi and clink our martini glasses in a toast to one hundred years of cinematic representations of the 1950s. To the best of my knowledge, this centenary ought to be celebrated in 2024 to mark the 1924 release of a rather terrible science fiction film, *The Last Man on Earth*. Set in 1950, it imagines a future in which all but one man is killed off by the dreaded disease "masculitis." Other cinematic incursions into a future 1950s followed in the late 1920s and mid-1930s. Then, in the 1950s, prospection gives way to self-mythologization and, by the early 1970s, retrospection when the 1950s surges as a subject of cinematic—and other— fascination. The 1950s has since sustained filmmakers' interest, becoming the focus of more than seven hundred works of film and television, with more than one hundred English-language screen fictions released since 2015.

What follows is not a catalogue raisonné of these releases. I take a good number into account in order to categorize the general tendencies apparent in this vast corpus, but then concentrate on a selection of dominant tendencies exemplified by films saturated with analytical richness and social or political significance. Some of these are nuanced interventions into postwar history, while others are deeply problematic in several regards. I briefly consider a few examples from television, primarily "quality" long form series, and make mention of a few other representational and leisure practices that summon the 1950s. My efforts, however, are concentrated on the cinema. I do so to present a two-pronged argument that (1) cinema has helped define the 1950s by contributing in considerable and meaningful ways to the process of periodization and thus a general conception of the decade, and (2) cinema has fractured our sense of the 1950s. It challenges a reductive and fairly cohesive set of tropes with a complex amalgam of representations that also intervenes in debates about historiography, historicity, cultural memory, mediation, nostalgia, and periodization. In other words, cinema has fractured our sense of the 1950s, yielding in the process a series of 1950s types or kinds as well as a wealth of critical insights into the past(s), present(s), and relationships between them.

These are easy claims to make if our purview includes the global corpus of films devoted to the 1950s. From *Ayla: The Daughter of War* (Turkey, 2017) to *Rahenge Sadaa Gardish Mein Taare* (India, 2017), the regional perspectives and range of cinematic practices yield a deeply variegated portrait of that decade. However, the focus here is on the specifically American 1950s, long aligned in numerous discursive registers with a simplistic, politically inflected, *dominant* construct of white, middle-class prosperity and mores. Indeed, there is a special relationship between the two—America and the 1950s—long nurtured by social conservatism, consumer capitalism, and insular foreign policy. But the privileged status of this entwined object is also maintained by progressive forces that regularly summon it for the purpose of demystification or to spur activism in the present. The 1950s has long functioned as a foil to the 1960s and as a carefully manufactured construct invoked repeatedly during the 1970s, 1980s, 1990s, and throughout the twenty-first century for a variety of ends.

During each of these decades, scholars, journalists, and cultural critics have felt compelled to reflect on the prevalence of the 1950s in their own contemporary moment. My first attempt to come to terms with this practice was during the late 1990s. I wanted to take stock of how quintessentially postmodern filmic practices engaged—through pastiche, parody, self-reflexivity, and so on—with the 1950s. My concern was with the aesthetic trappings of a cinematic practice that generated strident critiques of the past and mythic representations of the postwar period. However, this morphed into a concern with how an American 1950s accrued vitality in British film and television productions invested in Thatcherism and Americanization. I returned again to this phenomenon ten years later but abandoned any sole focus on the 1950s for nostalgia itself, keeping the 1950s in suspension throughout, but primarily insofar as it helped articulate a brand of cinematic nostalgia. Here's hoping the third time's a charm.

The 1950s has surged with astonishing force at various junctures over the last half century. Such moments of cultural and political investment in the postwar era are, of course, heavily determined by the desires, anxieties, ideologies, technologies, and whims of the contexts in which they surface. Therefore it is necessary to explore how contextualizing factors shaped the 1950s in different ways, and especially how cinematic representations spearheaded, challenged, or intervened in our cultural memories of it. Although I briefly chart the respective evolutions of the dominant 1950s types at issue by considering the vicissitudes of the 1970s, 1980s, or 1990s that gave them form, I privilege recent releases. Specifically, I account for how twenty-first-century cinema advances these earlier modes of representing the 1950s and cultivates their aesthetic and narrative strategies for the purposes of engagement, veneration, critique, or departure.

Indeed the examples to which I give the most attention have been released since 2010, with a majority dating from 2015. As such I foreground the 1950s types most relevant to our contemporary moment rather than those quantitatively dominant. This methodology requires regard for two facets of the present of this writing that are imbricated with one another and which, independently, hold a degree of explanatory power for the examples I pursue: (1) the continuing shifts away from postmodern precepts as the determining logic for cultural production and (2) the political context entrenched—though by no means originated—by the 2016 presidential election. The first has inflected the affective character of cinematic representations of the 1950s while the second is responsible for, among other things, its latest surge. I offer a cursory sketch of each here but aim to complicate and expand on them in the chapters that follow.

From Post- to Metamodernism

Around the turn of the twenty-first century, we started to hear a rumbling about the death of postmodernism. Much of it was hyperbolic and required the homogenization of an often contradictory set of discourses. Indeed our shift away from certain postmodern tenets might be described better as a gradual one—in turns incremental, torrential, incomplete, and tainted by a profusion of relapses. Many of its aesthetic strategies remain prevalent throughout visual culture today and show few signs of dissipating in the face of something new or a return to things even older. Intertextuality continues to abound in popular visual culture, and in the typically postmodern way that effaces reverent connections to source materials, favoring instead explorations of the self-reflexive or ironic charges of different representational practices.

We also continue to witness repeated attempts at constructing deliberately archaic images, a variant of pastiche that seeks to recreate the look of old media forms. From the televisual black and white of *Pleasantville* (1998) that transforms into a polished Technicolor to the monochromatic newscast aesthetic of *Good Night, and Good Luck* (2005), the revival of these visual templates has increased, especially over the last twenty years as new technologies render such pictorial returns to the past more convincing.[1] This approach continues to be popular in the recent releases considered here. However, since the turn of the twenty-first century, it also has been mobilized in the service of otherwise more deferential approaches to the past and not as part of a program of postmodern parodic indifference that questions whether the past was even knowable in the first place. This is not to suggest that incisive political or social critique was not also at the heart of several quintessential postmodern films. *Walker* (1987) or, again, *Pleasantville*, like much postmodern cinema, also sought to engage with "real" historical problems. Nor is it to suggest that such a postmodern vein could account for all historically oriented films produced since the 1970s or that all of these films addressed history in a specifically postmodern way. This is clearly not the case.

A different affective inflection to some of the more recent works seems to preserve certain postmodern aesthetic tendencies while it fuels a greater urgency in reporting on truths about the past and recuperating individual and collective experiences that were once elided. I am interested in this cohabitation of tendencies here. In my search to give it form, I turn to Timotheus Vermeulen and Robin van den Akker's concept of metamodernism.[2] Briefly, metamodernism is characterized by an oscillation between modern enthusiasm and commitment and postmodern irony and detachment but, in the end, seeks to replace the latter's penchant for deconstruction with an investment in reconstruction, sincerity, and authenticity.

Examples include the cinema of Michael Gondry and Wes Anderson that "attempts to restore, to the cynical reality of adults, a childlike naivety" or the romantic conceptualism of artists Tacita Dean and Mona Hatoum, who inject a sentimental charge into the calculated, rational conceptualism of earlier years.[3] Vermeulen and van den Akker also note a spike in curatorial projects foregrounding a neoromantic sensibility and thus a structure of feeling that comes closest to exemplifying metamodernism's play of opposites. They cite Olafur Eliasson's "The Weather Project" (2003) as an instance of the "commonplace ethereal," Catherine Opie's investment in the "quotidian sublime," and architectural designs by Herzog and De Meuron that negotiate between "culture and nature, the finite and the infinite . . . a formal structure, and a formalist unstructuring (as opposed to deconstruction)."[4]

Throughout this study I will return periodically to metamodernism, advancing—and sometimes retracting—the analytical power of its features in relation to (some of) the cinematic tendencies at work in my corpus. My intention is not to use metamodernism as a grand contextualizing force within which to situate cinema of the twenty-first century. I do not wish to claim we are living in some kind of "metamodern" world. Instead, I extract those contentions I find instructive for making sense of certain films. At the core of metamodernism—if indeed there is one—is a desire to grasp something meaningful, to move forward, to believe in the virtues of hope, and to be genuinely moved. This smacks of nostalgia for a certain strain of modernity, and that is definitely part of it. Again, the cinema of Wes Anderson, touted by Whitney Crothers Dilley as "hyper-nostalgic," comes to mind.[5] However, Vermeulen and van den Akker warn that the reintroduction of these "modern" virtues should be framed by a Kantian as-if-ness. That is, our cultural expressions ought to proceed as if these things were possible, all the while filtering our efforts through a (postmodern) skepticism that recognizes the pitfalls of doing so. In other words, we ought to see the ideals and possibilities inherent in what we esteem or the pasts we cherish, but recognize the limitations and complexities that necessarily remain in our efforts to pursue and represent them. Still, this seems to overstate the way in which postmodern strategies supposedly effaced meaning, feeling, and truth. However much irony and parody may have reigned, their prominence did not occlude an investment in a kind of deeper affect or historical reality even in the most quintessentially postmodern films.

Nostalgia for the 1950s (Again) in Contemporary Political Discourse

Postmodernism's obituaries may already be archived, but its ghosts continue to haunt cultural and political life in the United States. They do so in frighteningly strange ways. For instance, we are currently at a point where the relativity of the truth expounded by proponents of postmodernism—invested in challenging certain power structures, entrenched metanarratives, and histories marred by exclusions—has been put to use in the service of ends very much at odds with the ethos of the proponents of postmodernism. We are witnessing attempts by the center—of capital and politics—to once again erase the experiences of the margins, taking away any powers that might have been accrued by appealing to a bastardized relativity ascribed to postmodernism. From the term "truthiness"—offered by Stephen Colbert in 2005 to reflect the absurd pronouncements by George W. Bush—to Kellyanne Conway's "alternative facts" in 2017 to describe the debacle around the size of Donald Trump's inaugural crowds, to bizarre rejections of scientific discoveries throughout the Covid-19 pandemic, now it is the Right adopting postmodern challenges to truth as a tactic to bolster their power at the expense of many still-disenfranchised groups. In fact, the unabashed spewing of lies that marked Trump's presidency on everything from immigration to the pandemic has left many with mouths agape and a new fervor to defend the importance of truth, fact, and data. This questioning of truth and its subjectivity has resulted in much hand wringing about the extent to which Donald Trump was a "postmodern" president and thus the extent of postmodernism's continuing relevance for our present. Articles to that effect abounded after his inauguration. Writing in the *New Republic* Jeet Heer turns to Fredric Jameson and others to show how closely aligned Trump or, rather, Trump-as-cipher is with certain postmodern forces:

> These writers describe a world where the visual has triumphed over the literary, where fragmented sound bites have replaced linear thinking, where nostalgia ("Make America Great Again") has replaced historical consciousness or felt experiences of the past, where simulacra is indistinguishable from reality, where an aesthetic of pastiche and kitsch (Trump Tower) replaces modernism's striving for purity and elitism, and where a shared plebeian culture of vulgarity papers over intensifying class disparities. In virtually every detail, Trump seems like the perfect manifestation of postmodernism.[6]

Heer continues by surveying the "propagation of fictions," the multiple and dubious claims to reality, the many moments of simulation (Trump as "simulacra of a businessman"), and the economics of late capitalism that made a Trump presidency possible. Truth and facts remain at the heart of such assessments, with writers from *Time*, *The Globe and Mail*, *The New York Times*, and the BBC asserting the death of truth and objectivity when it is really starting to matter in the face of catastrophic changes to our climate, the toll of Covid-19, and horrendous assaults on voting rights. In some ways, however, this characterization of Trump's presidency as postmodern goes only so far. Perhaps it is best seen as a surface alignment, one that starts to falter the deeper we dig.

This is not to say that the alignment between Trump and postmodernism isn't productive. It is. Especially if we take time to unpack Heer's brief description of nostalgia in order to see how nostalgia itself is being understood. As cited above, Heer writes that "nostalgia (Make America Great Again) has replaced *historical consciousness* or *felt experiences of the past*" [emphasis added]. This conception of nostalgia is grounded in Jameson's view that "History" proper has been replaced with the history of nostalgic aesthetic styles. Pastiche and parody have effaced meaningful connections to the past, leaving in their place inauthentic longings manufactured by the desire economies of consumer culture. For instance, thanks to cinema, the 1930s and 1950s have been replaced by a general sense of pastness, or what Jameson calls "1930s-ness" and "1950s-ness."[7] This pastness is depthless, ahistorical, and predicated on little more than the surface trappings of style and fashion. There are several problems with this perspective that Heer replicates. Many scholars, starting with Linda Hutcheon, have demonstrated the faults with Jameson's own nostalgia for the possibility of an unproblematic access to history and, particularly pertinent here, the idea that aesthetic strategies cannot generate genuine feeling. Nostalgia is, in part, about a felt experience of the past. Such a feeling can still be incredibly strong even if the trigger for it is mythic or invented. Likewise, such triggers can originate from the worlds of style and fashion which themselves, contra Jameson, have strong links to actual material histories and realities.

As defining as Jameson's account of postmodernism is, his explanation of postmodern nostalgia, adopted by Heer, does not help us see the powerful ways in which this sentiment has been harnessed by the Right. I would argue that a certain kind of "historical consciousness" and a "felt connection to the past" are precisely what the Right's nostalgia mobilizes and feeds on, and it does so in a way that alternates between myth and reality. The campaign slogan "Make America Great Again" is, of course, nostalgic in structure. It implies that the present is somehow deficient and that the past is much preferred and thus the model for future action. But the past that was once "great" in the minds of its adherents, is one steeped in both historical reality and myth and one multifaceted enough that different constituencies can find their own distinct nostalgic longings potentially fulfilled by its promises. While expressions of this nostalgia may be lacking the critical currency of their postmodern antecedents, like many instances of postmodern nostalgia they are nevertheless also deeply indebted to the 1950s. It is this form of 1950s nostalgia to which I now turn in order to make a case for the

8   FRACTURED FIFTIES

persistence of the postwar past in political discourse and to provide a sketch of the context in which many of the films surveyed here are produced and with which they engage.

For many observers, nostalgia was a key ingredient in the election of Trump. His victory was secured by what Robert P. Jones describes as the transformation of evangelical "value voters" into "nostalgia voters."[8] Although this suggestion of transformation obscures the way particular evangelical "values" have been part of a much longer Republican campaign grounded in nostalgia, it certainly highlights the effectiveness of how "Trump's promise to restore a mythical past golden age—where factory jobs paid the bills and white Protestant churches were the dominant cultural hubs—powerfully tapped evangelical anxieties about an uncertain future."[9] Jones's observations are based on surveys that demonstrate just how strong the pull of nostalgia for the 1950s is among the white evangelicals who voted Republican. It was a very deeply felt connection that spoke to the essence of their identities. For instance, immediately before the 2016 election, the Public Religion Research Institute (PRRI) "American Values" poll found what was at stake were two irreconcilable visions of America, dependent on whether or not respondents thought that the 1950s were worse or better than the present.[10] The unsurprising results, that white men preferred the 1950s to the present while women and people of color preferred the present to the 1950s, were covered widely in the media. Jones explains that people were not motivated by "concrete policy issues," but by the way the "campaign painted a bleak portrait of America's present, set against a bright, if monochromatic, vision of 1950s America restored."[11]

Nancy Letourneau of the *Washington Journal* reinforces these points about nostalgia through her contention that:

> [T]hose who argue over whether Trump supporters were motivated by racism or economic anxiety continue to miss the point. The issue at play was more broad than either of those assumptions capture. It was about nostalgia for the mythical golden age of the past that, fueled by anger, became a defense of "the divinely ordained way things are supposed to be." Included in that stew are the intertwining fears about changing demographics, immigrants, Muslims, women, LGBTQ, globalization, the impact of the Great Recession, the decline in religious affiliation and racism. In other words, nostalgia voters (i.e., confederate insurgents) were reacting to the perceived changes in their established social order.[12]

But these nostalgia voters, fearful and resentful of the slight gains made by marginalized communities, were responding to more than just a vision of a "mythic golden age." Their "historical consciousness" is fueled by a "deeply felt" connection to real historical circumstances that defined the 1950s, facets held in abeyance in the subconscious of even some of the most reductive nostalgic tropes. The different constituencies making up the nostalgia-voting bloc can latch onto much about the historical reality of the 1950s. White supremacists are drawn to the 1950s because the United States was still deeply segregated and overtly anti-Semitic, and racially motivated crimes could go unpunished. Of course, this remains the case still today despite a series of legal victories, some of them dating to the 1950s. Economically disenfranchised, under- and unemployed white men yearn for the 1950s because they were all but guaranteed a job and the social mobility and prestige that came with it. Social conservatives gravitate toward the 1950s because those years comprised the last decade before women's rights and gay rights took hold in any kind of concrete way that challenged the power held by the patriarchy and heteronormativity. The religious right also esteems the 1950s for these reasons and because the 1950s represented a time when "White Christian America" defined the core, normative culture for the nation. Patriots of many stripes also could be proud of America's unparalleled military might on the international stage; never mind the global human cost at which this strength was achieved.

This appeal to the 1950s by Republicans is not by any means new. It is part of a long-standing political strategy dating back to Ronald Reagan's campaigns in the 1980s. Then already, the 1950s was used as a partisan pawn, celebrated as a nostalgic object by the Right while condemned as such by the Democrats. Daniel Marcus tracks Reagan and George H. W. Bush's rhetorical uses of the 1950s and, later, Bill Clinton's own brand of decade nostalgia, one that feted the progressive social movements of the 1960s as an antidote.[13] In some ways, Barack Obama's "yes we can" and "hope" slogans that looked more forward than back stand as a rather metamodern injection into a near half-century of nostalgia-infused presidential campaigns. In fact, Vermeulen and van den Akker began their essay on metamodernism with an excerpt from Obama's "Yes, we can change," speech to the Democratic national assembly in January 2008.[14] With the presidential election of 2016, there seemed to be a return to business as usual—almost. Defenses of the postwar past during this contest were mounted with a high degree of aggression and hyperbole. Moreover, there was little attempt by some constituencies to hide their relish of 1950s inequities behind an alibi of nostalgia for "kinder, gentler times." Though this, too, is not entirely new. For even during the Reagan and Bush Sr. years that made much use of seemingly benign televisual images of the postwar years, certain repressions of the 1950s were surreptitiously highlighted in ways that appealed to their supporters.

The reality of the circumstances of the 1950s was also in part responsible for the first eruption in the nostalgia economy of the 1970s. These circumstances represented what was lost by the gains made through 1960s social activism. The racism, misogyny, and homophobia that fueled the nostalgia economy were not often named as such. Instead, this nostalgia was seen as induced by simply a "better" time, allowing enthusiasts of this era to disavow their bigotry. There were other driving forces of this nostalgia as well, but however much at a remove from these ideological triggers they seemed, they remained imbricated with them. For instance, a decidedly consumerist bent flavored the nostalgic appeal of the material and visual culture of those who had come of age during the 1950s. Fashions and toys tapped into the nostalgia market and became indispensable to the process of mystification. However, the significance (in the sense of signifying power) of these products was bestowed, in large measure, by narrative forces that erased the experiences of those on the periphery. Poodle skirts and hula hoops, for example, were contextualized by the blindingly white worlds in the advertisements, magazine covers, and television programs in which they reappeared. Moreover, these nostalgic objects circulated in a consumerist economy with structural injustices that continued to disadvantage many in the 1970s: women could not have a credit card in their name, and people of color continued to face overt discrimination in many financial sectors.

Those occupying the purported center of American culture—white, middle-class, heterosexual, Christian men—were also the subjects of mystification, some specific to their station (e.g., patriarchal or hegemonic masculinity) and others shared—though experienced differently—by their neighbors on the periphery. One particularly powerful force to which all were subject was the Red Scare. This had implications reaching far beyond political alliances and even the end of the House Un-American Activities Committee's official mandate. McCarthyism, among other factors, generated a lot of anxiety in the postwar era. And as Alan Nadel observes, it was an era marked by great difficulty reconciling an unhappy citizenry with the imperative to be happy, to unabashedly celebrate the unprecedented wealth and security of 1950s America. A pithy section heading spells out the implications of this imperative: "Not being happy is not being normal is being un-American."[15] Nadel thus reveals the broad disjuncture between a discontented American populous that coped poorly with massive societal shifts while being forced to live happy lives to "demonstrate that the American way of life, from day to day and year to year, was the most attractive in the world."[16] As he further explains:

> Achieving normality, however, was virtually impossible. Perhaps the biggest absurdity of 1950s normativity was the fact that the "norms" of Cold War America, like its postwar prosperity, were totally anomalous. Most simply, Americans could not become cheerful exemplars of the joys of capitalism by returning to normal life because from a historical, social, technological, and especially demographic perspective, *nothing* about postwar America was normal.[17]

This demand to be happy goes a long way to explain the proliferation of those ridiculously uninhibited expressions of glee, if not outright *jouissance*, in advertising that have become the fodder for contemporary memes. It also explains those beaming smiles in 1950s domestic sitcoms, the model for appropriate postwar familial behavior. In this way, the era seems to have destined itself to become future fuel for nostalgia and parody.

When the Right alludes to a mythic golden age, this is the image that most often comes to mind. Indeed media coverage of Trump's campaign and presidency have all but permanently entrenched the 1950s as his preferred object of nostalgia despite his own caginess when it comes to committing to an era. For instance, on the eve of the 2016 election, Dana Nuccitelli observed that "Donald Trump's goal is to make America *Mad Men* again by reversing the progress we've made over the past half century and returning the country to a 1950s era-style society dominated by white men."[18] She itemizes the litany of injustices against women, people of color, and science, commonplace and institutionalized in 1950s—and the AMC television drama—that Trump and his supporters wish to reinstate. Whereas Nuccitelli concentrates on the misogyny and white supremacy that Trump seeks to normalize, writing in *The Atlantic* more than a year earlier, Ester Bloom unpacks the consequences of the "Make America Great Again" slogan by recounting the nostalgic appeal of the privileges enjoyed by white, heterosexual, middle-class men during the postwar years. Her aim, too, is to pinpoint the "golden era" to which Trump's vague rhetoric alludes, and she suggests that "[r]egardless of when it ended, it would not be unfair to use the '50s as shorthand for this now glamorized period of plenty, peace, and the kind of optimism only plenty and peace can produce."[19] The point of her piece, however, is to remind his supporters that such plenty was a direct consequence of big government, strong unions, and high taxes. Danielle Fernandez, who seemed to predict a Republican win when most thought it impossible, also argues that "lacking as it does an historical referent, the era of American greatness the Trump campaign heralds as ideal—perhaps the one that will come (again) when Trump ascends—remains unclear, but most people who are moved by this myth likely imagine the 1950s."[20] To succeed, however, the voting public must first be convinced to "buy into his 1950s-nostalgia campaign."[21] Admittedly, this is not too difficult to do for some constituencies. As noted above, 1950s nostalgia campaign has been waged by various political, economic, and social interests for nearly fifty years, and Trump certainly isn't the first—or likely the last—political candidate to invoke the 1950s in this way.

After the 2016 election, the 1950s became even further entrenched both in Trump's rhetoric and in the journalistic responses to his presidency. In *Fire and Fury*, Michael Wolff's best-selling, gossipy exposé, the 1950s returns again and again as a frame to make sense of Trump and his actions.[22] Wolff's aim may have been to spin a tantalizing narrative around the daily absurdities originating from the White House in 2017, but his frequent alignments of Trump with the 1950s reached a vast readership and thus did much to cement this connection. It was a connection also repeated in more studied reflections. Writing in *Foreign Policy*, Charlie Laderman reminds us that Trump was a child of the 1950s and "just as his domestic agenda is a nod to that era's vision of the American Dream," his view of America's role in the world reflects a "nationalist critique of American liberal internationalism that might have been dormant in policy circles since the 1950s but which has never really gone away."[23] But it is a view without nuance and without knowledge of the specific historical circumstances that first generated this perspective or sustained it. Instead, promises of domestic and foreign policy remained extremely vague.

However much such vagueness was a byproduct of a mind with little to no grasp of history, this noncommittal approach continues to work to the Republican's benefit, permitting followers to fill in the blanks with their own nostalgic object. But this past is not without some grounding. It finds expression through a series of tropes and ideas that we recognize as part of a national imaginary, to be celebrated or condemned, inflected or developed, depending on one's political persuasion. And regardless of use, each iteration simply serves to reinforce the centrality of the 1950s in the broader cultural consciousness.[24] These reductive tropes have their roots in the 1950s, emerging from postwar television: the *Leave It to Beaver*-esque, white, patriarchal, middle-class family gathered around the dinner table in their suburban bungalow. They emerge from advertising: a stylish, young couple swooning over the latest tail-finned car. Sometimes this car is parked at a diner in a nod to an emerging youth culture. Sometimes it is parked against the backdrop of a rocket launch site, suggesting that its technological supremacy and futurity are inherited from America's advances in the space race.

The Fractures

Taken together, these reductive visual tropes coalesce into a simplified impression of the 1950s, one that has enjoyed much currency and power in a range of contexts from politics, film, television, and advertising to the broader nostalgia economy. But however simplified it may seem, often consciously so in an effort to ascribe an idyllic simplicity to the period itself, this vision also holds deep within it a series of often unspoken contradictions and questions. If we excavate the history of each trope and subject its components to a close analysis, fractures start to show. In so doing, we find ways to access the nuances of the historical realities of the decade and especially its countercultural forces that do not often register on the surface. Other fractures also start to show if we track, chronologically, the uses of different 1950s types through the 1970s, 1980s, and up to the present. The seeming dominance of white suburban domesticity as definitive of the 1950s begins to erode, opening up space for competing, complicating, and more densely layered versions of this decade.

In other words, this book ultimately is about how cinema helped fracture—in the sense of splintering and fragmenting into parts—what was once a somewhat coherent *construct* into a multifaceted collection of constituent types despite the unending pressure from certain political circles to the contrary.[25] Taxonomies of this nature certainly have their pitfalls, some of which bear similarities to those suffered by periodization itself, as detailed in Chapter 1. Classificatory schemes end up privileging various features at the expense of others, writing off as marginal what through a different lens is vitally important or defining. They also artificially reinforce boundaries that are in reality quite porous. In fact, some films could just as easily be slotted into one type as another. That said, I use this classificatory scheme to highlight some of the key intensities and concerns driving a selection of recent releases to show how they are mobilized in the service of periodizing the 1950s, engaging historiography, performing historicity, and intervening in the production of cultural memory.

Before delving into case studies that itemize the ways in which film has helped fracture the 1950s into distinctive types, I offer two chapters that perform a different kind of work in Part I, "Theory and History." Chapter 1 excavates a series of theoretical concerns in relation to this project, dealing specifically with periodization as a process, the significance of the decade as a historically specific measure of time, and the cinema as a phenomenological vector embroiled in the machinations of the first two. I also reflect on the contributions made by discussions around "period films" and consider the relationship between the 1950s and the Fifties, surveying the various ways in which this distinction has been articulated and used. In fact, as I describe the contents of each chapter below, I start to use Fifties in place of 1950s to indicate the mediated nature of a construct of pastness. In the context of these discussions, I bring into the fray a number of theoretical and historical projects that have had a hand in determining the questions I pose in relation to my own case studies. In particular, I look to Michel Serres and Penelope Corfield's work on periodization and time, Fred Davis and Jason Scott Smith's isolated studies about the decade, and Susan Buck-Morss's analysis of the phenomenology of cinema in relation to mass events. Scholarly contributions by Mary Caputi, Michael Dwyer, Daniel Marcus, David Haven Blake, Eleonora Ravizza, and others prove indispensable in understanding the resonance of the 1950s across the American political and cultural landscape.[26]

Chapter 2 launches from the assumption that there is a wide "image envelope," to borrow Victor Burgin's suggestive term, which includes all the visual and material detritus that comprises our "picture" of the 1950s.[27] Although much of this picture was generated in earnest during the postwar period's commitment to self-mythologization and subsequent and often, nostalgic, representations of the 1950s—produced since the late 1960s—our first images of the 1950s emerged much earlier. Due to the prognosticating efforts of filmmakers like Maurice Elvey, fascinating images of the 1950s surfaced as early as the 1920s and 1930s. This chapter, therefore, examines how the 1950s were imagined in *Last Man on Earth* (1924), *High Treason* (1929), and *Transatlantic Tunnel* (1935). The point here is not to itemize instances where films got it right, so to speak, but rather to acknowledge that such predictive efforts—also the domain of a World's Fair—have contributed to our vast repository that is the 1950s and thus should not be ignored in a project concerned with engagements with that decade.

Part II of this book, "The Foundational Fractures," contains three chapters dedicated to the "Leave It to Beaver Fifties," "Jukebox Fifties," and "Cold War Fifties." The term "foundational fractures" may sound a bit like an oxymoron, but the Fifties that emerged in cinema of the mid-to-late 1960s and early 1970s was already fractured into these three main types, each with its own additional layers of complexity that reflect a series of upheavals around race, class, sex, gender, politics, psychology, and science. In fact, even some of the most seemingly benign nostalgic fare had embedded in its narrative, aesthetic, or sonic structures the critical potential to engage in meaningful ways with the 1950s, its construction and legacy.

Chapter 3, "The Leave It to Beaver Fifties" is concerned with cinematic representations of suburban life and domesticity, particularly in relation to gender and race. I pirate the title of this postwar sitcom because of its continued currency as a shorthand in political and cultural realms, an expression that invokes a certain vision of family life in the 1950s, both for those who idealized its power structures and relations and for those who sought to critique its internal oppressions and external exclusions. In this chapter, I start with a few examples from the 1990s and 2000s that deserve mention, but then concentrate my analysis on *Revolutionary Road* (2008) and *Suburbicon* (2017), concluding with a consideration of the television anthology series, *Them* (2021).

Chapter 4, "The Jukebox Fifties," speaks to youth culture and the privileging of music within it. Teenagers, a relatively new identity category that became entrenched in the 1950s, and the popular music geared toward them, were a dominant force in some of the earliest cinematic representations of the postwar era. Despite my insistence above that this book focuses on recent releases, this chapter devotes space to one early example, namely, *Grease* (1978), to survey the internal fractures that in many ways defined this film and set it apart from other Fifties revivals of the 1970s. What's more, as a cult film, *Grease* thrives in the popular imaginary, continuing to circulate in various forms, restagings, and fan practices. I also show that it harbored a critical edge, sometimes in spite of itself, and one that depended in large part on various nascent postmodern strategies invested in cultural memory. These concerns continue to dominate *Grease*'s progeny, even if these later films diverged quite substantially from it. My aim is to follow one key thread to demonstrate the ways in which its legacy persists.[28] Specifically, I will track how the "greaser," a working-class identity construct, continues life not just through various film roles but through rockabilly culture, itself of recent interest to photographers and documentarians, including Jennifer Greenburg. This work is noted after an analysis of April Mullen's independent film, *Badsville* (2017).

Chapter 5, "The Cold War Fifties," is fairly expansive in scope and includes three definitive subcategories that concern the first phase of the Cold War between 1947 and 1962: The Korean War Fifties, The McCarthyite Fifties, and The Atomic Fifties. The Korean War Fifties offers us the first instances of retrospective representations of the 1950s in several films released during the first few years of the 1960s. Recently, an international resurgence of interest in this conflict has reflected itself in films such as *Operation Chromite* (2016), *Retreat!* (2016), *Ayla: Daughter of War* (2017), *Hal King* (2021), and *Lost Bastards* (in production as of this writing). While each of these represents a very different approach to the "Forgotten War," my focus will be on Steve Wallace's independent R&B opera film, *Hal King*. I conclude this section with a few observations on the role played by the Korean War in the television series *Lovecraft Country* (2020).

The McCarthyite Fifties focuses on the trials and consequences of the House Un-American Activities Committee, often in an effort to shed light on contemporary ideological conflicts. Such was the case for the 1970s cycle of films, for example, *The Way We Were* (1973), *Fear on Trial* (1975), *The Front* (1976), and *Tail Gunner Joe* (1977) that challenged that decade's Fifties nostalgia boom. Another wave of interest in McCarthyism dates to the end of the Cold War, reflected in *The House on Carroll Street* (1988), *Guilty by Suspicion* (1991), and *Citizen Cohn* (1992). *Good Night, and Good Luck* (2005) and *Trumbo* (2015), however, occupy the center of this analysis.

The Atomic Fifties includes a body of films concerned primarily with the space race during the 1950s and early 1960s. This topic manifested itself across a range of genres and includes films as diverse as *The Reflecting Skin* (1990) and *Blast from the Past* (1999), considered elsewhere in this book. Although such films may warrant attention here too, the focus in this section is on *Hidden Figures* (2016). This film not only invokes questions about historicity but also provides a point of contact with *Hal King* through the situation of the civil rights movement in relation to the Cold War. The ways in which

Hidden Figures negotiates this relationship—and also the ways in which it fails to—are particularly instructive for thinking through the connections between the new civil rights movement (Black Lives Matter) and the new Cold War, both of which are implicitly acknowledged by the film.

The third and final part of this book, "The Liminal Fractures," concerns itself with Fifties types in relation to borders, ones that circumscribe subjectivities, spaces, and representational practices. An interest in the porosity of boundaries guides this part, inspired partially by an adapted view of Serres's thoughts on periodization and time as explored in Chapter 1. Chapter 6, "The Retromediated Fifties," examines films that are ostensibly about other media practices in the 1950s and often tell their stories through the aesthetic lenses of these media. As such, they are engaged with the mediation of historical periods and the role of film and photography in shaping our conceptions of earlier moments. I begin with brief analysis of *Hail, Caeser!* (2016) and *La La Land* (2016) as instances of what might be called a "Hollywood Fifties" subtype for their investments in both the aesthetics and practices of postwar cinema, that is, an engagement with a kind of deliberate archaism.[29] In a marked departure, *Sylvie's Love* (2020) fully and unabashedly inhabits its genre of choice, melodrama. I briefly consider this approach before turning to an example of retromediation that leaves film behind: *Carol* (2015). Directed by Todd Haynes, the film documents the developing love affair between a socialite and shop girl, but does so through an aesthetic template borrowed from 1950s street photography.

Chapter 7, "The Fifties Reframed," is less a distinctive type than suggestive of an approach, an investment in expansion that builds on retromediation in certain regards. It is one that seeks to admit into the purview of postwar engagements both hitherto neglected subjects and modes of representing them. Here I explore how the Fifties have been reframed in two ways: by moving the camera's lens to focus on subjects often excluded and by recalibrating the lens itself to see its subjects differently. That is, I focus on films that account for experiences that fall outside the mythical purview of white, middle-class, patriarchal consumer capitalism in different respects. In some cases, this shift in focus is realized in geographical, gendered, or class terms as in the harrowing *Bastard Out of Carolina* (1996), set in the poverty-stricken rural south or *The Reflecting Skin* (1990), set in the prairies. While *Fences* (2016) contends with the intersection of class and racialized identities, another boundary rendered porous by this film is one between art forms: cinema and theater. International borders are at stake in *Brooklyn* (2015). My concern, though, is not with the vast number of Irish and British films set in 1950s in the British Isles, but rather instances where a British heritage or Irish period film texture has been transplanted into narratives defined by an American experience.[30] That is, I consider how *Brooklyn* imports select heritage conventions into a film about a young Irish woman's postwar migration to America.

Several dominant themes bind these chapters, uniting productions that enjoyed tremendous box office success and awards recognition with more obscure independent films. For instance, most chapters address civil rights struggles in both postwar and present-day America. The context of the production of these films, up to and including Black Lives Matter, plays an important role in situating these films and unpacking their contributions to political discourse. Gender and sexuality, closely regulated during the 1950s, also are at issue here, not just in the films discussed but also in relation to other cultural practices (e.g., rockabilly events) brought into the fray through their particular ways of reviving the Fifties. Indeed a through-going concern, articulated first in relation to periodization, is with boundaries. I am interested in how Fifties types have been circumscribed and their borders then ruptured by time, geography, aesthetics, and media.

Of course this is a study with many limits, and several possible and even popular Fifties types are not addressed. Biopics could constitute their own chapter, if not a book, in order to shed light on how the personal is figured in relation to the broader social or political realities of the time. While I do spend time with the odd film that borrows from biographical traditions, many others could be further subdivided along the lines of artist biopics (e.g., *Pollock* [2000] and *Big Eyes* [2014]); musician biopics (e.g., *Walk the Line* [2005], *The Last Ride* [2011], and *Mario Lanza: The Best of Everything* [2017]); literary biopics (e.g., *Sylvia* [2003], *Capote* [2005], and *Set Fire to the Stars* [2014]); celebrity biopics (e.g., *Accidental Icon: The Real Gidget Story* [2010], *My Week with Marilyn* [2011], *Joshua Tree, 1951: A Portrait of James Dean* [2012], and *Life* [2015]); and sports biopics from *Raging Bull* (1980) to the proposed *Sweetwater* (in preproduction as of this writing). Biopic strategies are also at work in cinematic forays into the lives of the Beat Generation, another potential Fifties type in its own right: e.g., *Neal Cassady* (2007), *Kill Your Darlings* (2013), and *Big Sur* (2013). A series of other biopics, on both well- and lesser-known individuals, reveals the postwar worlds of politics and science.

There is no shortage of homage to 1950s B-movie creature features. A staple of horror cinema, these films have persisted since the 1950s, virtually without interruption. Films such as *Attack of the Atomic Zombies* (2011), *The Atomic Attack of the Son of the Seaweed Creature* (2013), and *It Came from the Desert* (2017) have continued this hallowed tradition into the 2000s. We might include *Lovecraft Country* (2020) and *Them* (2021) in this vein too, but these television productions exceed this category in many respects as we shall see. Quaint 1950s towns also provide the setting for thrillers and crime dramas: *The Violent Kind* (2010), *The Killer Inside Me* (2010), *The Diner* (2014), *Take Me Out* (2015) and *Alice Fades Away* (2021). In an entirely different vein, a series of children's and animated films pay homage to postwar material and television culture, for example, *Toy Story* (1995) and *The Iron Giant* (1999). Others seem to consciously defy categorization by blending multiple cinematic traditions and paying homage to a range of cultural practices and histories, *The Ghastly Love of Johnny X* (2012) and *Agent Frank Skuddler and Project Blue Book* (2018) to name but two.

Across this range of hundreds of films invested in the American 1950s, we find varying degrees of historical engagement, mystification, concern with mediation, and challenges to cultural memory. These films were produced against a half-century-long backdrop of constantly shifting terrains that reconfigure and recontextualize the many tumultuous facets that characterized the 1950s as well as the deeply fractured visions that constitute its representations. The broader Fifties nostalgia economy that many of these films seek to complicate certainly persists across our visual and political culture, often in reductive and ideologically motivated ways. But this is an interesting moment for cinema (and television) and the Fifties, especially insofar as how the former periodizes the latter as well as how the latter might fare—as a mythic construct—in an age deeply concerned with threats to truth and historical fact. Decade periodization itself—in American popular and journalistic realms—seems to be waning. A few key factors contribute to this fading. First, a simple awkwardness mars attempts to name these first few decades of the 2000s, leading to both outright avoidance and hand-wringing about what to call them. In all likelihood, the 2020s will fare no better because "The Twenties" is still firmly anchored to the 1920s due to that decade's continuing popularity in our cultural imagination. Periodization in the United States now seems to be falling back on the older historical practice of naming eras after political figures (for instance, the Obama Era, the Trump Era, and perhaps, most recently, the Pandemic era).

A broader cultural shift from postmodernism to something else (e.g., digimodernism, altermodernism, hypermodernism, metamodernism, etc.)

underpins this shift from a decade to a leader as a marker of an era. Although such epistemic transformations have explanatory potential for much narrower bands of reality than they claim, these attempts at categorization necessarily lead to reflection on periodization itself—as it does in Chapter 1. These reflections, in turn, lead to a kind of fetishistic disavowal about how we encapsulate vast space-time realities: I know perfectly well that a period designation (e.g., the Fifties, Postmodern, etc.) can never adequately capture the vicissitudes of a particular moment or era, but I continue to use them anyway because of a need to organize the past and to draw attention to key or dominant forces. This kind of soul searching can be found in some of the films at issue here, films that knowingly periodize, while still confronting the pitfalls of doing so. In fact, a major concern of this book is how films focused on the Fifties do important historiographical work. They do so by engaging problems of periodization, representation, mediation, memory, and nostalgia. They also perform important historical work by recognizing history's exclusions, marginalizations, and (re)colonizations. In a postmodern vein they challenge how we come to know the past through its "textualized remains," and, in a—for lack of a better word—metamodern vein, they recognize the political power of difficult truths long suppressed.[31] They also recognize the affective power of aesthetic strategies of all stripes to both challenge history and produce histories in myriad ways. The films I analyze are, in turn, troubling, inspiring, problematic, critical, challenging, thoughtful, moving, hollow, incisive, and muddled. Taken together, they track the complex evolution of a period in time, shaped and continually reshaped by its past, present, and mobilizations across political and visual culture.

Notes

1. These returns are not focused exclusively on the 1950s. Many other decades have received this treatment, for instance, films (or parts of films) set in 1920s. Martin Scorsese's *The Aviator* (2004) and *Hugo* (2011) mobilize a two-strip Technicolor look as a way to aesthetically engage with cinema history. I unpack the specifics of this approach, also known as "deliberate archaism," in more detail shortly.
2. See Timotheus Vermeulen and Robin van den Akker, "Notes on Metamodernism," *Journal of Aesthetics and Culture* 2.1 (2010): 1–14. http://www.tandfonline.com/doi/full/10.3402/jac.v2i0.5677
3. Ibid., 7.
4. Ibid., 8–11.

5. Whitney Crothers Dilley, *The Cinema of Wes Anderson: Bringing Nostalgia to Life* (New York: Wallflower Press, 2017), 1.
6. Jeet Heer, "America's First Postmodern President," *New Republic*, July 8, 2017. https://newrepublic.com/article/143730/americas-first-postmodern-president.
7. Fredric Jameson, *Postmodernism: Or, the Cultural Logic of Late Capitalism* (Durham, NC: Duke University Press, 1991), 19.
8. Robert P. Jones, *The End of White Christian America* (New York: Simon and Shuster, 2017), 246. In some ways Jones is compelled to argue this. His book is about the end of "White Christian America" as the dominant force and its power to define the nation's core cultural and moral principles. His remarks on Trump are part of an epilogue, which sometimes erodes the arguments earlier in the book. Overall, it is an odd text. A promising chapter foregrounds race, even if it fails to deal with the depth and complexity that the topic deserves. A chapter then follows that ostensibly undoes this by betraying his nostalgia for this "end." Nevertheless, I cite it here because the Public Religion Research Institute (PRRI) surveys, typically sound in methodology, give insight into the impact of nostalgia and the 1950s on Trump's campaign and victory.
9. Jones, *End of White Christian America*, 246.
10. The ensuing report was titled "Better or Worse since the 1950s? Trump and Clinton Supporters at Odds over the Past and Future of the Country." The results are available on the Public Religion Research Institute's website at https://www.prri.org/press-release/better-worse-since-1950s-trump-clinton-supporters-odds-past-future-country/. The results were reported by numerous media outlets including the *New York Times*, *Salon*, *Huffington Post*, *The Economist*, and even the *Daily Mail*. Of course it seems that some of these voters responded based on their mediated conception of the 1950s.
11. Jones, *End of White Christian America*, 246–47.
12. Nancy LeTourneau, "Dear Trump Voters: The 1950s Aren't Coming Back," *Washington Monthly*, July 5, 2017. https://washingtonmonthly.com/2017/07/05/dear-trump-voters-the-1950s-arent-coming-back/.
13. Daniel Marcus gives an instructive account of how a Fifties vs. Sixties dynamic structured political debate of the 1980s and 1990s in *Happy Days and Wonder Years: The Fifties and Sixties in Contemporary Cultural Politics* (New Brunswick, NJ: Rutgers University Press, 2004). I wish to extend this to the 2000s to show how certain films have played a significant role in the political mobilization and circulation of historical tropes situated in America's postwar past.
14. Vermeulen and van den Akker, "Notes on Metamodernism," 1.
15. Alan Nadel, *Demographic Angst: Cultural Narratives and American Films of the 1950s* (New Brunswick, NJ: Rutgers University Press, 2017), 7.
16. Ibid., 4.
17. Ibid., 10. Nadel also lists the following demographic shifts that "radically reorganized the size, location, composition, interactions, values, and pastimes of the American population, making a resemblance to America before the stock-market crash at best a metaphor and more appropriately a mix of nostalgia and whimsy. The end of World War II; the return of more than half of the male population between the ages of twenty-two and forty-six, two-thirds of those in their twenties and thirties; the rapid

creation of large suburban populations; the exodus of women from significant roles in the workplace; the baby boom; court-ordered desegregation; the explosion in college attendance; the rapid expansion of the white-collar class; the vast technologies of domestic life (cars, highways, televisions, home appliances); and the proliferation of mall consumerism created a world in which 'normal' American life—for which deviance was a political and social anathema—was an inherent and profound deviation" (10).

18. Dana Nuccitelli, "President Trump Would Make America Deplorable Again," *Guardian*, November 6, 2016. https://www.theguardian.com/environment/climate-consensus-97-per-cent/2016/nov/07/president-trump-would-make-america-deplorable-again.
19. Ester Bloom, "When America Was 'Great,' Taxes Were High, Unions Were Strong and Government Was Big," *The Atlantic*, September 28, 2015. https://www.theatlantic.com/business/archive/2015/09/when-america-was-great-taxes-were-high-unions-were-strong-and-government-was-big/407284/.
20. Danielle Fernandez, "The 1950s, American Greatness, and Trump's Brand of Nostalgia," *Public Seminar*, August 3, 2016. http://www.publicseminar.org/2016/08/the-1950s-american-greatness-and-trumps-brand-of-nostalgia/.
21. Ibid.
22. To list just a few of many references to the 1950s, Wolff speaks of Trump's "business and military 1950s-type cabinet choices" (4), his "unique political virtue was as an alpha male, maybe the last of the alpha males. A 1950s man, a Rat Pack Type, a character out of *Mad Men*" (23), his efforts to model himself on a "1950s businessman sort of ideal" (90), his brand of fiftiesness as opposed to Pence's, who is described as "the husband in *Ozzie and Harriet*" (124), and Trump and the alt-right's desire to restore, as an ideal, "the virtue and the character and the strength of the American workingman circa 1955–65" (141). This book is deeply flawed in many ways, but nevertheless serves as an example of how Trump's alignment with certain facets of the 1950s proliferate through the public consciousness, becoming ever more firmly entrenched through repetition.
23. Charlie Laderman, "Donald Trump's 1950s Self-Help Foreign Policy," *Foreign Policy*, February 10, 2017. http://foreignpolicy.com/2017/02/10/donald-trumps-1950s-self-help-foreign-policy/.
24. In fact, as I left my work here to procrastinate a little, the first thing I saw—no subtle sign telling me to get back to work—was the following meme: "Aren't time zones fascinating? Australia is already in 2018, Europe is still in 2017, and the US is currently in 1950."
25. There are multiple definitions of the term "fracture." In medicine, the term denotes a break in a hard object or material, like bone, in response to an outside force. While this meaning has some resonance here, I am using "fracture" in the sense of a series of splits leading to fragmentation.
26. Eleonora Ravizza's published dissertation *Revisiting and Revising the Fifties in Contemporary US Popular Culture: Self-Reflexivity, Melodrama, and Nostalgia in Film and Television* (Berlin: Metlzer, 2020) is the most recent study to address

representations of the 1950s in popular culture. Ravizza advances an argument quite different from mine here, claiming that "contemporary cultural artifacts attempt to rework and rewrite the fifties cultural imaginary but cannot ultimately succeed in this process" (2). While I think she makes a compelling case for why this is so with respect to certain titles, I see this rewriting as an ongoing process that is succeeding in certain regards, especially if we cast a wider net, especially one that includes recent independent titles and long form television series.
27. See Victor Burgin, *The Remembered Film* (London: Reaktion, 2004).
28. Although we might locate the origins of certain high school musical films, television series, or television episodes in *Grease*, many of these works do not engage with the Fifties and as such, I do not discuss them here.
29. Many films fall into this category, as I've discussed elsewhere. For instance, *Far from Heaven* (2002) recreates the look of Douglas Sirk's 1950s melodramas. *Pleasantville* (1998) bases its aesthetic on 1950s domestic sitcoms, and *LA Confidential* (1997) plays the looks of 1950s film noir. Specifically, this term was coined by Marc Le Sueur to speak to the production of films in ways that recreate the look of older media. See Marc Le Sueur, "Theory Number Five: Anatomy of Nostalgia Films: Heritage and Methods," *Journal of Popular Film* 6.2 (1977): 187–97.
30. I'm not suggesting that British and Irish period films are an undifferentiated lot. A vast and ever-growing set of strategies are contingent on the period represented, source material, and preferences of directors and cinematographers. That said, certain tendencies unite much of this fare, as recently argued by Belén Vidal in *Figuring the Past: Period Film and the Mannerist Aesthetic* (Amsterdam: University of Amsterdam Press, 2012).
31. "Textualized remains" is Linda Hutcheon's term for describing what history leaves behind, including archival evidence and documents. Linda Hutcheon, *A Poetics of Postmodernism: History, Theory, Fiction* (New York: Routledge, 1988), 96.

PART I
THEORY AND HISTORY (OF A PAST FUTURE)

1
Periodization, Cinema, and the Decade

Periodizing, the act of circumscribing and foregrounding a set of features to define a particular era such as the "Enlightenment" or the "1950s" is, of course, a highly fraught exercise. For many, our modern practice of periodization begins with Johann Gottfried Herder's 1774 work *Auch eine Philosophie der Geschichte zur Bildung der Menschheit* (One More Philosophy of History for the Edification of Mankind).[1] Later, Michel Foucault, Raymond Williams, and historiographically minded thinkers test its efficacy and expound its limitations. Some commentators, typically in special issues devoted to periodization in relation to their disciplines, are fairly meticulous in itemizing the many faults of this enterprise and its applications, though they often conclude with the reluctant admission that there is little to offer in its place.[2] In part, this is because of its deep entrenchment as an organizing principle for both scholarship and pedagogy. Periodizing, of course, has epistemological consequences for a range of fields from history to art history, literary studies to philosophy, and film studies to classics.

The critiques are incisive, and some of them are worth describing here. In an oft-cited remark, Bruno Latour bluntly suggests, "It is the sorting that makes the times, not the times that make the sorting."[3] In other words, periodization is an exercise in which an action committed in the present determines, if not overdetermines, our understanding of the past. This is a fairly basic historiographical point, to be sure. And yet, despite concerted attempts to address periodization in its own right, the consequences of its use are not always as fully articulated as they should be when period terms are wielded in the context of case-study analyses.[4] There persists a tendency to revert to period designations whenever they help lend coherence or give weight to claims about a researcher's set of examples. Nevertheless, we cannot deny the classificatory force that some sets of objects of study might have. The consistencies between certain groups of things do and perhaps even ought to have consequences for periodization. "Rococo," for instance, describes a fairly coherent set of aesthetic practices at a given point and place in time, which helps us engage with specific iterations of constructs of class and leisure.

A few studies of periodization acknowledge the contextually specific—and thus, period-specific—ways in which this process might be evaluated. For instance, Robert S. Baker describes how the problems of periodization seem to align with those raised in the context of postmodern debates about "historical knowledge and its representation." He lists "relativism, narrativity, master narratives, objectivism, rhetoricity and the linguistic turn, ideology and contextualism" as points of issue and critical connection between periodization and postmodernism.[5] Scholars attending to the deep structural assumptions that underpin their own discursive practices note how a consideration of these consequences can yield trenchant critiques and uncomfortable truths about how we categorize the past. For instance, eliding inconvenient anomalies for the sake of imposing coherence and perpetuating the exclusion of marginalized peoples by privileging historical narratives that reinforce hegemonic power structures are two fairly typical byproducts of the process.[6] As such, the politics of periodization—the ideological forces that shape the telling and classification of histories—must always and necessarily inflect our reading of the contextualizing work that period designations do.[7]

The practice of naming periods evokes related concerns and also has been subject to a degree of scrutiny. For instance, designations based on "politico-dynastic," "cultural," and "aesthetic" categories, to borrow Meyer Shapiro's kinds, have assumptions about what ought to be singled out and heralded as distinguishing of an era written into their nomenclatural fabric.[8] The consequences of an assumption become immediately apparent with the deployment of a term like "Victorian." This familiar shorthand for the stretch of time between 1837 and 1901 carries with it the belief that "a ruler or a family of rulers can embody a period; it is as if the one who heads the state holds together disparate historical phenomena in an extension of that role."[9] Likewise, the "Roaring Twenties," the "Fabulous Fifties," the "Swinging Sixties," or the "Turbulent Sixties," tell us in no uncertain terms how we ought to feel about the period in question.

Although the roots of these names are certainly distinctive, both "Victorian" and "Fabulous" also alert us to the ways in which period designations are not just temporal, but spatial. The "Victorian" experience of the British aristocracy was, of course, quite different from the Victorian experience of the British working classes. It was deeply at odds with that of the peoples violently colonized under British imperialism. The Fifties may have been "fabulous" for white, Christian, middle-class, heterosexual men in the United States. It often was not fabulous for people excluded from this privileged contingent on the basis of their race, religion, gender, ethnicity, class, or sexual orientation. These individuals faced a litany of exclusions and brutal aggressions.[10] The geography of periodization—where one might have lived through "Victorian" or "Pre-Columbian" times and thus the historiographical ramifications of having had period terms imposed from afar—perhaps should be recognized as an additional form of recolonization.[11]

Further consequences emerge as we define periods in relation to segments of time that are even shorter, such as a decade. I return to the specific ramifications of this temporal unit later in this chapter, following two broader, somewhat divergent and, in their own way, quite radical critiques of periodization that I hope inform how we think about the decade and the periodizing work that cinema does. The first, issued by Penelope Corfield in *Time and the Shape of History* presents a productive—if contentious—point of contact with the "metamodern" concerns presented in my introduction, whereas the second, grounded in Michel Serres's conception of time, prepares us for thinking about the porosity of period boundaries—the structuring thread of the third section of this book. Beyond Corfield's and Serres's critiques of periodization, their reflections on time and history also inform my analyses in the chapters that follow.

Corfield would be the last to admit an affinity between her approach and metamodernism, in part because of her detailed itemization of the faults of such terms and the epistemic claims proponents of their use seem to make. She subjects modernity and postmodernity, especially, to withering critique for their internal contradictions and inefficacy at advancing historical understanding. Her interest lies in expanding theories of historical continuity—like Ferdinand Braudel's—to admit cosmic, biological, and geological histories into the fray.[12] She argues that we ought to look at history through what she calls a "trialectical" framework that acknowledges deep structural continuities (i.e., things that persist), micro-change (i.e., the momentum of gradual shifts and evolution), and macro-change (i.e., the turbulence and upheavals of revolutions and natural catastrophes).[13] Periods, whose start dates, end dates, and names must be subject to rigorous analysis, ought to be studied through a lens that accounts for the interconnections between these three "dimensions" of time. For Corfield, doing so would reintroduce the force of continuity, something she feels has been too long neglected in historical scholarship that privileges short periods of time and significant events. This urging certainly aligns with her critique of postmodernism and claims by its philosophers of history that the past cannot be knowable or accessible in any kind of direct or unproblematic way. For her, it is and, necessarily, must be so if we are to identify and track changes across a continuum from those minor in impact to those expansive and universal in nature. Indeed, Corfield's point is that long-term processes are vital to historical understanding and within the scope of our comprehension.

This point, perhaps to her chagrin, accords with some of what Timotheus Vermeulen and Robin van den Akker attribute to metamodernism. Corfield's stance represents the increasing vocalization of a belief in historical fact, in the capacity to know something concretely, in a desire for access to truths. However, unlike the metamodernism of Vermeulen and van den Akker, Corfield's return to this rather "modern," objectivist sentiment is not tempered by a postmodern skepticism, a vital check especially insofar as it alerts us to the representational, mediated nature of history. Nevertheless, what is of particular value here beyond a healthy challenge to one's own preconceived notions about best practices in evaluating our past and its uses, is a reminder of the different shapes (linear, cyclical, end time, etc.) that history can take, as well as the interlacing of different registers of continuity and discontinuity, of persistence and upheaval. The latter is particularly important for thinking about the 1950s, a period defined *visually* as deeply discontinuous with its predecessors and successors. The fetishization of the new around color, materials, technologies, and media that sources its visual distinctiveness in popular cultural representations must be acknowledged in its own right, but also in relation to the deep historical structures that persist. And this is especially important if we are to carve out a space for films that eschew this 1950s visual signature to reflect on continuities, not as deep as the cosmic ones Corfield accounts for, but broader political, economic, and social consistencies that have escaped notice as contextualizing forces in representations of the postwar period.

Such attempts to understand periods as containers for multiple registers of change and types of complex processes are evident in Michel Serres's thinking as well. Serres reminds us that historical eras, however much defined by structuring events or certain dominant social intensities, remain "polychronic" and "multitemporal." They retain marked traces from a variety of pasts, ones that emerge and then recede again as present circumstances dictate. They draw "from the obsolete, the contemporary, and the futuristic."[14] Indeed for Serres, time itself is not to be understood as linear or chronological, as "geometrically rigid," but as a turbulent and chaotic force that percolates. He expresses a particular fondness for what he calls "the theory of percolation," and returns to its Latin roots (*colare*) to show how the French verb (*couler*) accounts for flow and filtering, and thus a process whereby some things pass while others are held at bay.[15] In historical terms, percolations rupture the boundaries that circumscribe temporally defined eras, to the point that the integrity of those borders starts to fail altogether.

This idea of percolation is richly suggestive and reveals perhaps even more than Serres intends, especially when we acknowledge both its signification of a chemical process and its application to making coffee. Arguably, the latter metaphor may prove more robust than the former and thus one worth the tedium of its unpacking. Serres appeals to the process that involves water passing through a permeable substance. To introduce additional layers of density, he invokes the irregular trajectories of river currents, specifically those of the Seine, with its turbulence, countercurrents, and multiple lines of flow, only some of which terminate in the English Channel. This potamological metaphor helps us envision, on the one hand, how the boundaries between periods—like filters—function as gate-keepers that allow some things to pass and, on the other hand, it accounts for the twists and returns that characterize the nature of time itself.[16] Coffee percolators, first invented in the nineteenth century, complicate things even further, especially as far as our understanding of periodization is concerned. They work by heating water to a boil, forcing the bubbling liquid up through a central tube and then down through a fixed basket of grounds (the sediment), and back into the source water. This newly flavored water follows the same cycle repeatedly until the coffee is ready.

So, what resonances might be gleaned from this process for comprehending time and its segmentation into periods? Let's start out somewhat clumsily and treat the coffee percolator as a decade. And, let's assume that the incomprehensibly large number of molecules of the water in the base of the percolator represents the incomprehensibly large number of personal and collective experiences, objects, and events that constitute a ten-year span.[17] This water doesn't materialize ex nihilo. It has a history and a source and bears traces of its origins. Once inside the percolator, it is forced upward by the activating force of heat and then passes down through the sediment (e.g., ground coffee) that gives it flavor. These grounds are akin to the narrative and contextualizing forces that give a period its essence. Each granule functions like a context that inflects the molecules that pass through it. Like the water, these granules, too, have a cyclical history involving the cultivation of seeds, planting, nurturing, harvesting, processing, and traveling. Moreover, coffee originates from various sources and thus carries traces of its origins deep within its genetic structure.

Unlike a river system, the percolator is a self-contained unit, one that continually processes and reprocesses its contents in a cycle of infusion. However, its contents do ultimately escape, and they do so in two distinct states. Scent diffuses into the air, and liquid is decanted into other containers and drains. Here the metaphor risks going a bit too far. So, rather than follow the biological trajectory, instead follow the criminal act of dumping some of this precious liquid down the drain. This act, just like the other digestive one, eventually requires the assistance of a water treatment facility before returning it to the water table, where it might again be accessed through municipal sources for that next pot of coffee. Admittedly, this metaphor is imperfect at points and is more adept at explaining the circulations that produce periods than how different periods relate and intersect. Nevertheless, a concrete example from the postwar era might help us see what this mode of percolation adds to Serres's geological one.

Consider the poodle skirt as one of those molecules that forms part of the lived reality of the 1950s. Its "atomic" structure might include things like fabric, dye, thread, design, labor, and so forth. It has been one of those objects activated and ultimately privileged by the dominant forces of the 1950s, for instance, the "heat" of the mass media. It has been forced to rise above other objects and has been singled out for further contextualization and narrativization. The specific cluster of grounds it passes through on the way back down does just that, imbuing it with their essence and significance. These grounds might include things like book cover illustrations, specific television episodes, gendered social practices, political discourses about teenagers, different fashion economies (e.g., dressmaker pattern covers, fashion magazine articles, store displays), and sites of youth cultural expression (e.g., diners, dances, concerts, and schools). The poodle skirt travels this route alongside other objects/molecules, too: jukeboxes, cars, films, and so forth. Indeed, some of these molecules insert themselves into the grounds, and the distinction between Fifties' objects and a Fifties' contextualizing force becomes blurred, as in the case of a particular film like *Rebel without a Cause* (1955) or *Life* magazine. Each is a privileged Fifties' object in its own right, but each also has done much to contextualize other things, practices, and experiences aligned with the 1950s.

The coffee percolator is an odd sort of contraption. I vividly remember staring at the reflections cast on its shiny chrome shell, listening to its rhythmic bubbling, and inhaling the strong scents that ultimately robbed the liquid of some of its flavor. I can see in its design the nineteenth-century forces writ small, the aesthetic trappings that made my model a paragon of 1950s design, and the quirkiness of its technology that eventually spelled its eventual obsolescence. It was very much a product of its admittedly lengthy time. And in this way, it shares much with what I've enlisted it to represent: the decade. The decade, too, is an odd sort of contraption, its peculiarities becoming more evident the longer you contemplate it; though as an object of study, it has received surprisingly scant attention.

Fred Davis's 1984 article on decade labeling and Jason Scott Smith's 1997 text on the history of the decade stand out as critical investigations into the decade in its own right. These analyses were followed by a smattering of short reflections in journalism studies, fashion studies, and sociology, but ones that rarely extend the issues raised by Davis and Smith. Davis's interest lies in why decade labeling occurs and what its implications are for collective life and memory.[18] He is concerned with how a "symbolic texture" or "symbolic profile" becomes attached with a degree of fixity to a decade, and how these in turn "help foster a people's living sense of history."[19] Davis ascribes the predilection to compartmentalize in roughly ten-year segments of time to the prevalence of decimal number systems in Western societies but explains their historical entrenchment through Proppian morphology.[20] Davis writes,

> [T]he initial popular characterization proves strangely resistant to subsequent thematic revision . . . because the psychological fixity of a decade's image inheres not only in the events and personalities peculiar to that decade but . . . in its narrative-like linkages to characterizations bestowed on decades antecedent and subsequent to it. . . . [Therefore it] is difficult to change the thematic representation of one without markedly altering the definitions of others as well.[21]

In other words, "the symbolic hegemony of the jazz age imagery" is reinforced in part by the imagery that constitutes the popular vision of the teens (dominated by World War I) that preceded it and the imagery that constitutes the popular vision of the 1930s (dominated by the Depression) that followed it—from trench to flapper to dustbowl. Likewise, one understands the "Turbulent Sixties" through characterizations of the Fifties and Seventies, resulting in the narrative arc of "social quiescence–outward rebellion–inner absorption."[22] Although Davis attributes the seeming permanence of such "symbolic hegemonies" to their position in multidecade, narrative-plot structures, he concludes with the admission that other forces also are likely at play, including the mass media.[23] I think Davis is correct in alerting us to the media's role in initially solidifying a reductive vision of a decade. However, in the chapters that follow, I argue that these same media are also responsible for complicating our conception of decade periods. In particular, I aim to show how cinema is at the heart of challenging the "fixity" of the Fifties.[24]

Smith's study is concerned with the history of the decade's emergence and its historiographical consequences. The decade, he argues, is a peculiar and decidedly American invention, one that while "representative of the practice of periodizing history," does not fit into previous linear or cyclical conceptions of time. Instead, it "represents thinking about time in a punctuated, discontinuous manner."[25] His interest lies in how a "decimal-oriented chronological marker" came to prominence over periods defined by more traditional historical events, for example, wars, dynasties, and depressions.[26] The root causes for the emergence of the decade are found in "the development of generational thinking, a widely shared sense that time itself was speeding up, and a growing preoccupation with the 'new' in American culture."[27] Much of this began with radical shifts in conceptions of time itself in the late nineteenth century. Some of it was philosophically induced by reflections on the Civil War, the fin-de-siècle, modernity, individualism, and the reorientation of nostalgia away from home as its object of longing toward a more general, recent past. Shifts in time were also technologically generated through inventions predicated on standardized time like the railroad, telegraph, and organization of labor in the factory system.

The decade was also fashioned, in part, through the narrativization of these forces in the popular writings of Walter Lippmann and Frederick Lewis Allen. Both sought to come to terms with the new quotidian realities of the 1920s and, in the process, cemented that decade as a period.[28] Indeed, for Smith, the 1920s is the first period decade, "the first decade truly to legitimate a ten-year span of time as a historic category."[29] And, thanks to Lippmann and Allen, it was the 1920s' own discursive constructions that laid the template for future decade periodization. Allen's writing, in particular, legitimized popular culture, leisure pursuits, and fashion as history and as necessary constituents of our picture of the past. But as Smith points out, this portrait of the "American mind" of the 1920s was severely limited, focusing only on the experiences of rich, white, male, northeasterners. Moreover, it emphasized discontinuities over continuities, isolating a set of events and experiences bookended, conveniently, by the Great War and the stock market crash.[30] The image of the 1920s that Allen constructed—and that still persists today—was thus profoundly exclusionary and carelessly excised from longer-term historic processes.

The decade, as an organizing principle, has gathered steam throughout the twentieth century in large part due to popular journalism.[31] So, too, have its problems: it helps obfuscate longer and more gradual developments,[32] it overemphasizes a catalog of events predisposed to media representation, and it privileges visual practices that register marked and rapid change like fashion and design. None of these things is inherently problematic in its own right. Short-term processes are worth documenting, many media-ready events deserve representation, and fashion and design have tremendous historical and social importance. The problem lies in the way decade periodization foregrounds one at the expense of the other, a critique Corfield would certainly support.

Smith also addresses the question of *why* decade periodization persists. As noted, the early twentieth century witnessed a series of world-changing events such as World War I and the stock market crash that fringed the 1920s. Each of these crises made the life that preceded them seem so fundamentally different and, therefore, made them feel so long ago. As a result, nostalgia now attached to much more recent pasts; the deep depression of the early 1930s triggered longing for the mid- or even late 1920s. As Smith points out: "Nostalgia's role in driving cultural cycles, in conjunction with a media industry that would have been inconceivable before World War I, has only grown during subsequent years, continuing to lend credence to periodizing in ten-year segments."[33] And, yet, despite the continuing cultural resonance of designations like "the '70s," "the '80s," "the '90s," and so on, historians have been quick to admit the limits of decades to encapsulate the era in question. This is why "the 1950s" often ends in 1963 with the assassination of John F. Kennedy, or the 1960s is divided into "good" and "bad" years. Oliver Gruner makes use of this rift and the dialogical relationship in his analysis of representations of "the Sixties" in cinema since the 1970s, a companion study to this one.[34]

There is another fairly common practice in relation to decade periodization that Gruner, I, and others (e.g., Mary Caputi, Daniel Marcus, and Michael Dwyer) have employed to signify a deeper complexity ingrained in this practice.[35] We all have sought to make a distinction between the 1960s and the Sixties, the 1950s and the Fifties, or between, on the one hand, an actual lived reality rife with complexity and contradiction and, on the other hand, a mediated, mythic, and often nostalgic construct. This tendency originates with Jameson's claim that postmodern nostalgia has transformed the 1950s into 1950sness and, in the process, effaced history proper by replacing it with the pastness of aesthetic styles.[36] Marcus, Caputi, and Dwyer look especially to the Reagan era to explore the mobilization and implications of this distinction and the role played by the Fifties in the rise of neoconservatism. Indeed, all three studies are incredibly important for the work they do in tracking the cultural and political formation of the Fifties through a range of media, showing the complex ways in which a seemingly oversimplified, nostalgic construct is ultimately activated to a variety of ends. Marcus offers a meticulous reading of the intersections between the cultural and political realm, often writ large in popular journalism, the uses of nostalgia across a spectrum of media, and the multiple ways in which the Fifties and Sixties were conscripted to different ends by politicians and the press. Dwyer's scope is equally vast, focusing on film and popular music, but involving a range of other cultural texts and practices to survey instances of "pop nostalgia" for the competing ideological uses to which the Fifties of the Reagan era was put. Like Marcus, Dwyer also aligns the 1950s with the decade and the Fifties with multiple fantasy ideals or myths, depending on which side of the political spectrum one might fall.

Caputi, writing from the domain of political science, makes this partisan divide explicit in how she attends to this naming practice. For those on the left, "the Fifties," often encased in scare quotes, is an invented, mythic construct. For those on the right, the numerical designation suffices. In their estimation, the "1950s" unproblematically corresponds to a purportedly real history that is knowable and, from their perspective, ideal.[37] However, Caputi does not suggest that neoconservatives are wholly mistaken in their vaunting of this period. There was something about postwar America—its political and economic successes domestically and internationally—that was easy to latch onto and celebrate. However, Reaganites exaggerated these successes, failed to acknowledge who and how many were excluded from this bounty, and then proceeded to weave them into self-aggrandizing

Cold War narratives that pitted a benevolent United States against godless communists.[38] For these reasons, "the Fifties," continue to function as a powerful cultural metaphor, one that "bristle[s] with an array of ideological connotations, a swirl of aesthetic resonances, a battery of moral implications so highly charged and emotionally laden that any mention of the decade in the current context far exceeds literal, historical references."[39]

These Reagan-era contestations over the Fifties are certainly important to acknowledge. So, too, are the ways in which the Fifties evolved through its discursive mobilizations across a political, media, and consumer landscape prior and since. Most of us are likely to admit that the 1950s, despite the rhetoric that positions it as a "kinder," "gentler," "simpler" time, are endlessly complex and constantly changing. But I think more can be said about why complexity adheres to the Fifties and what motivates its process of perpetual reconfiguration with recourse to its media representations. Starting with Davis, scholars certainly note the presence of the mass media in defining decades and the Fifties in particular. Previously I also have suggested that the distinction between the 1950s and the Fifties is reductive and often artificial for the ways in which it fails to accommodate the reciprocity and dialogical relationship between them, one sustained by the ways in which the 1950s sourced the Fifties by providing, among other things, the period's images of itself.[40] This is something reinforced by the fascinating triangulation of presidential politics, Madison Avenue, and television in relation to General Eisenhower's 1952 and 1956 presidential election campaigns as recently brought to light by David Haven Blake's dedicated archival research for *Liking Ike: Eisenhower, Advertising, and the Rise of Celebrity Politics*. The manufacture of a fairly uniform and, ultimately, mythic vision of postwar domesticity for television screens that offered a "common and coherent viewing experience" did much to "sell" the president as a desirable commodity.[41] In the process, it cemented a set of images and tropes that carried with them what it meant to be a patriotic American consumer/citizen.

Although these images continue to hold sway, these films also appear to confront periodization *itself* as well as the role of cinema and television in this process. In what appears to be a higher-level reflexivity, films not only contribute to the fracturing of the Fifties into the constituent types that structure the following chapters, but also reflect on the extent to which these types evolved cinematically and through other media representations. Especially in films produced since 2010, we start to see how references to the past become part of an intertextual grammar. These references—once used to parodic, satiric, nostalgic, or critical effect—now are used to consider how tensions between the 1950s and the Fifties reveal our current historiographical imaginary. They also bring to light views on cultural memory.

Cinema and Periodization/The Period Film

To further unpack the relationship between the Fifties and the 1950s with respect to cinema, we must venture beyond cinema to admit the vast stores of imagery and representations that either directly attend to this period or are in some kind of proximity. We ought to acknowledge the degrees to which the Fifties is foregrounded—from entire films focused on the postwar past to sweeping historical or biographical narratives that include in their scope the Fifties as a temporal slice. Such films, in turn, may be reflective, surveyed through the lens of the present, like *Forrest Gump* (1994) and Lee Daniel's *The Butler* (2013), or prognostic, like *Things to Come* (1935). We also might consider what provides the sources for these cinematic images. What informs the set design, cinematographic filters, costumes, props, architecture, and cityscapes that surround actions set in the past or a present aesthetically aligned with the Fifties? What kinds of historical records, materials, and representations were consulted? Is there a dominant visual logic that dictates the Fifties on offer, like Douglas Sirk's color palette in Todd Haynes's *Far From Heaven* (2002), or 1950s street photography in Haynes's *Carol*?

Are the consumer products that graced magazines of the period on full display, or are these eschewed to suggest something about the class inhabited by the protagonists? Do characters, sets, and narratives channel film's postwar competitor, television, through domestic sitcoms like *Father Knows Best* (1954–60) or *Leave It to Beaver* (1957–63)? Were episodes of these programs directly consulted by directors and production designers? Are memories or the subsequent parodies of these sanitized middle-class lives, which exploded across the visual cultural landscape starting in the 1970s, the driving force? Has a different national sensibility infused what ultimately is a very American construct? For example, how has the feel of a British period film infused the American Fifties in *Brooklyn* (2015)? Can the dominant source of Rockabilly even be located now that it has dispersed across advertising, photojournalism, music videos, concerts, and the personal stylistic trappings adopted by people of all ages?

These questions take us in many directions, depending on whether we follow their historical, political, material, aesthetic, or phenomenological consequences. For instance, consider the phenomenological route. A different kind of work is performed by *Life* magazine issues that nostalgically commemorate the Fifties, by window displays of vintage goods in secondhand stores, and by films that recreate the worlds of the Fifties. Each interpellates us differently. And, depending on the medium that sources the cinematic Fifties, we are likely to see a disparate range of references, inferences, and inflections at play. This is not to suggest that *Life* photographs, vintage store displays, and films don't intersect and inform each other in modulating and complex arrangements. Nevertheless, in what follows I isolate the cinematic phenomenological vector for a moment to foreground the impact of cinema on periodization. To do so, I turn to Susan Buck-Morss's claim that a cinema screen is a "prosthesis of perception." The astute observations she makes in the service of this argument help us further unpack the nature of the relationship between the 1950s and the Fifties.[42]

After recounting D. W. Griffiths's disappointment at the reality of a World War I battlefield that spurred him to recreate the French front in Hollywood for *Hearts of the World* (1918), Buck-Morss observes that "[m]odern warfare cannot be comprehended as raw experience. Like many of the realities of modernity, war needs the prosthetic organ of the cinema screen in order to be 'seen.' "[43] Other mass phenomena, like the modern city and the crowd, are equally beholden to the cinema for their existence, so much so that they are almost impossible to excise from their representations on film.[44] Buck-Morss explains that in the case of the crowd, "the screen as a cognitive organ enabled audiences not only to 'see' this new collective protagonist, but (through eidetic reduction) to 'see' the idea of the unity of the revolutionary people, the collective sovereignty of the masses, the idea of international solidarity, the idea of revolution itself."[45] This simulated entity, which gave audiences a "prosthetic experience of collective power," is, despite the montage effects that represent it to us, at heart a spatial one.[46] Cities and crowds are defined by their spatial magnitudes and the multiple vantage points that are required to convey spatial realities and intricacies.

However, if spatially mass phenomena require the cinema to be seen, perhaps an argument can be made that certain temporally "mass" phenomena— like historical periods—do, too. In other words, we could begin to adapt Buck-Morss's claims by first suggesting that the past can be visualized only as a temporal unfolding on the space of the screen. History, involving a contained space of action within which past events play out sequentially seems possible only with the aid of some kind of moving image technology.[47] From there—and depending on how it is cinematically and ideologically inflected—the Fifties, for instance, becomes virtually impossible to separate from its cinematic representations and, through its own "eidetic reductions," we "see," for example, "domestic bliss" or "domestic servitude," consumerist bounty, Cold War superiority, Jim Crow segregation, the origins of teenage culture, and so on.

Another point that Buck-Morss makes here speaks to a further dimension of cinema's role in helping to periodize the Fifties. She writes, "In the prosthetic cognition of the cinema, the difference between documentary and fiction is thus effaced. Of course we still 'know' that they are different. But they inhabit the screen as cognitive equivalents. Both the real event and the staged even are absent."[48] The real material objects of the 1950s, mediated images of the 1950s, postwar rock and roll, cinemascope filters, documentary footage, CGI cityscapes, aged stars from the 1950s, contemporary actors "period cast," and even anachronistic flourishes that percolate through the film's construct of the past, all coalesce on screen, to be reduced to their function in the service of the Fifties. And if all these things are cognitive equivalents (with the help of our fetishistic disavowal) and imbued with the same persuasive force, we must examine the effects of their dispersal and circulation beyond the cinematic screen. In fact, we often find them deployed with great effect in political circles. Leaders and candidates since the 1970s, like Ronald Reagan, have been quick to incorporate filmic lines and realities into their rhetoric. In this way, cognitive equivalents on the screen threaten to become entrenched as actual equivalents in political discourse.

Buck-Morss's argument is predicated on the realities of a particular moment in film history, on the productions of the early twentieth century that filmed their street demonstrations in certain sociopolitical contexts and that exhibited them in newly built movie houses offering conditions of (mass) reception. But like "war" or "the crowd," the cinematic manufacture of the Fifties is a process without end. Each of these entities is continually reconfigured by its re-presentation and re-definition according to various historical, imaginative, technological, and predictive forces. In this way, the cinema contributes to periodization and keeps periodization alive as a *process*. It refashions the Fifties in ways that manifest the undulating cycle of new and old images, sounds, and stories that inform our perception of the decade. Through this, the cinema builds and perpetually reforms our visual registry of the Fifties that subsequent image-makers might turn to, not just for entertainment purposes, but political, consumerist, and even historical ones too.

Dealing with how cinema periodizes the 1950s invites at least a brief foray into the world of "period films." There are certainly affinities and productive intersections, primarily due to how certain scholars have evolved our conception of the uses of cinema, but also some important differences that become starkly apparent when we attempt to import its concerns to case studies that evoke the Fifties. What they share is a deep investment in the visual and a desire to engage the past through visual means. Belén Vidal makes a compelling case for how affective histories and projections of contemporary historical imaginations are activated through the dispersal of particular "figures of meaning" (e.g., the house, the tableau, and the letter) across a range of period films released since 1990.[49] Equally pertinent is Vidal's argument that these figurations come to us through a mannerist aesthetic. She explains that "[m]annerism as a mode allows us to conceive *both* conformity and deviation within narrative films that trade on the conventional realism of period reconstruction—a realism built on intertextual (and intermedial) iterations. Historical, literary, architectural, pictorial, but also technological citations make the period film image a layered construct."[50] Likewise, many Fifties films operate according to this logic and similarly produce, in the process, a complexly layered image that mines a range of sources. However, the degrees to which and the ways in which realism and fantasy are engaged represent a point of departure. For Vidal, contemporary period films veer toward the latter whereas it is the former that seems to be making a reappearance in a good number of the films of the Fifties.

A national inflection also circumscribes the films of the Fifties as peculiarly American and period films as quintessentially British. This is not to negate the international range of these films nor their transnational appeal, both of which are meticulously calculated at various stages of production and distribution. As Claire Monk suggests, something is "*particularly* British"[51] about the period films that form an integral part of British cinema, so much so that these film are often equated with Britain's national cinema.[52] But the range of genres represented by period films, the temporal range of pasts resurrected, and the enduring interest in historic reconstruction beginning with (British) cinema's earliest years has necessitated an expansive definition of the term. For Vidal, it is an umbrella term that subsumes historical films, classic adaptations, heritage films, and costume dramas.[53] For Monk it is composed of a series of diverse subcategories that include:

feature films and television dramas; literary adaptations from contemporary novels or plays set in the past, and from older novels and plays with once-contemporary settings, including those that have accrued the status of "classics"; productions based more or less loosely on "real" historical figures or events, well-known or not; productions which claim authenticity to "fact" or the source text and those which foreground imaginative license; productions which reconstruct a distant past and those set within living memory.[54]

I cite Monk's itemization in full because much of this resonates with the diversity of Fifties offerings. Just as period films can't be reduced to the heritage cycle that took off during Thatcher's conservative Britain, the Fifties can't be reduced to the conservative nostalgic offerings that took off during Reagan's America. This forces us to acknowledge that cinematic periodization does not produce a homogeneous entity, a stable sense of the past, however reductive some of its representations might be. When cinema participates in defining a period, it does so through a complex array of different genres, degrees of reverence to a particular past, degrees of critical engagement with the history in question, and different approaches to national identity and the subjectivities that constitute a complex and forever-changing cultural matrix.

Another key difference between the decade periodization that happens in American cinema and the multiple periodizations performed through British cinema is worth considering because, in the end, it is a difference that paradoxically brings them together. Building on the work of Amy Sargeant, Monk, and Julianne Pidduck, Vidal observes a shift in the global image market economy to explain how the period film has evolved from a specifically British entity to a "fully fledged international genre."[55] This genre enjoys a transnational appeal that stems from the mobilization of a shared set iconographic conventions, shared in part due to the political and cultural reach of British colonialism. Thus, what started as an attempt to grapple with the British past, with questions of heritage, Englishness, quality, class, and so forth has extended its reach beyond national borders. Interestingly, this reach has extended to America too and to the Fifties, and what is, by contrast, an inward-looking practice. That is, Fifties films tend to look inward to national realities rather than outward to consider America's place in, and relation to, the world. It is for this reason that I devote a section in Chapter 6 to the creation of a geographically American Fifties through a

British (or internationally coproduced) lens that often imports what Vidal calls the "aesthetic texture" of certain British period films.[56]

Nostalgia is, of course, an integral part of representations of the Fifties and thus impossible to ignore in attempts to chart the evolution and uses of this construct. I have argued elsewhere that contemporary understandings of nostalgia, and especially cinematic nostalgia, are in fact contingent on their imbrication with the Fifties. I briefly state my prior argument here and request that the reader hold it in abeyance as we proceed through the case studies that follow. That said, I return in dedicated ways to the question of nostalgia in instances where we see evidence of its mutation into new forms, uses, and understandings. My prior work tracked the evolution of nostalgia across various national and disciplinary terrains, attending to its oft-neglected emergence as a cultural phenomenon in the United States in the early twentieth century and then concentrating on the social and political factors that determined the formation of its dominant American strain in the early 1970s.[57] This dominant strain, deeply invested in visual and commodity culture, nurtured at its center a privileged object—the Fifties. This object of longing became so potent that it started to inflect understandings of the experience itself, determining decades of scholarship that conflated nostalgia with the Fifties. I examined the consequences of this conflation and the origins of the forces that facilitated the emergence of the Fifties in the 1950s (e.g., shifts in the institutional structures of postwar television and consumer capitalism). I argued that cinematic nostalgia for the Fifties provided a template for other expressions of filmic nostalgia, shaping—and privileging—the *visual* contours and strategies of representations of the 1920s, 1930s, and 1940s.

I raise the issue of nostalgia in relation to the Fifties here in part to reinforce a point central to this study; Lisa Gitelman states it simply: media is "essential to periodicity." She explains that "the material forms of communication—printed texts, broadcasts, whatever—are instrumental to a sense of temporality that underwrites the present of the public sphere and by implication all of the pasts that it invents for itself."[58] This is a fairly straightforward point to be sure but one that often must be restated in the specific context that Gitelman issues it: the field of history. Indeed it seems that the contributors to several subfields of this discipline need gentle reminding that mass media—and not just concerted scholarly efforts—have an important role to play in periodizing. Media do not simply reflect the character of periods as others have defined them, but participate in a variety of complex and often critical ways in their articulation. Perhaps this is an uncomfortable truth as it wrests a degree of epistemological power away from historians. Nevertheless it bears repeating that visual mass media played a significant role in our conception of the Fifties, in mediating the relationship between the 1950s and the Fifties, in turning the 1950s into the Fifties, and in subjecting it to a process of chronic reinvention that has fractured—and will continue to fracture—our image of the Fifties. These representations remind us of our obligation to attend to the complex relationships between events and their representations, archival facts and the historiographical imaginations that filter them. They also remind us of the full range of fears and desires that impress upon the various subjectivities that necessarily experience those pasts very differently. Cinema and television provide us a special kind of (analytical) access to these pasts, in its own terms and in ways that open up for consideration the vicissitudes of history and of the present.

Conclusion: "Balham Is About as Close as You Get, in 2015, to the 1950s"

In 2015, Melissa Kite wrote a short, nostalgic lament about her inability to find the perfect house. By the end of the piece, she comes to realizes that she has "not been looking for a place in a place." Instead, she has "been looking for a place in a time. I have been house-hunting for somewhere in 1956."[59] Her vision of community, one that includes small shops, a local post office, and a culture of conversation among neighbors, is not to be found in places like the Cotswolds, which actually trade in precisely such images. Villages there, she finds, announce themselves as distinctively twenty-first century. Image industries may have done much to entrench a degree of pastness in these storied places, but the reality is one where rich Londoners abscond behind their electric gates without even the curtest of waves. Instead, this type of village existence is more likely to be found in one of the many communities that constitute London, Balham in particular.

Kite's article, however, is more than simply a tongue-in-cheek account of 1950s nostalgia. It points to a few broader elements worth considering by way of conclusion here, each of which can be accessed through the "utopian" ad she scripted:

For sale: exceptional example of an interesting, secure period set in beautiful standards of human behaviour. From the lack of aggression and impeccable manners of citizens generally to the ability of everyone to stand together in the face of adversity, this truly will be the time of your dreams. Social cohesion and moral consistency are complemented by full religious tolerance and legal rights for all, including those in the majority. Non-violent, interesting culture. Space race, Golden Age, rock'n'roll, Elvis, Hitchcock, Fellini, Liz Taylor and Marilyn Monroe complete the stunning feel. Planning permission for Kim Kardashian denied.

Of course, what is interesting about her utopian listing is the way in which it exceeds multiple borders and boundaries: spatial, geographical, national, temporal, fictional, medial, mythic, historical. The period here is one that folds and is intruded upon by various different types of objects, realities, and temporalities. It recalls Serres's and our expanded sense of percolation in its polychronicity, in its flows and filters. It alerts us to the power and limits of the decade, the appeal and repulsions of the Fifties. A clear sense of historicity infuses her ad as do the forces of nostalgia. And it primes us for thinking about Balham....

Notes

1. See Victoria Jackson, "Introduction: On Periodization and Its Discontents," in *On Periodization: Selected Essays from the English Institute*, ed. Victoria Jackson (Ann Arbor: University of Michigan Publishing, 2010), n.p. https://quod.lib.umich.edu/cgi/t/text/text-idx?c=acls;idno=heb90047.
2. See Jackson, *On Periodization*; and special issues dedicated to the topic by *New Literary History* (1970) and *Clio* (1997).
3. Bruno Latour, *We Have Never Been Modern* (Cambridge, MA: Harvard University Press, 1993), 76.
4. Donald Wesling suggests that reflexive work on periodization is "notably skimpy," in part because it is "an enabler of thinking" in several historical disciplines, providing an external—and validating—frame with "seductive force." Donald Wesling, "Michel Serres, Bruno Latour, and the Edges of Historical Periods," *Clio* 26.2 (Winter 1997): 189. Ludmilla Jordanova offers a related critique when she argues that "period terms seem to hamper fresh thinking." Ludmilla Jordanova, *History in Practice* (London: Bloomsbury, 2016), 115.
5. Robert S. Baker, "History and Periodization," *Clio* 26.2 (Winter 1997): 135.

46   FRACTURED FIFTIES

6. For instance, Ania Loomba confronts periodization in relation to race and colonialism in early modern English plays in "Periodization, Race, and Global Contact," *Journal of Medieval and Early Modern Studies* 37.3 (2007): 595–620. These byproducts also are sometimes acknowledged in projects that seek to expound major cultural or social shifts. For instance, Jonathan Crary admits in his study of the nineteenth century that his "broad temporalizing is not in the interest of a 'true history,' or of restoring to the record 'what actually happened.' The stakes are quite different: how one periodizes and where one locates ruptures or denies them are all political choices that determine the construct of the present." Jonathan Crary, *Techniques of the Observer: On Vision and Modernity in the Nineteenth Century* (Cambridge, MA: MIT Press, 1992), 7.
7. For an effective critique of "context," see Mieke Bal and Norman Bryson, "Semiotics and Art History," *Art Bulletin* 73 (June 1991): 174–208.
8. Meyer Shapiro, "Criteria of Periodization in the History of European Art," *New Literary History* 1.2 (Winter 1970): 113.
9. Jordanova, *History in Practice*, 117.
10. For a highly refined account of the "spatial" dimension of collective memory and periodizing practices, see Eviatar Zerubavel's concept of "sociomental topographies of the past." He explains: "A 'sociomental topography' implies a pronouncedly cognitive focus, and this book indeed looks at how the past is registered and organized *in our minds*. I am thus much less concerned with what Jesus, Columbus, or Nebuchadnezzar actually did than with their roles as 'figures of memory.'" Eviatar Zerubavel, *Time Maps: Collective Memory and the Social Shape of the Past* (Chicago: University of Chicago Press, 2004), 2. In other words, he is more interested in our memory of the past than in what actually transpired, a concern for this study, too.
11. The result of this, according to Wolfgang Reinhard, is that "historians from nations with a broken historical tradition are more inclined to reflect on periodization than others whose national identity has never been put to the test." Wolfgang Reinhard, "The Idea of Early Modern History," in *Companion to Historiography*, ed. Michael Bentley (London: Routledge, 2003), 283.
12. For Braudel, short-term events are "'delusive' as guides to understanding history." Braudel, paraphrased in Penelope Corfield, *Time and the Shape of History* (New Haven: Yale University Press, 2007), 32.
13. Corfield questions this balance between constancy and change and addresses the need to account for how they interconnect: "Given the force of continuity, underlying and comingling with the rival pressures of change, it can be hard to decide which is the more powerful. Which constitutes the default system: persistence or mutability? This problem recurs again and again when trying to disentangle the permanent from the evanescent, showing how closely intertwined they habitually become" (31). For Corfield, "persistence" amounts to deep continuities and structures, including climate, geography, environment, historic trackways, laws of physics, rules of mathematics, and common biological identity (41).
14. Michel Serres with Bruno Latour, *Conversations on Science, Culture, and Time*, trans. Roxanne Lapidus (Ann Arbor: University of Michigan Press, 1995), 60.
15. Ibid., 58.

16. There are, of course, many metaphors to explain time. Marshall Brown, for instance, counters the idea that time is a quiverful of arrows shot in multiple directions with a snowball that accrues detritus as it rolls on. He adds to this: "It is a boat with a wake, an eddying current, a ramifying organism, a maturing individual. All such images have elements of truth." He reflects that these concepts show us that time is, in the end, pluridimensional, thus echoing Serres. Marshall Brown, "The Din of Dawn," in Virginia Jackson, *On Periodization*, n.p.
17. One drop of water is composed of a sextillion molecules. I think the comparison is apt.
18. Fred Davis, "Decade Labeling: The Play of Collective Memory and Narrative Plot," *Symbolic Interaction* 7.1 (1984): 16.
19. Ibid., 16–18.
20. In 1928 Vladimir Propp surmised that all narratives can be reduced to a few basic structures in *Morphology of a Folktale*, rev. ed. (Austin: University of Texas Press 1968).
21. Davis, "Decade Labeling," 19.
22. Ibid., 20.
23. Ibid., 22.
24. Michael Dwyer uses "fixing" in a double sense to allude to how the Fifties, in *Back to the Future* (1985) is both repaired, and thus "made to more closely represent a vision of a bygone period that embodies particular values perceived to be absent or under threat in the present," and frozen or halted, by cutting the "historical 1950s off from the years that preceded and followed, treating the era as if it existed in a historical, cultural, and political vacuum, wholly disconnected from the social and cultural potentials of the 1940s and 1960s." Michael Dwyer, *Back to the Fifties: Nostalgia, Hollywood Film, and Popular Music of the Seventies and Eighties* (New York: Oxford University Press, 2015), 22.
25. Jason Scott Smith, "The Strange History of the Decade: Modernity, Nostalgia and the Perils of Periodization," *Journal of Social History* 32.2 (Winter 1998): 263.
26. Ibid., 263. Smith explains that whereas centuries as periods already have been subjected to criticisms similar to those aimed at other periodizing practices, the decade has received scant mention except in a few popular magazines.
27. Ibid., 265. Smith later explains that "generation" had been reimagined during the 1920s when it became a term to denote a "category of culturally shared experience" (271).
28. Ibid., 268–69. Lippmann wrote journalistically for the popular press. Allen penned the best-seller *Only Yesterday: An Informal History of the Nineteen-Twenties* in 1931.
29. Smith, "Strange History of the Decade," 269.
30. Ibid., 273.
31. See, for example, the work of Carolyn Kitsch and, in particular, "'Useful Memory' in *Time Inc.* Magazines: Summary Journalism and the Popular Construction of History," *Journalism Studies* 7.1 (2006): 94–110.
32. For Smith, these include the ascendancy of conservatism and the fate of the labor movement (Smith, "Strange History of the Decade," 277).

33. Ibid., 276. The early 1930s witnessed the first instance of decade nostalgia, with articles published in the *New York Times* that lamented the passing of "The Twenties" and, in particular, the styles of the 1920s.
34. Oliver Gruner, *Screening the Sixties: Hollywood Cinema and the Politics of Memory* (New York: Palgrave Macmillan, 2016).
35. For example, see Daniel Marcus, *Happy Days and Wonder Years: The Fifties and Sixties in Contemporary Cultural Politics* (New Brunswick, NJ: Rutgers University Press, 2004); and Dwyer, *Back to the Fifties*.
36. Fredric Jameson, *Postmodernism: Or the Cultural Logic of Late Capitalism* (Durham, NC: Duke University Press, 1991).
37. Mary Caputi, *A Kinder, Gentler America: Melancholia and the Mythical 1950s* (Minneapolis: University of Minnesota Press, 2005), 23–27.
38. Ibid., 12–18.
39. Ibid., 1.
40. For instance, I argued that "[t]hroughout the 1950s, mass media representations of everyday life were part of a remarkably intensive and astute self-mythologizing effort that continues to hold sway, even today, over impressions of the decade. As such the Fifties were in part created during—and are thus contemporaneous with—the 1950s." Christine Sprengler, *Screening Nostalgia: Populuxe Props and Technicolor Aesthetics in Contemporary American Film* (Oxford: Berghahn Books, 2009), 39.
41. David Haven Blake, *Liking Ike: Eisenhower, Advertising, and the Rise of Celebrity Politics* (New York: Oxford University Press, 2016), 9.
42. Susan Buck-Morss, "The Cinema Screen as Prosthesis of Perception: A Historical Account," in *The Senses Still: Perception and Memory as Material Culture in Modernity*, ed. Nadia Seremetakis (Boulder, CO: Westview Press, 1994), 48.
43. Ibid., 51.
44. Ibid. Buck-Morss explains that this argument is made at various junctures by Walter Benjamin in relation to crowded public spaces, by Vsevolod Pudovkin with respect to the multiple viewpoints necessary to capture the essence of a street demonstration, and by Russian philosopher Valery Podoroga in terms of how "the mass can *only* inhabit the simulated, indefinite space of the screen" (51).
45. Ibid., 52.
46. Ibid., 52–53.
47. Theater and living history demonstrations are other viable candidates, but with phenomenological differences, some made clear by Buck-Morss's consideration of the "infinite reproducibility of cinematic experience" and "audience as a massified 'one'" (55).
48. Ibid., 50.
49. Belén Vidal, *Figuring the Past: Period Film and the Mannerist Aesthetic* (Amsterdam: University of Amsterdam Press, 2012), 9–15.
50. Ibid., 32.
51. Claire Monk, "The British Heritage-Film Debate Revisited," in *British Historical Cinema*, ed. Claire Monk and Amy Sargeant (London: Routledge, 2002), 176.

52. Ibid. See also Claire Monk and Amy Sargeant, "Introduction: The Past in British Cinema," in *British Historical Cinema*, 1.
53. Vidal, *Figuring the Past,* 9.
54. Monk, "British Heritage-Film Debate," 176. In terms of the distant past vs. set within living memory, we might adapt that to say those that position the Fifties as long ago, vs. those that integrate the Fifties into a sense of the lived presence.
55. Vidal, *Figuring the Past*, 20.
56. A certain kind of "aesthetic texture" is drawn in part from the literary source materials of these films, ones that necessitate particular settings, architectural spaces, interiors, costumes, and activities central to the articulation of specific types of class experience. These templates then come to inform subsequent period films that find themselves outside of a British aristocratic or bourgeois milieu. Andrew Higson addresses this in the context of his analysis of heritage films, which, as a subset of period films, share certain aesthetic tendencies. He notes the prevalence of a "museum aesthetic" that gives way to a particular visual style, explaining that "[t]he concern for character, place, atmosphere and milieu tends to be more pronounced than dramatic, goal-directed action. Camerawork generally is fluid, artful and pictorialist, editing slow and undramatic. The use of long takes and deep focus, and long and medium shots rather than close-ups, produces a restrained aesthetic of display." Andrew Higson, "The Heritage Film and British Cinema," in *Dissolving Views: New Writing on British Cinema*, ed. Andrew Higson (London: Cassell, 1996), 233–34.
57. See Chapter 1, "Setting the Stage: The History of Nostalgia," in Sprengler, *Screening Nostalgia*.
58. Lisa Gitelman, "Ages, Epochs, Media," in Jackson, *On Periodization*, n.p.
59. Melissa Kite, "Balham Is About as Close as You Get, in 2015, to the 1950s," *The Spectator*, September 26, 2015. n.p. https://www.spectator.co.uk/2015/09/balham-is-about-as-close-as-you-get-in-2015-to-the-1950s/.

2
The Futuristic Fifties

"Remember this is 1950 and you're not in Balham!"

This instruction was issued to Maurice Elvey's "crowd players" as they prepared for their futuristic dance scene in *High Treason* (1929). According to Nerina Shute, Elvey urged them to "be more abandoned," a directive supported by costumes that "display[ed] elegantly the more, shall we say, unexploited portions of female undergarb."[1] While the dresses may well have supported the "gentle art of distributing sex appeal," the choreography hardly represented an instance of "abandon."[2] In a strategy that prefigures John Cage's elevation of silence over sound in music, these dancers privilege stillness over movement. Awkward pauses frequently interrupt a series of uninspired waltz moves, freezing dancers in place in what reads like a game of Red Light/Green Light. The orchestra that provides the soundtrack for this minimalist dance is equally minimalist in its staffing. A conductor is the sole performer who manipulates a fully mechanized set of keys, trumpets, trombones, and saxophones through two podiums featuring a smattering of knobs and switches. Though physically arranged in a neat rainbow formation behind this proto-DJ, the multiple wind instruments are superimposed over one another in a brief sequence as if to suggest their collaboration in the production of richly layered sounds. Their keys and buttons are animated by some unseen force and with a dynamism that recalls Fernand Léger's Cubist exploration of objects, momentum, and light in *Ballet Mécanique* (1923–24). The conductor then relinquishes the controls and begins gesturing in a way we would more readily expect of his position. However, doing so clears the dance floor for two women who engage each other in a fencing battle (Figure 2.1).

This is just one sequence unrelated to plot advancement that puts the future of 1950 on display in *High Treason*, a film about the narrow aversion of a second world war. Released as both a silent and sound film, it imagines

Figure 2.1 Fencing in front of an automated orchestra, *High Treason* (1929)

a world divided into two political entities—The Federated States of Europe (headquartered in London) and the Atlantic States (headquartered in New York).[3] A group of cigar-smoking weapons manufacturers hatches a scheme to spark a global conflict between these two entities by bombing the tunnel train between England and France. The Peace League, presumably established in the aftermath of World War I, does all it can to ease tensions. However, it falls to the heroic efforts of Evelyn Seymour (Benita Hume) and a group of conscripted women to prevent the bombers at the Aerodrome from taking flight. It also requires the pseudo-ethical murder of the war-bent president of the Federated States of Europe (Basil Gill) by her father, Peace League president, Dr. Stephen Seymour (Humberston Wright).

It is difficult to see *High Treason* now as anything more than a historical curiosity and visual wonder, or to hold one's critical faculties in abeyance in order to invest emotionally in the intermittent melodrama on offer.[4] Human relationships are mostly secondary here, overshadowed by the inventive forecastings of a future 1950, realized not just technologically, but socially, artistically, politically and, most remarkably, through the gestures and objects of everyday life. *High Treason*'s futurity reaches into nearly all facets of existence. There are several things the film managed to get right, if not about the

1950s, then later in the twentieth century: video calling, the Chunnel, the European Union, congested air traffic, push-button technologies, automation, electronic news tickers, the proliferation of screens, new practices in the performance of music, and creative movement strategies in dance. Certainly much thought went into constructing a detailed vision of 1950. And attending to what the filmmakers got right is necessarily a significant part of the spectatorial experience and pleasure of the film today. But, as satisfying as such an exercise is, the film should be treated as more than a prophetic spectacle. Through its richly layered evocation of the future, *High Treason* enables us to formulate a series of questions about periodization—and indeed even the role of speculation in periodizing enterprises—that can then structure subsequent analyses, including of Elvey's later film, *The Tunnel/Transatlantic Tunnel* (1935). While *The Tunnel* will constitute the bulk of my analysis in this chapter, I also briefly survey another 1950s-set film, *The Last Man on Earth* (1924), for the ways in which it marshals fine art in its rather odd articulation of the future, a strategy we see in all three films at issue here.

High Treason's futurity was met by some critics with a degree of ridicule and incredulity. Writing about the sound version—set in 1940 as opposed to the silent version's 1950 setting—Ernest Marshall writes: "Maurice Elvey does not convince anybody that the pictures he presents so admirably are likely to be a correct forecast of conditions that will prevail in such a short space of time... [*High Treason* is] so fantastic and far-fetched that there is no possibility of illusion being created in the mind of the audience to whose eyes and ears appeal is made."[5] A few positive reviews did emerge, though under special circumstances that likely had as much to do with appreciation for the film as it did the moral indignation elicited in response to the film's censorship in two states. When the film was banned for fear that it might incite crime in New York and Pennsylvania, the Roehrich Museum, at the behest of the National Board of Review, invited five hundred prominent individuals to a special screening in order to solicit their responses to the film. They found it "an intelligent, artistic and entertaining production."[6] Certainly, this broad-based reason for the ban obscures the details of the "crimes" imagined, likely ones of protest against war, government, and military powers. Indeed, the fear that prompted the bans speaks to the extent to which the film dealt with some very real preoccupations of the day, charting what *might* transpire soon, given developments already underway.

Although this ban did have an impact on profits, Elvey's film still fared considerably better than the reactionary 1928 play by Noel Pemberton-Billing on which it was based. While some of Pemberton Billing's anxieties inflected Elvey's production, the filmic version departs in many substantial ways, not least of which is its futuristic setting. In fact, *High Treason* bears a greater similarity to Fritz Lang's *Metropolis* (1927), borrowing liberally from this earlier film. For instance, shots featuring uniformly clad workers amassing or performing a perfunctory operation in unison led to *High Treason*'s moniker "The British Metropolis." While *High Treason* aimed high in terms of production, vision, distribution, and impact, it often fell short of its comparators. It also failed to secure the honor of the first British sound film. Despite Elvey's best efforts, Hitchcock completed and released *Blackmail* (1929) shortly before *High Treason* hit the theaters. This may well have been for the best, as the silent film was, and continues to be, heralded by critics as a much greater cinematic achievement than the sound version, which is incomplete.

Watching from the vantage of the twenty-first century, we are perhaps struck by how the practices, fears, desires, social changes, and nascent technologies of the 1920s become entrenched realities in *High Treason*'s 1950. According to Lucie Dutton, *High Treason* is ultimately and primarily about the Great War and the (correct) fear of another one. Moreover, the "New Woman" of the 1920s gives rise to *High Treason*'s gender parity in global political organizations, something still very much an anomaly today. Described by Christine Gledhill as a proto-feminist film for placing women at the center of the resistance and in positions of political power, it nevertheless characterizes individuals as vain and infantile.[7] Indeed it is wrought with contradictions in this regard as Evelyn is in turn weak and fierce, swooning over Michael Deane (Jameson Thomas) and then turning her unarmed faction of women against his armed regimen of soldiers. It is her resolve that stood out for audiences of the time and prompted reviewers like Shute to conclude: "In 1950 I understand that ladies are to be both fearless and fearsome."[8] This ambivalence suggests an attempt to chart how increased agency and autonomy might yield tangible results with respect to gains in power and an inability to escape the entrenched gendered assumptions and expectations of the time. It also seems to look back to the Great War as a model of women's engagement in war efforts, anticipating even more significant participation in future conflicts.

In *High Treason*, rudimentary and limited forays into television broadcasting in the mid-1920s give rise to a fully integrated system of screens for multiple communicative purposes. The inhabitants of *High Treason*'s future watch sports, access news, and regularly engage in video conferencing with one another through small screens that adorn their walls or emerge from desks with the touch of a button. The early automations developed for factories in the 1920s become domesticated and personalized in the homes and leisure spaces of *High Treason*. For Richard Koeck, architecture too has a key role to play in this regard, as the film addresses several key architectural debates of the 1920s through its futuristic London. Art director Andrew Mazzei happened to be a practicing architect and thus intimately familiar with the slew of articles in British architectural journals of the time that discussed new planning possibilities for the city and a Channel Tunnel.[9] According to Koeck, this is one of many ways in which the film did not offer a "daring forecast" of the future, but what he calls a "near future" vision grounded in actual technological developments for building, communication, and transport.[10] This near-future extended to a set of fears both answered by technology (e.g., hygiene concerns due to urban density solved by an elaborate showering setup that includes a full body drier) and exacerbated by it (e.g., new potential targets for warfare).[11]

Through these, *High Treason* reminds us of a key critique of technological determinism: inventions do not materialize ex nihilo, nor do they necessarily precipitate significant change. They often reflect already deeply held aspirations and visions. This is a critique worth considering for the work it might do in expanding our sense of what periodization ought to account for. That is, our conception of a particular period is typically a product of hindsight and, thus, a retrospective exercise, or one attuned to forcing a logical coherence on the present we find ourselves in. It tends to be bookended by perceived ruptures, events, or paradigm shifts that signal a new reality. But what might be gained if we attend to continuities or include another temporal vector that looks to the time before the period in question? What role do speculative efforts play in the construction of a later period and, perhaps more importantly, how do they exist alongside the usual retrospective representations of an era and thus as part of a larger field of images that, in this instance, form a visual registry of the 1950s? Furthermore, what is the significance of these early cinematic visions, ones produced by a still relatively new medium? How do they borrow and diverge from other image cultures from which they draw, like painting, for instance, with its own very specific set of relationships to representing history, capturing the present, and foretelling the future?

These are the questions I would like to ask of Elvey's subsequent 1950s-set film, *The Tunnel*, with a brief interlude that first considers a much earlier silent film, *The Last Man on Earth*, directed by John G. Blystone and based on John D. Swain's short story of the same name that appeared in a 1923 issue of *Munsey Magazine*. This film will allow us to think through the significance of the "near future" and the ways in which its articulation relies on forms of visual culture to suggest social developments and in a way that sets further groundwork for considering *The Tunnel*'s futurity. *The Last Man on Earth* is a ridiculous comedy suffused with gender panic that itemizes the consequences of a world without men and what happens when one lone survivor, the hermit Elmer Smith (Earle Fox), is reintegrated into this society. Its odd nature was even the subject of contemporary reviews that called it "a boisterous and frivolous fantasy."[12] The film opens with a pastoral scene of rural life, reminiscent of the John Constable's *The Hay Wain* (1821). Sunlight filters through the leaves of lush trees in a bucolic setting, rendered even more picturesque and nostalgic by the haze that encircles the frame. We see healthy livestock enjoying the fresh air and a moment of levity as a dog pulls a calf by a leash. The scene is permeated by a kind of simplicity and innocence, soon reinforced by visions of a quaint childhood. For it is within this setting that we are first introduced to an awkward 8-year old Elmer Smith (Buck Black) who pines for the young Hattie (Jean Johnston) and comes to her aid when she becomes stuck on a fence. He is kind, good-natured, a bit mischievous, but also tormented by other kids, a device that elicits our sympathy. Elmer's mother (Fay Holderness), who keeps a neat cottage, bakes, and sews, and thus exemplifies a "correct" domestic femininity, is eminently competent and confident in her assigned role. Elmer's father (Harry Dunkinson) however, is not. He fails to live up to the expectations of his position as "head of the household": he cannot chop wood and refuses to assume responsibility for his own childish behavior. He blames poor Elmer for sampling and thus ruining the cake baked by Mrs. Smith. Mr. Smith's failings and weaknesses hint at the downfall of men to come, suggesting perhaps the reason for their susceptibility to "masculitis," a dreaded disease responsible for eradicating the adult male population by 1950.

This future world is effectively a cautionary tale about what happens if the New Woman of the 1920s (clearly the target of the film) becomes the normative femininity in the absence of a corrective patriarchal masculinity. The president is a cat lady, the White House and Capitol Hill are overgrown with weeds, the stock exchange has closed, tough gals (code for lesbians) form gangs, and women have forgotten their domestic responsibilities and resort to dumping cans of beans onto a plate for dinner. There is an odd tension evident in the clothing too. On the one hand, many of these futuristic women are prone to a kind of nostalgia for masculine dress: bow ties, vests, top hats. On the other, some are overtly sexualized in this pre-Code film: low cut tops, exposed frilly underwear, extremely short skirts and shorts. One starts to wonder if the primary impetus for the film's futuristic setting was to function as an excuse for the unending parade of ostentatious underwear. Such dualities extend to behavior as well: boxing matches are organized to settle things between senators, but technologies, like cars, are feminized through the addition of flowery decorations. Some women are accomplished physicians, while others are wholly ineffective leaders. In the case of the former, success is attributed to "masculine" tendencies whereas in the latter, ineffectiveness stems directly from "feminine" traits.

Within this jumbled mix of gendered paradoxes and overwrought binaries, one overarching juxtaposition between culture and nature does emerge. Culture, clearly the domain of men here, is under threat by nature, aligned—though not always consistently—with women. In many cases, the art and architecture of classical antiquity is involved in articulating this conflict. Reference to this period is established early on with the very first intertitle that frames its text with relief statuary featuring twisting Hellenistic bodies. Variations of this frame decorate all subsequent intertitles too and offer numerous opportunities for juxtaposition between "culture" and scenes of "nature" that follow. Later, we see Neoclassical symbols of American political power (e.g., the columns of the White House and the Capitol) encroached on and subsumed by tangled vegetation; that is, nature run amok. The interiors of certain spaces are also fully adorned with classical statuary, though typically only when the women who inhabit them exhibit stereotypically masculine traits. Dr. Paula Prodwell (Marie Astaire), a logical, somewhat severe and no-nonsense scientist who managed to capture sun rays in a can, has Myron's *Discobolus* on prominent display in her office. The president, by contrast, is marked by a certain version of "feminine irrationality"; she is clumsy (trips up the stairs), disheveled, immature, overly emotional, and surrounded by an army of cats. In Congress, she quickly and sychophantically gives up her seat to Elmer. She then sits down next to him in a much lower chair, symbolically transferring her power.

But in Dr. Prodwell's space, classical antiquity also meets futuristic moderne, as her patterned walls and other décor point to an emerging Art Deco style. That we only see this latter aesthetic in the context of the doctor's office is significant. After all, this is the site that holds the promise of a rational future, one that sees the reintroduction of men. On the contrary, the Tea

House Gang's hideout, "The Chicken Coup," is a rustic and dilapidated structure deep in the woods and wholly devoid of all signifiers of modern life. The film often moves between the rural sites like this and the urban environment. At times, the characters do too, traveling in a biplane piloted by the Amelia Earhart–inspired Furlong (Pauline French). Indeed, her name too perpetuates this clash of culture and nature and, in this case, technological pasts and futures. Her name refers to the unit of measure that emerged in medieval times to suggest the length of an average plowed furrow. And yet, she flies a plane, something that would have resonated with audiences used to press coverage of Earhart's feats, including her altitude record of 14,000 feet established in 1922 and the resulting opinion pieces on women's suitability in the world of aviation. The film finally ends in the city, a stage set that features modern design and buildings that seem to anticipate the pared down aesthetic of the Bauhaus, then still in its nascent stages. It is here that we learn about the future for *Last Man on Earth* through a ticker tape parade celebrating the birth of Elmer and Hattie's aptly named twins, Romulus and Remus. Elmer and Hattie are thus reconciled at the end, as are the classical and the modern. Nature (i.e., Elmer's "natural" immunity to masculitis and procreation) may be responsible for humanity's survival, but the film ends with the architectural triumphs of modern culture.

These tensions between past and present, nature and culture, classic and modern may not always abide by their own logic (which is not a forte of this film), but they persist throughout in marked ways that harness and often depend on visual culture for their articulation. Some of this illogicality stems from the inherently unstable and deeply problematic gender binaries to which the film appeals. Other instances are perhaps a product of an attempt to define a near future world in a relatively new medium and in ways that depend quite heavily on past representational forms. After all, this is a moment before synchronous sound and thus before filmmakers could harness the myriad acoustic possibilities of cinema to indicate another time (past or future). For instance, it is the visual culture of sculpture, architecture, painting, design, and fashion that are integrated into the aesthetic and narrative fabric of *The Last Man on Earth* to constitute a near future. They register radical change (e.g., fashion) and continuities (e.g., classical sculpture). As such the film gives us insight into a certain way of periodizing that accords surprisingly well with Penelope Corfield's account of the process and into how this process was envisioned through visual means at a time before decade periodization took hold.

These concerns also arise in Maurice Elvey's *The Tunnel*. This film, too, is structured by an odd sort of tension between traditional and modern art, mobilized to articulate a near future and to suggest the possible ways in which historical continuities—ones that register gradual shifts in cultural practices and technological applications—might play out. Although Elvey refused to date the time of the film, saying vaguely that "you can best say it is 'tomorrow,'" he explains that "it is near enough in present time in which habits and customs and, above all human feelings, have not changed much from those we know and love."[13] Despite this evasiveness, *The Tunnel* offers enough concrete indications of time and its passage to establish its start in the early 1940s and focus on the final stages of the completion of its grand engineering marvel, a transatlantic tunnel, in the early 1950s.[14]

Based on the 1915 English translation of Bernhard Kellermann's 1914 novel *Der Tunnel*, the film follows the technological trials and moral tribulations of American engineer Richard (Mac) McAllen's (Richard Dix) decade-long endeavor to build a suboceanic rail route connecting the United Kingdom to the United States in an effort to secure world peace. It also foregrounds his marital woes, leading Sarah Street to suggest that Mac's relationship with his British wife, Ruth (Madge Evans), is "symbolic of the tortuous collaborative relationship between the two countries" and that the tunnel itself is "symbolic of Anglo-American cooperation both in terms of contemporary discussions about reciprocity between the film industries and in relation to the developing European crisis."[15] Although Kellermann's novel was written in response to maritime disasters, like the sinking of the *Titanic* in 1912, the various filmic versions produced during the 1930s are concerned, though in decidedly different ways, with the rise of Hitler in Germany: the 1933 German version is fully fascist in its construction of an Aryan "proto-Fuhrer," whereas Elvey's British version foregrounds the tunnel's capacity to "unite the English-speaking world" in the face of a fractured Europe and set of rising threats from the (unspecified) "East."[16]

Like *High Treason*, *The Tunnel* is eminently typical for its time, supported by what Jeffrey Richard's identifies as the two pillars of 1930s mainstream thinking: hatred of war and dedication to long-term planning.[17] This latter principle is well served by Elvey's decision to situate the narrative in the foreseeable future. The film opens in the early 1940s, which we glean from dialogue cues (e.g., chatter about the completion of the Channel tunnel in 1940) and slightly odd cultural practices. In fact, the very first shot frames an orchestra playing Beethoven, fully traditional in its sound and presentation.

This is how the English translation of the novel opens too. But whereas the novel sets its concert in a newly opened "Madison Square Place," as the camera pulls back, we realize the film situates this concert in someone's private home. Moreover, when the performance ends, Ruth claps enthusiastically. This gesture, expected and commonplace in the 1915 novel, but a clear faux pas in the film's future 1940s, is received with horrified stares. Then, with the push of a button, elaborately painted doors slide shut, concealing the musicians. This room and the adjoining one provide the setting for the first twelve minutes of the film and the camera cuts between these two spaces with some regularity. In the second room, the background is dominated by a curious image that reads as a tapestry featuring a unicorn and a stag, a throwback to a medieval visual culture. However, this tapestry is not at all traditional but involves modern geometric forms, ones that appear to mimic a map, aligning the stag with the United States and the unicorn with Europe. These modernizations of traditional art forms, and their peculiar modes of consumption in the case of the Beethoven performance, alert us to a future world where things have changed . . . somewhat.

New technologies are also revealed as markers of the future in a series of novel ways. Some are subtly integrated, as when Mac presses a button to illuminate the planned trajectory of his tunnel on a large half globe that sits atop a mantel. Others are revealed with a degree of cinematographic fanfare. The "ultrawave and [worldwide] television broadcasting system" is first introduced by a close-up of a loudspeaker. As the camera slowly tilts down, it reveals an enormous television screen, certainly a significant technological advance over what was then, in 1935, possible but still very rudimentary and anomalous (Figure 2.2). Video calling—between homes, homes and aircraft, homes and subterranean train cars—is featured with increasing regularity as the film progresses through its ten-year stretch. These "televisors" appear in virtually every room of every house and, in one case, two of them hang alongside small framed paintings on an office wall, forming a rather odd but analytically productive juxtaposition between two distinct but interrelated forms of visual representation. All images here are framed, arranged together in a salon-style formation and thus draw attention to their own representational status, eschewing the differences in each mode's relation to the reality it purports to convey. That is, this scene establishes an equivalency between the painted portraiture and the "portraits" of the callers seen on the televisors, suggesting perhaps, something of an evolution of forms.

Figure 2.2 Giant "televisor" broadcasting to the city, *The Tunnel* (1935)

Cultural forms, communications devices, and transportation vehicles are objects of attention in terms of defining the future. Various examples from each of these categories are aesthetically and technologically evolved, which often means automated and complicated by new layers of function. Unsurprisingly, vehicles are privileged and offered up in several forms: cars are super-streamlined, like the actual 1933 Tatra used in several scenes; wheelchairs are motorized; airplanes, encountered only in toy form, are not yet aerodynamic, but are remote controlled. However, Mac's helicopter/gyrocopter is aerodynamic to a degree, and thus looks nothing like the nascent helicopters of the 1930s. The individual train car is perhaps the most fully futurized object in the film, not in terms of aesthetics, for trains themselves were already highly streamlined by the mid-1930s, but in terms of its structural reconfiguration. Here the train car is individualized, the size of a large automobile. It is automated, driverless, and runs on what we imagine to be the electrified tracks of the tunnel at high speeds. As such, this future effectively collapses two transport technologies into one. The train, long a symbol of progress implicated in social and political ideologies of expansion, colonialism, trade, leisure, and development, becomes personal here and unhinged (literally) from its mass incarnation. In this way, it remains very much entrenched in the film's program of entwining old and new in technological, operational, and aesthetic ways.

Scenes involving the construction of the tunnel also register this entanglement of past and present. Although the tunnel walls, tracks, spectacularly sophisticated radium drill, and command center boasting multiple screens and control panels certainly speak to the future, images of work harken back to earlier forms of backbreaking labor, drawing on well-known visual traditions of painting. Mac may occasionally don what looks like an astronaut helmet to protect him from heat and mysterious vapors that cause "tunnel blindness," but laborers are typically seen shirtless, sweating, dirty, and with tattered hats and trousers. Images of work performed by exhausted older men using pick-axes and other surprisingly rudimentary tools to accomplish such a sophisticated engineering feat take place in an environment defined by danger and discomfort. Oppressive steam and darkness permeate this subterranean space that claims many lives. The film tallies the thousands lost to disease and accident, including Mac's own son. Depictions of the physical mechanics of work in this environment draws on the iconography and, by extension, critical thrust of nineteenth-century Realism, like Gustave Courbet's 1849 *The Stonebreakers*. In this painting, as in *The Tunnel*, hard labor remains inescapable in the pursuit of "modern" advances in transportation (e.g., roads in the painting; tracks in the film) despite the promise of new technologies to ease the plight of the exploited working classes. Again, past and present intermingle here, and they do so through appeals to former practices of visual representation.

Doing so reinforces a kind of developmental trajectory of invention, innovation, and adaptation. In other words, it articulates forms of continuity. Continuity between technologies, between technology and its cultural and social uses. In the realm of transportation, this meant both connecting people and disconnecting them in fairly immediate ways. While the tunnel promised to connect nations, the helicopter always seemed responsible for distancing Mac from his family, taking him away from his home. And so too does the televisor. In other words, the film sought to both uphold the wonder of new technologies and chart their effects on bodies and social relations, ones grounded in certain 1930s realities as well as imagined 1950s ones. It considered how cultural forms from music to art, from maps to telephones, might not just be aesthetically reconfigured but explored in terms of their impact on people. Thus, like *High Treason*, *The Tunnel* offers us an opportunity to consider how a near future and series of incremental cultural and technological shifts grow out of the preoccupations of a time just prior. Both films remind us that fears and desires articulated through prognostications in film, literature, and art also have value in shaping understandings of an era, and not just the canonical objects and events that have been retrospectively heralded as symbolic of it, objects and images that often only fetishize "newness."

I think the Fifties, especially, would benefit from this more expansive—and admittedly experimental—approach. It would also enable us to consider some challenges to periodizing practices and thinking, and the ways in which these align with that odd unit of time, the decade. Decade periodization, as discussed in the previous chapter, is a curious twentieth-century phenomenon, a process that values rupture over continuity, according to Jason Scott Smith and Fred Davis. While Smith is interested in the emergence of this peculiar and decidedly American invention during the 1920s, Davis is concerned with the entrenchment of a decade's character by the narrative arcs foisted upon it, stories that tell of how the "roaring twenties," for example are discursively constructed in opposition to the war years that preceded it and the depression that followed.[18] Such emphasis on discontinuity, however, fails to account not just for important continuities but also for process, development, and evolution as well as returns, reclamations, and resistances that mark the character of any period. It is in this respect that Corfield's interest in continuities and Serres's concept of time as something that percolates introduce some necessary complications. The multitemporality of historical eras—ones marked by myriad pasts, contemporary concerns, and even speculations of futures to come—ought to be acknowledged, according to Serres, in order to challenge the reductive conceptions of decade identities, for example, that have come to dominate the popular imagination.[19]

In their own way, *High Treason*, *The Last Man on Earth*, and *The Tunnel* each enable us to think through forms of continuity and visions of futurity and perhaps even to see how exercises in speculation can contribute to period constructions. They register some of the ways in which the concerns and desires of the late 1920s and mid-1930s might, with the aid of technological advancements, shape the near future, from its look to its cultural practices, social relationships, and political alliances. On another level, they also register shifts in decadal thinking itself. *The Last Man on Earth* and *High Treason* were released at a time of the decade's own formation and entrenchment, thanks to the popular writing of Walter Lippmann and Frederick Lewis Allen. Both these films carefully root their near futures in the foundations of the films' presents: socially, technologically, and aesthetically. *The Tunnel*, however, seems itself to be structured by a more pronounced decade logic, produced at a time when decade-thinking would have already been exported overseas. The Chunnel is invented in 1940, the start of a new decade, while the Transatlantic Tunnel, a 10-year project, is completed sometime in the early 1950s, presumably starting yet another new era of "world peace."

As such, we might venture a claim that there are multiple temporal vantage points from which period identities are crafted and that we should do more than simply reflect on the years contained by the designation in question. Understanding the complexities of a decade, for instance, would benefit from a consideration of its retrospective, contemporary, and prospective constructions as well as how its identity is variously and continuously reconfigured. Fictions, realities, and fantasies all have their own roles to play in shaping impressions of a period and should all be considered. For instance, if we wish to grasp the 1950s as a historical period, we should consider what of its own past this era conserved, invented, foregrounded, and mythologized. Moreover, we should also consider the ways in which the decades prior to the 1950s imagined their near future to see how and why certain forces and investments persisted, becoming embedded in the social and aesthetic fabric of that decade's identity.[20] We ought to acknowledge that however more significant a hand the lenses of the 1970s, 1980s, 1990s, and 2000s have had in constructing our perception of the 1950s, we likely owe certain elements to the forecasting efforts of the 1920s and 1930s too. Indeed, these earlier representations of the 1950s now coexist with the latter ones, each contributing to our "picture" of the postwar period.

To reiterate, this is not to suggest that the films in question here have anything near the periodizing force of the retrospective constructions that followed the 1950s. Nevertheless, they remain part of a visualization of the postwar period and can assist in formulating questions about periodization itself, ones that might complicate thinking about the machinations of this process when we turn to its more conventional operations in the chapters that follow. For instance, these earlier films showcase the ways in which cinema plays a key role in articulating visions of the future not only by imagining how things may look but also by identifying which objects will be marshalled in the effort to register change. That is, they define a cache of privileged objects capable of clearly indicating stylistic evolution or technological innovation. Films like *The Last Man on Earth*, *High Treason*, and *The Tunnel* certainly helped entrench a collection of reliable visual indices of change: hair styles, clothing, vehicles, art, and architecture. In a much broader sense, this serves as an effective reminder of the fairly obvious importance of production design in communicating to audiences the experience of another time, future or past. While a future (or past) aesthetic is necessarily imbricated with the social and political uses of the object tasked with signaling this other time, the larger point is, again, the significance of the visual and the increasing reliance on certain types of objects to remove us from the film's present. This is a structuring assumption for what follows as well. Indeed I hope to retain this focus on the visual throughout this book and track the ways in which the initial and somewhat tentative interventions into periodization itself become increasingly complex as we begin to foreground twenty-first century representations of the 1950s.

Notes

1. Nerina Shute, "Ungentle Women of 1950," *The Film Weekly*, June 3, 1929, p. 5.
2. Ibid., 5.
3. Curiously, the silent version is set in 1950 and the sound version is set in 1940. The sound version, once thought lost, is currently incomplete and therefore the following analysis references the silent version.
4. For film critic Ernest Marshall, "[t]his story is really such a farrago of nonsense that one is sorry Maurice Elvey could not find better material to his expert hand." Marshall, "The Pros and Cons of Two British Talking Films," *New York Times*, August 25, 1929. https://www.nytimes.com/1929/08/25/archives/london-film-notes-the-pros-and-cons-of-two-british-talking-films.html.
5. Ibid.
6. "National Board Attacks State Censored Action," *National Board of Review Magazine* 5.4 (April 1930). https://nationalboardofreview.org/award-years/1930/.
7. Christine Gledhill, "An Ephemeral History: Women and British Cinema Culture in the Silent Era," in *Researching Women in Silent Cinema: New Findings and Perspectives*, ed., Monica Dall'Asta, Victoria Duckett, and Lucia Tralli (Bologna: University of Bologna Press, 2013), 142.
8. Shute, "Ungentle Women," 5.
9. Richard Koeck, "Modern Life in High Treason: Visual and Narrative Analysis of a Near-Future Cinematic City," in *Cities in Transition: The Moving Image and the Modern Metropolis*, ed. Andrew Webber and Emma Wilson (London: Wallflower, 2008).
10. Ibid., 73.
11. Ibid., 81.
12. Mordaunt Hall, "A Boisterous Fantasy," *New York Times*, December 13, 1924. https://www.nytimes.com/1924/12/13/archives/the-screen-a-boisterous-fantasy.html.
13. John T. Soister and Henry Nicolella, *Down from the Attic: Rare Thrillers of the Silent Era through the 1950s* (Jefferson, NC: McFarland, 2016), 16.
14. That said, there is one curious marker of futurity absent: clothing and hair. However, as Soister and Nicolella astutely surmised, this may have had to do with the ridicule Elvey faced for what was considered too outlandish in terms of fashion in *High Treason*. Ibid., 17.
15. Sarah Street, *Transatlantic Crossings: British Feature Films in the United States* (London: Continuum, 2002), 77.

16. Jeffrey Richards, "*Things to Come* and Science Fiction in the 1930s," in *British Science Fiction Cinema*, ed. I.Q. Hunter (London: Routledge, 1999), 24.
17. Ibid., 19.
18. Ibid., 20.
19. Michel Serres with Bruno Latour, *Conversations on Science, Culture, and Time*, trans. Roxanne Lapidus (Ann Arbor: University of Michigan Press, 1995), 60.
20. To reinforce this point further, I'm making a distinction here between the way in which the past persists in the present and the way in which past imaginings of the future persist in the present they imagined. It is a slight, but important difference, a difference in temporal orientation. In one case, it is about how the present carries things forward from the past. In the other, it is how the imagined future of the past is borne out in a new or subsequent present.

PART II
FOUNDATIONAL FRACTURES

3
The Leave It to Beaver Fifties

In his history of Levittown, David Kushner opens with an anecdote from a conference reflecting on "Suburbia at Sixty." One presenter showed four slides: a black-and-white photo offering an aerial view of a generic suburban development; a black-and-white photo from the 1950s of a white nuclear family standing in front of their new home; a promotional photo from *Leave It to Beaver* (1957–63), and a recent photo of a McMansion, situated in a new twenty-first-century suburb. The speaker queried the audience about which photo didn't belong and their unanimous answer was the McMansion. Somewhat hesitantly, the presenter challenged the consensus by explaining that it really ought to be the *Leave It to Beaver* image, given its fictional status. However, as Kushner suggests, with a conference designed to look back on sixty years of suburban development and, specifically, Levittown, "the audience couldn't help but blur the line" between reality and representation.[1] The suburbs—and Levittown especially—is as much a physical place as a mediated one.

In fact, I first thought to title this chapter, "The Levittownesque Fifties," a cumbersome nomenclature, but one that nevertheless could allude to the troubling histories and myths that remain associated with this vision of suburban life. Levittown, named after William Levitt, describes a series of sprawling neighborhoods first built in 1947 to provide (exclusively white) World War II veterans with detached homes outside urban centers. This was the quintessential site of suburban domestic life and all that entailed for commuting husbands, stay-at-home wives, and their children. I then thought "The Suburban Fifties" might be a more encompassing term and one with the potential to indicate its postwar constructions of whiteness in subdivisions beyond Levittown. However, it failed to reflect one key aspect of this type of Fifties, namely, the extent to which a particular image of suburban life was also shaped and reinforced by media. As such, I opted for "The Leave It to Beaver Fifties." This term not only locates its origins in television and, specifically, the domestic sitcom, but continues to circulate in political circuits

Fractured Fifties. Christine Sprengler, Oxford University Press. © Oxford University Press 2023.
DOI: 10.1093/oso/9780190067342.003.0004

in ways that acknowledge its prevalence in discourses surrounding race and patriarchy.

Network television became the primary incubator of a vision of white, Christian, patriarchal domesticity that seemed far removed from urban and geopolitical realities through shows like *Leave It to Beaver*, *Father Knows Best* (1954–60), *The Donna Reed Show* (1958–66), and others.[2] Of course, it wasn't. However inward they looked, these images of family life remained deeply implicated in broader political ideologies, narratives of nationalism, and anxieties around demographic shifts. For instance, Levittown and other suburban neighborhoods were imbricated as much in civil rights struggles as they were Cold War politics, not to mention the nexus between the two. Bill Levitt, a staunch anticommunist and segregationist, saw his work building suburbs as deeply political and stated: "No man who owns his own home and lot can be a Communist. He has too much to do."[3] In fact, while several domestic sitcoms defined and circulated (though syndication) this construct of postwar suburban domestic life, "Leave It to Beaver" has become a reliable shorthand. It invokes this vision of family life in the 1950s, both for those who idealized its power structures and relations and for those who sought to critique its internal oppressions and external exclusions. And it continues to do so. A *New York Times* headline about the 2016 presidential election that reads, "Voters Who Long for Leave It to Beaver," confirms its twenty-first-century resurgence. The term reappeared again during the 2020 election with Trump's appeal to "suburban voters."[4] More recently, a 2021 *Salon* headline, "The new GOP 'Southern Strategy': Civil War or Leave It to Beaver?" is appended with a byline that renders explicit the white supremacy at the heart of this construct: "How long will it take Republicans to call racism by its name?"[5]

This chapter will begin with a brief survey of a few late 1990s and early 2000s films and then focus on twenty-first-century releases, *Revolutionary Road* (2008) and *Suburbicon* (2017). I conclude by looking beyond cinema to television, with an examination of *Them* (2021). While all three generate suburban realms as constructs to critically dissect, they do so to different ends: *Revolutionary Road* deals with the disenchantments of strictly defined gender roles while the latter two engage with the integration of neighborhoods. However, all deal as much with certain postwar realities—and ostensibly so—as they do with the mediated constructions of Fifties suburban living: their tropes and the structuring sensibilities through which these tropes are cinematically offered up to us. In other words, *Revolutionary*

Road, *Suburbicon*, and *Them* seem to engage as readily with postwar suburbia as they do with their predecessors' framing of this construct (and horror genres more broadly in the case of *Them*), whether unreflexively nostalgic or irreverently postmodern.

Blast from the Past (1999), a film suffused with certain postmodern intertextual tendencies, is centered on the suburban home's meaning, destruction, and replication. However, while parody and irony abound, it is not an exercise in *critical* postmodern deconstruction. It opens with a cocktail party hosted at the height of the Cuban missile crisis by Calvin (Christopher Walken) and Helen (Sissy Spacek), who is nine months pregnant. News reports of escalating nuclear tensions spark fear in Calvin, who drags Helen into their fallout shelter. As they enter, a wayward jet crashes into their house, wrongly convincing them that an attack has occurred. They set the locks for thirty-five years. Their shelter is not only fully stocked but also a precise replica of their home on the surface, and thus provides, in outward appearance anyway, a bastion of domestic comforts and a protected oasis in which to raise their son. For Andrea Vesentini, the film's representation of the fallout shelter accords with how cinema showcased such shelters as spaces of "retreat from upsetting historical processes in which the present could be brought to a standstill and preserved from complete annihilation." They were "mirror spaces" of suburban homes, "domestic utopias" immune from "dangerous" social forces or, in other words, progressive movements that were feared as challenges to heterosexual white male privilege.[6]

Calvin's first foray into the 1990s confirms this. Upon leaving his "domestic utopia," one in which he and Helen reproduce in their son all the virtues of patience, respect, education, good manners, and graces, he encounters a character who embodies several 1960s social movements at once: a Black sex worker who offers "If you want a boy, I can be a boy. If you want a girl, I can be a girl." Calvin describes this person as a "mutant" and part of a landscape of degeneracy, crime, and countless other moral failings. This is just the beginning of the film's deeply problematic representations of race, gender, and sexuality. By the end, when Calvin and Helen finally return to the surface, they are whisked to the countryside where their son has recreated their original home. Like their fallout shelter, it is a perfect simulation of their early 1960s dwelling, one that permits them to remain in the past. As such they enact not only a geographical kind of "white flight," but a temporal one as well.

In *Pleasantville* (1998), the suburban home is a 1950s domestic sitcom construct and not, for the most part, an object of longing. Home as a site of comfort and plenty is parodied through an overabundance of chintz, knickknacks, décor, and breakfasts that could feed a crowd. It is a space whose (mock) sanctity requires protection: a conversation between father and son about dating cannot take place inside its walls. Consciousness—of sex and of gender inequality—bring all this crashing down. This is signaled most forcefully by the distinctly cinematic clap of thunder that follows the father's cheery refrain "Hi honey, I'm home!" and the burning tree that erupts with the mother's first orgasm, a conflagration that threatens to engulf the entire house.

Far from Heaven (2002) similarly deconstructs a mythologized construct of home. Initially a picture-perfect suburban dwelling and site of familiar routine, its underbelly is revealed through Sirkian stylistic maneuvers that foretell its unraveling. Increasingly violent clashes of complementary color signal growing unease while its design perfection signifies its unhomeliness. It is a stage set, a function made clear by the photo session that captures Cathy's (Julianne Moore) artificial poses in what we are prompted to read as an artificial environment. She and her home are little more than images for the consumption of others in a desire economy. In this way, *Pleasantville* and *Far from Heaven* perform that quintessential postmodern function of deconstructing representations of home, showcasing the suffocating effects of oppressive patriarchal structures. In each case, these late postmodern nostalgia films offer highly mediated constructs of home that play reflexively with the signifying elements that constitute them, the ideological discourses in which they have been activated, and the mythic images of postwar America at whose service they have been mobilized.

More recent critiques of suburban domesticity can also be found in "quality" television, specifically *Madmen* (2007–15) and *The Marvelous Mrs. Maisel* (2017–). Both begin their series in the late 1950s, oscillate between the city (New York) and its suburbs, and gradually, as the seasons pass, take us into the 1960s to document radical social transformations. For instance, shifts in conceptions of gender and work are structuring concerns in both, sexuality receives minor cursory attention, and race, insufficiently acknowledged in *Mad Men*, does play a larger role in the *Marvelous Mrs. Maisel*. The suburbs are represented by Betty and Don Draper's (January Jones and Jon Hamm) Ossining home and Midge Maisel's (Rachel Brosnahan) in-laws, Shirley and Moishe Maisel's (Kevin Pollak and Caroline Aaron) Queens home. While the Maisels' abode is a bit grander, both exceed the quintessential Levittown-style bungalow; they are large symmetrically Colonial

Georgian estates, with decorative columns flanking a front door, perched slightly above a tree-lined street.

This home functions as the quintessentially suffocating prison for Betty as it does for Midge and her parents, Rose and Abe Weissman (Marin Hinkle and Tony Shalhoub), as they are forced to vacate their upper West Side apartment. It is clear that while the aspirational but rather coarser Maisels are enamored with their home and all it represents, the urbane Weissmans and their daughter are driven mad by their stay in suburbia.[7] Although much of this plays out in comedic terms, as Lawrence J. Siskind suggests, through an exaggeration of "the gap between these two Hebraic varietals," Germanic Jews and Eastern European Jews, it positions the true "home," and the feelings home is ideally supposed to engender, as an urban apartment. Their feelings for this space are authentic, they are deeply upset when required to leave it, and Midge, at the end of season 3, spends an emotional moment back in her apartment as she is about to reacquire it. By positioning the urban in contrast to the suburban, both series account for the failures of the latter to live up to expectation as promised through discourses on the American Dream. The *reasons* for these failures, suggested in *Mad Men* and *The Marvelous Mrs. Maisel*, are more fully explored in a number films focused on postwar suburbia, including *Revolutionary Road*.

Based on Richard Yates's 1961 novel of the same name, Sam Mendes's *Revolutionary Road* presents a vision of suburban life in 1955 at odds with those conjured by domestic sitcoms of the postwar era and subsequent nostalgic constructs of white, patriarchal, heteronormative bliss. The couple at the center of this world, the Wheelers—April (Kate Winslet) and Frank (Leonardo DiCaprio)—are "special." But what makes them special in their own estimation is often opposed to what makes them special in the eyes of others. They attribute their distinctiveness to a refusal to conform to 1950s expectations; Frank is perceptive enough to acknowledge his white-collar city job as a sham and both he and April plan to leave their monotonous middle-class existence behind for a more unrestricted life in Paris. Their friends, coworkers, and neighbors, however, attribute the Wheeler's superiority to their ability to embody the image of postwar suburban success: Frank's job in the city, a meticulously kept house in the suburbs, a gray suit for him, a fully put together ensemble for her, two children, trips to the beach, dinner parties with friends, and the training to know when to utter the right rote phrase with precisely the right artificial inflection. In other words, they've mastered how to inhabit a Leave It to Beaver vision of white middle-class perfection. Yet, their "reality," one that reflects the postwar "underbelly" well-known since the 1950s itself through the Beat Generation in literature, Sirkian melodrama in cinema, Sloan Wilson's *The Man in the Gray Flannel Suit*, and Betty Friedan's *The Feminine Mystique* in popular treatises, is what fuels the narrative and drama in the film.

Fights between April and Frank dominate *Revolutionary Road*, screaming matches with raw, unrestrained emotion that lead Eleonora Ravizzo to classify it as a type of melodrama.[8] Both April and Frank are scarred in their own ways and encounter failures, tragedy, depression, and feelings of insufficiency and self-doubt. They think of themselves as above needing to conform to social expectations, yet both are hindered by their failure to live up to them—from April's failure as an actress to Frank's (initial) failings as a salesperson to their unfulfilling affairs, contempt for each other, and the monotony of their lives. It all ends with April's death, following a botched abortion in a last-ditched effort to resurrect their abandoned Paris dream, one dealt a double blow by Frank's promotion (an alibi for his cowardice) and April's pregnancy. In many ways the film—and novel—are a catalog of the disappointments faced by a suburban life predicated on strictly defined gender roles.

This "underbelly" of a Leave It to Beaver suburbia is a well-worn trope and has been since the 1950s. Often touted as the "reality" obfuscated by Technicolor visions of the decade, filmmakers like Mendes have made much of avoiding a certain aesthetics of nostalgia for something ostensibly more authentic. However, there are several problems with this approach. First, this is simply the obverse of a limited nostalgic vision of the period. As such, it excludes the vast complexity and extent of the "underbelly," addressing only in oppositional terms the experiences and subjectivities that constitute the corporate and televisually manufactured Leave It to Beaver realm. As such, there is no acknowledgment of experiences outside a white heteronormative existence. The experiences of people of color and same-sex couples are completely erased from this world. Some commentators have defended such exclusions in subsequent cinematic representations as reflective of the actual historical exclusions perpetrated by a deeply racist and segregated society. For instance, Pablo Gómez Muñoz notes the ways in which Terence Malick represents people of color and other marginalized individuals in *The Tree of Life* (2011) as "nearly invisible," appearing and disappearing abruptly without ever uttering a single line. This is Mendes's approach as well. Fleeting glimpses of a single person of color at a party in the village or walking among the mass of commuters at Grand Central station constitute the extent of racial diversity in the film. While for Muñoz, this can be read as an editing practice that "plays on the invisibility of certain groups by highlighting the 1950s suburban discrimination in visual terms," it is insufficient in both films and, in *Revolutionary Road*, represents an unwillingness to confront the privileges enjoyed by the Wheelers precisely because of their whiteness.[9]

Indeed, the novel even provides a few opportunities to acknowledge racialized identities and constructions of whiteness, opportunities that could have been harnessed to further complicate the ways in which Mendes mobilizes a contemporary consciousness—as he does with respect to gender—to frame his engagement with the past. Yates often describes his protagonists' skin and accounts for Frank's office and colleagues as "a great silent insectarium displaying hundreds of tiny pink men in white shirts, forever shifting papers and frowning into telephones, acting out their passionate little dumb show under the supreme indifference of the rolling spring clouds."[10] Yates also introduces one Black couple in a scene omitted by the scriptwriter, Justin Haythe. When Mrs. Givings visits her institutionalized son, John, at Greenacres, Yates observes "[a] t the table nearest the door a young Negro couple sat holding hands, and it wasn't easy to identify the man as a patient until you noticed that his other hand was holding the chromium leg of the table in a yellow-knuckled grip of desperation, as if it were the rail of a heaving ship."[11] Although this one and only acknowledgment of race positions the Black husband as having a mental illness, questions are immediately raised as to whether this is actually the case. He is not readily identifiable as "the patient," according to Yates, and his peer at Greenacres, John, is the only character with insight into—and willing to speak—the truth of postwar discontentment. John's mother, Helen Givings, is his antithesis (and antagonist) in many respects and it is she who utters the only (disparaging words) that acknowledge class, not the middle-classness of the Wheelers, but rather the working-classness of those who inhabit the street before theirs, whose presence confirms the superiority of the homes and families on Revolutionary Road. She dismisses these smaller houses as "these little cinder-blocky, pickup-trucky places—plumbers, carpenters, little local people of that sort." These missed opportunities mean that the film ends up conforming to the whiteness of the Technicolor version of the Leave It to Beaver Fifties. It fails to show what it means for Frank to be one of those hundreds of "pink faces" doing nothing of substance for a good salary and therefore able to afford to move out of the city as part of the white flight to the suburbs *because* of the labor performed by and continued marginalization of people of color and the working classes.

A second issue with Mendes's justification for supplanting a Technicolor vision of the 1950s with his more muted palette involves Yates's desire to evoke precisely this kind of artificial world for the Wheelers to rebel against. The very first pages of the novel describe the chromatic vibrancy of the suburbs and the objects that populate it: automobiles are "unnecessarily wide and gleaming in the colors of candy and ice cream" and these cars were finally were able to "relax" in the suburbs where they fit in to the "long bright valley of colored plastic and plate glass and stainless steel."[12] These brightly colored objects are emblems of the consumerism that trapped April and Frank. The color, design, and materials, touted in the advertising and television of the 1950s as symbolic of progress, futurity, and happiness, invest these objects with much signifying potential in this regard. However, the film eschews this, replacing the cars Yates envisioned with ones in muted tones with decidedly less chrome. Likewise, the Wheeler's house in the film boasts a "country kitchen" feel which, while fairly popular in postwar interior design, permitted Mendes to avoid the colorful plastic housewares and rainbow of appliance hues that dominates the image of middle-class suburban domestic life (Figure 3.1). What is more, even in pine-clad country kitchens, the Formica and appliances often provided dashes of the "colors of candy and ice cream," which is not the case for the Wheelers. While Maureen Grube's (Zoe Kazan) apartment echoes the Wheeler house in terms of décor, styles, and color, the Campbell's house offers an interesting contrast. It makes use of a version of the film's palette, but the look is much darker and decidedly

Figure 3.1 Country kitchen in *Revolutionary Road* (2008)

less modern. Country kitchen pine is replaced by dark brown oak, "clean" lines and solid colors are replaced by patterned rugs, chintz wallpaper, and busy upholstery. The house is messier, more disorganized and reads as more "authentic."

Mendes and scriptwriter Justin Haythe address their decision to eschew a Technicolor look and base *Revolutionary Road* on "source material of the period."[13] Specifically, Mendes explained that he "didn't want to base the look of this movie on other movies from or about the 1950s."[14] They also did not look at paintings, presumably the types of Edward Hopper canvases that have inspired a good deal of cinematic representations of the postwar period. Instead, they turned to documentaries and photographs, specifically those by Saul Leiter, a source of inspiration for Todd Haynes's *Carol* (2015), as we shall discuss in Chapter 6. For instance, Mendes and cinematographer Roger Deakins not only screened documentaries of the time, but even restaged some of their scenes: the establishing shot of the Wheeler house and one foregrounding Frank's car's side mirror to show him approaching his vehicle (Figure 3.2). Likewise, certain photographs by Saul Leiter were cinematically recreated, specifically the masses of commuters in their gray flannel suits or Frank leaning on the railing of the concourse level of Grand Central Station, surveying the crowds below him. The unstated assumption here is that Mendes aimed to eschew an inauthentic mediated vision of the postwar era in favor of a more authentic one, failing to acknowledge the equally constructed nature of his source material.

Figure 3.2 Frank (Leonardo DiCaprio) approaching his car in *Revolutionary Road* (2008)

Mendes and his crew did more than base shots on these documentary sources, they also recreated the aesthetic template of Saul Leiter's images. His street photography thus both provided a framework for staging scenes on New York's streets and train stations and also supplied the film's color palette, its distinctively non-Technicolor aesthetic. Leiter's color photographs—long an unacknowledged part of his oeuvre—sourced the film's subdued look, one heavily reliant on beiges, pale blues, soft greens, and shades of cream. While variations in lighting modulate these hues, this palette applies to the entire film, to a range of spaces from streets to homes, bars, and the beach. As such, Mendes (and Deakin) achieve an affective flourish through color just as manufactured as the supposedly inauthentic Technicolor aesthetic they seek to supplant and challenge. Put another way, this color scheme, tasked with helping reveal the "truths" of postwar suburban life, is problematic, for Mendes's vision of the 1950s is just as steeped in a constructed visual image as its foil.

This extends beyond the aesthetics to the dialogue involving marital arguments which, as Ravizza rightly points out, are reliant on conventions of theater.[15] April and Frank's arguments always feel too precisely scripted, their movements and gestures too carefully choreographed as though designed to conjure the spatial logic of a stage. This makes sense thematically, insofar as engagements with performativity support the film's construction of April as a failed actress and April's performances of domestic femininity.[16] It also reinforces readings of their suburban house as a stage set to be read as evidence—by neighbors and the film's audience—of their conformity to a Leave It to Beaver world. Indeed, Mendes reflects on the importance of the house, which he describes as a character in its own right, and the practice of using the home's interior to indicate the degree to which April has control over the image of domesticity she knows she must present. What begins as a space "full of promise," and specifically the promises made by 1950s developers and ideologies of domesticity, becomes "a prison."[17] The must-have picture window, what Mark Nicholls aptly describes as a "1950s icon of domestic performance and surveillance,"[18] is scoffed at by April and Frank near the start of the film but begins to cast prison bar-like shadows toward the end. It also visually entraps April as she stands bleeding to death from her attempted abortion.

April is something of a polarizing figure in the scholarly literature on the film, generating divergent readings of the extent to which she either reinforces or subverts postwar patriarchal structures and expectations. For

Andrew Slade, *Revolutionary Road* problematically "recuperates a time when men were in control and the women who overstep those limits suffer and are punished for this."[19] As a case in point, April's death plays into "the cultural politics of abortion from a conservative point of view" for its punitive nature but also because mitigating factors are never introduced to explain her disenchantment with domesticity.[20] As Robert Sklar similarly observes, Mendes evacuates what insufficient cursory personal history Yates offered to develop April's backstory rendering her less sympathetic, more selfish, and neurotic.[21] Popular reviews of the film were equally concerned with this omission, asking how "revolutionary" Mendes's cinematic version really is in light of the ways in which his adaptation tempers Yates critique of 1950s masculinity by rendering Frank a "better man" and, even, "better father" by the end.[22] Mark Nicholls and Angela McRobbie, on the other hand, acknowledge the feminist intent of the film, specifically Mendes's concern with itemizing how the strictures of 1950s domestic life fueled deep discontent and thus sparked the next decade's women's movement. This is evident, if not always through dialogue and characterization, then at least through strategies of framing, lighting, and mise-en-scene that variously confine and oppress April in the space of her home. But as McRobbie rightly points out, this feminism is a decidedly liberal one for the way in which "the narrative bolsters a linear model of progress along with the idea of personal or individual liberation."[23]

This "profoundly liberal feminist 'structure of feeling,'" as McRobbie terms it, has consequences beyond funneling critiques of the film into a focus on the insufficiency of our understanding of April's psyche. This insufficiency is due to the "patriarchal voice" of Yates's novel, as Sklar puts it, refracted through the no less patriarchal vision of Mendes's film that concludes with the full recuperation of the doting father-figure. This is an odd ending to be sure given the almost complete erasure of the Wheelers' children from a film centered on domestic life. However, another consequence of the film's individualism is the exclusion of the broader social world in which April and Frank exist. This world may be visually present, but is never more than backdrop and rarely, if ever, acknowledged. Frank's commute takes us from the suburbs to the streets of New York, from Grand Central station to restaurants and the Knox building elevators. The Wheelers, as a couple, chart our path from apartment parties to the theater, the beach, and a bar. The only other character to take us elsewhere, which becomes the central "somewhere" (i.e., the Wheeler home) is Helen (Kathy Bates), the realtor, and April's friend. Early in the film and in flashback, she drives a pregnant April and Frank down a street that intersects with Revolutionary Road to see the "cute" house on a hill about to become theirs.

Revolutionary Road may focus on a domestic suburban existence, but at the expense of the world that surrounds such visions of home. While based on a novel from the time period represented, Mendes filters the film's reality through the present, constructing characters and situations with the hindsight of the social movements on the horizon for the Wheelers. Yet, despite the film's condemnation of the suburbs, it does not extend its critique nor its contemporaneity to the racist politics and segregating practices that generated such communities in the first place. As a film ostensibly formulated to critique postwar suburban life, to expose the underbelly of a Leave It to Beaver realm populated by the requisite commuting, white-collar father, stay-at-home mother, and two children, this is a notable failing. That is, *Revolutionary Road* seeks to remind us of a fairly widespread consciousness of the problems with the suburban dream well before this construct was co-opted by the nostalgia mills and political rhetoric of and since the 1970s and lampooned by postmodern irreverence in the 1990s.

For Stephen Rowley, *Revolutionary Road* is thus something of an "origin story" and a "classical anti-suburban text" that shares more in common with "*All That Heaven Allows, Rebel without a Cause* or *No Down Payment* than its immediate suburban film predecessors." It revives the "social commentary cinema of the 1950s that situates within this era a now stubbornly persistent suburban reality."[24] It is sincere—if narrow—in its critical aims and seeks to reveal truths since obscured by nostalgic constructions of American domesticity at mid-century. And, to do so, it returns to the literature of the period as its narrative source and the photography of the period for its visual source, subscribing wholly to the myth of photographic truth.

Suburbicon, on the other hand, may be antisuburban, but not in the sense Rowley means. Originally written in 1982 by Joel and Ethan Coen and later adapted and extended into new narrative terrain by George Clooney and Grant Heslov, *Suburbicon* was a failure by almost all metrics. A key problem, according to critics, was Clooney's inability to reconcile two distinct films into one. The first involves a Coen-esque absurdist crime comedy that tracks the collapse of Gardner Lodge's (Matt Damon) plan to hire two incompetent hitmen, Sloan (Glenn Fleshler) and Louis (Alex Hassell), to murder his wife, Rose (Julianne Moore), for the insurance money and the opportunity to continue his affair with her twin sister, Margaret (also played by Moore).

The plan unravels to such a spectacular extent that, by the end, Gardner considers murdering his own young son, Nicky (Noah Jupe). The second, based on actual events in Levittown, Pennsylvania, in 1957, foregrounds the racist violence perpetrated by the (all white) Suburbicon inhabitants against the first Black family to move into the community, Mr. and Mrs. Mayers (Leith Burke and Karimah Westbrook) and their young son, Andy (Tony Espinosa).[25]

This initial problem of narrative incongruity was exacerbated by edits during postproduction that sought to shift the tone of the film. Following the release of *Suburbicon*, Clooney admitted to cutting several comedic moments in the wake of Trump's election campaign.[26] He was particularly troubled by the slogan "Make America Great Again" for the ways in which it unabashedly resurrected the vision of white postwar suburbia that this film—and much visual culture of the last few decades—sought to skewer.[27] The more often Republicans vaunted this image in their rhetoric about domestic policies, the less funny and more sinister it seemed. That said, Clooney didn't purge all parodic evocations of the Fifties. The title sequence mobilizes it to announce the film's period setting and to establish the whiteness of the Suburbicon community as a structuring concern. Colorful, partially animated illustrations of postwar bungalows, shopping centers, and neighborhood gatherings flit by in a brochure-style book while a narrator celebrates Suburbicon as a "melting pot of diversity" for welcoming *white* families from Ohio, New York, and "as far away as Mississippi." Clooney explains how this sequence quickly establishes the film's engagement with a "Leave It to Beaver kind of world," one primed for ridicule.[28] But while this introduces the film's satiric tonality, one with similarities to *Pleasantville*, what follows are only a few isolated injections of humor, too sparse and subtle to sustain the film's comedic thrust. A heckler at a town hall meeting shouting "we won't pay for it" in response to proposals to build a fence around the Mayerses' property—a blatant nod to Trump's border wall refrain—is one early example designed to lampoon racist panic. As the film continues and the white mob grows increasingly violent, injections of humor in relation to the Mayerses' story line become difficult for the filmmakers to navigate. A distinct unevenness develops as criminal buffoonery continues to be lambasted, thus aligning the type of Coen-esque humor that pervades the film only with the Lodge family narrative. Eventually, even these intermittent absurdities begin to feel insufficient, if not woefully out of place, as scenes of racist mob violence intercut more frequently with Gardner Lodge's exploits toward the end, hinting at a potential (though ultimately insufficiently realized) merger of the two narrative trajectories.

This initial key problem of reconciling two plot lines also generated a much more significant one: the underdevelopment of the Mayers family's experiences. As several critics have pointed out, Mr. and Mrs. Mayers hardly ever speak. In fact, Mr. Mayers never utters a single line of dialogue. They are only ever on screen for brief periods of time, and their perspective is never offered, except through reaction shots that register fear, anger, or stoicism.[29] In this way, as Manohla Dargis observes, the movie "reproduces the inequality it's ostensibly outraged by."[30] And it is hardly alone in this regard; *Pleasantville* too targets 1950s racism without casting Black actors in its "Pleasantville" world. Likewise, as Wesley Morris points out, *Suburbicon* simply uses its Black characters without ever investing in their inner lives and thus only "flick[s] at progressivism."[31]

The film *uses* Mr. and Mrs. Mayers in several problematic ways. It does so to highlight the racism that structures the perspectives of *Suburbicon*'s white inhabitants. But while this permits access to what white characters feel and think and say about the Mayerses, the Mayerses themselves are never given any lines to articulate the complexities of their desires, values, and fears. Nor do we hear from them about their past lives or future aspirations. They are not afforded the particularities of individuals with life histories. We only know what Mr. Mayers does because other characters speak or, rather, speculate about him. He and Mrs. Mayers take on the burden of representing a generic but respectively gendered Black "bodies," ones both subjected continuously to white gazes in the film, and also constructed for a white audience of the film. Mr. and Mrs. Mayers appear formed from the rhetoric of "betterment," a deeply problematic ideology with long historical roots and one that continues to structure present-day discourse, specifically around urban revitalization that celebrates only the efforts of "good" Black citizens.[32] *Suburbicon* plays into this in order to play up the irony of the neighbors who reject integration until "the Negro shows he is ready." Mr. Mayers is more educated than his neighbors, and Mrs. Mayers shows far more poise and elegance than her fellow homemakers.

But *Suburbicon* only ever puts Mr. and Mrs. Mayers in situations where they are forced to assume an image of "dignified calm" or "stoic non-reaction" to the racist behavior of their neighbors: shouting chants, building fences, refusing services, staring belligerently (Figure 3.3). We only see Black people in spaces where they are subjected to white scrutiny and in situations where

Figure 3.3 Mrs. Mayers's (Karimah Westbrook) "stoic non-reaction" in *Suburbicon* (2017)

the former dare not challenge the indignities perpetrated by the latter out of fear. Andy's recounting of his father's instruction to "never show them nothing" is a survival strategy, often in response to racialized bullying, as much as "hands up" is in the context of Black Lives Matter. We never see Mr. and Mrs. Mayers in ways that aren't structured by their encounters with neighbors, that aren't performative for Suburbicon and *Suburbicon*—the fictional neighborhood *and* the film's audience. The absence of any private conversations between the Mayerses denies them the expression of the complexity of authentic emotions they might rightly feel in their situation: anger, frustration, contempt, disgust, revulsion, hatred. And in never expressing anything beyond stoicism and, on occasion, fear, they never appear as anything beyond the selves they perform for their white neighbors.

Suburbicon also uses the increasing violence committed against the Mayers family to aesthetic ends, specifically, to heighten the dramatic intensity of the events that transpire for Gardner Lodge toward the end of the film. The sequence begins with Gardner returning home to find protestors and emergency vehicles blocking his way. He is thoroughly unconcerned with what is happening to his immediate neighbors and feels only frustration at this inconvenience. When he finally arrives home, the following set of events unfold: Margaret poisons the insurance agent for trying to blackmail him; Gardner then bludgeons the fleeing insurance agent; Margaret prepares to poison Nicky but is killed by Louis; Uncle Mitch arrives and kills Louis, while Sloan dies in a gruesome car accident in pursuit of Gardner; Gardner returns, threatens Nicky, but consumes the poisoned sandwich meant for Nicky. These scenes are intercut with brief glimpses of the heightening violence perpetrated by the racist mob against the Mayerses. For example: the mob and law enforcement clash for 57 seconds, someone jumps on the hood of the Mayerses' car for 10 seconds, and people smash the Mayerses' windows for 29 seconds. At this point, scenes involving the Lodges shorten too, generating a rapid alternation between the two plot lines: Gardner speaks to Bud (30 seconds); the confederate flag is placed in the Mayerses' window (25 seconds); Gardner kills Bud (4 seconds); the mob sets the Mayerses' car ablaze (12 seconds). The screams of the frenzied crowd, their violence, the raging fires, and the terror experienced by the Mayers family are used here to bolster the dramatic impact of the Lodge events. When the latter is resolved and only Nicky is left alive, the film resumes its typical balance, spending the majority of the remaining ten minutes of the film on the Lodges. Sixty-seven seconds of this focuses on Mr. Mayers surveying the damage the next morning while another 90 seconds are devoted to witnessing the clean-up, with the help of some white neighbors. However, half of this time is viewed through the Lodge television set, as the previous night's event is now news.

This footage, which supplies the two newscasts that Nicky flips through before settling on a cartoon, is sourced from a single documentary, *Crisis in Levittown* (1957). It is one of several injections of media from the postwar period, each serving a specific narrative function. One of the very first involves an Orson Welles radio broadcast that Andy and Nicky listen to simultaneously, and affectively respond to in precisely the same way as they lie in bed preparing to sleep. Moreover, at this moment, both have reason for real fear: the crowds are starting to amass on Andy's lawn, and Sloan and Louis have already entered Nicky's house to kill his mother. All this cements a connection established earlier that day between the two preteens around a shared love of baseball and prefigures their lasting friendship that persists throughout the film, signaling hope for the (1960s) future.[33] In fact, Andy and Nicky's friendship provides the only real point of connection between the two families and, thus, the two distinct plots.

The myriad injections of media that follow take several forms and (inadvertently) point to yet another fault line between the Lodge and Mayers narrative trajectories. Specifically, they reveal a rift between two distinct sensibilities that structure the film: a postmodern and a metamodern one.

Children's programming and commercials from the 1950s on the Lodge television are played for laughs and familiarity, not likely for any kind of personal nostalgia for the film's middle-aged demographic, but as recognizable from a broader visual nostalgia economy.[34] Likewise, *Suburbicon* uses media references and cinematographic strategies to signal certain narrative developments. For instance, the film starts out as a highly saturated, colorful Technicolor world where houses, cars, and clothes all match, but gives way to a noirish dependency on tighter framing, less lighting, and more shadows as Gardner's plans start to go awry. As Clooney explains, *Suburbicon* borrows from a range of sources, including 1950s horror films for the chloroform murder scene and a Hermannesque soundtrack.[35] The *Vertigo* reference is reinforced with Margaret's decision to dye her hair blonde in an attempt to recreate her dead sister for Gardner. Julianne Moore and Matt Damon's performances are stylized in a way that recalls, if not directly draws on, their respective roles in *Far from Heaven* and *The Talented Mr. Ripley* (1999), both set in the 1950s. Mr. and Mrs. Mayers, on the other hand, are played by relatively unknown actors without the baggage of celebrity stardom. Finally, the Lodge house is carefully arranged to foreground late 1950s design: colorful glass vases with a sculptural flare, sleek modern wood or wood-accented furniture, crisp upholstery, a colorful kitchen, and ornately patterned drapes.[36] Everything is arranged for display: for Lodge family visitors and us, as viewers. Moreover, the décor is clearly brand new, a common tendency in 1950s-set films that, though likely the product of careful maintenance of retro memorabilia or newly manufactured props, effectively conveys the aspirational aims of the new middle classes setting up house for the first time in a commodity culture that fetishized newness and operated according to the logic of planned obsolescence. Together, these instances of intertextuality—and the parodic structure of feeling that inflects them—cast a distinct postmodern glow over the Lodge narrative.

The Mayers narrative, however, is inflected by a rather different sensibility. Arguably it appeals to a metamodern one for the way in which the histories harnessed through archival texts as well as documentary footage are done so with sincerity and what *seems* like an attempt to respect historical truth. Whereas the postmodern aesthetic strategies that framed the Lodges' exploits cycle through mediated references in a historiographic play with the past's "textualized remains" (as Linda Hutcheon would call them), the Mayerses' experiences recount an actual historical event critically important in the civil rights movement and do so with reference to extant historical materials. The first time the film draws on historical materials related to this event, however, satire is still the structuring force. Immediately upon realizing a Black family moved into Suburbicon, members of the neighborhood association launch a petition advocating for their removal. The text of this petition, based on the actual one circulated by Levittown residents, is patently absurd: "We defy the supporters of Mr. Mayers to say our fears are groundless. We favor racial integration, but only at such time the Negro shows he's ready for it. They don't seek to better themselves. This community has come too far to move backwards. We demand our civil rights to live where we want and with whom we want, and, with God's help, we will overcome!" This is both bafflingly ironic and deeply horrifying for the way in which it appropriates the language of the civil rights movement.

Subsequent incorporations of historical materials do not have this satirical edge. For instance, the mob's relentless singing of specific songs on the periphery of the Mayerses' property is particularly terrifying, but also done in a way that reminds audiences of their origins. For instance, "I Wish I Was in Dixie," may be perceived by some (white) communities as a generic anthem of southern pride, but its performance in this context aptly reminds viewers of its historical roots in blackface minstrelsy. Likewise, "In the Sweet By and By," a hymn, suggests the protesters belief that they have "God on their side." While these two aural instances reinforce what the petition establishes—the righteousness with which the white supremacists believe their rights have been impinged on—the satiric frame through which we experience the earlier instance is entirely absent here.

This earnest approach to representing history also structures the most prevalent way in which past media forms are mobilized in relation to the Mayerses' experiences, namely, through the integration of footage—both visual and aural—from *Crisis in Levittown*. Moments from this thirty-minute documentary film, composed mainly of interviews between Professor Dan W. Dodson (an active proponent of desegregation and Director for the Center for Human Relations and Community Studies at New York University) and Levittown inhabitants, are seamlessly woven into the diegetic world of the film to underscore the menace and stupidity of the community's racist members. This material is further coded as "truthful" through the aesthetic strategies used to integrate it into the film: as a newscast on television and on the radio. In one instance, an actual interviewee, filmed from the back, morphs into a character standing in front of the Mayerses' lawn. The film seeks to validate this event as history and ensure we hear the words as ones that were actually spoken in relation to the real Myers family in 1957. However, as with *Suburbicon* itself, *Crisis in Levittown* is composed entirely of white people speaking to other white people about Black people. There are no Black voices in the documentary, the source material for the Mayerses' narrative in *Suburbicon*.[37]

Although this footage documents the events happening in the Lodges' own backyard, the only way Margaret or Gardner become cognizant of the Mayerses' plight is through their radio and television, and thus in a mediated and distanced way. It may enter their domestic space in this regard, but there is little evidence that it fully registers in their consciousness. What is more, they have the power and the privilege—which they often exercise—to (literally) tune it out: Margaret turns off the television, Gardner changes the channel. At one point, Gardner insists to Bud that they keep the drapes closed, not out of fear, for they are nothing if not complicit in violence directed at the Mayers family, but instead because he'd rather both ignore what is happening *and* prepare to commit his own crime in secrecy. The (historically) "real" cannot seem to make inroads into the Lodge home.

Despite *Suburbicon*'s inclination to base the Mayerses' story on the actual Myers' experiences, history too has difficulty making inroads into the film.[38] Although my primary intention here isn't to highlight all instances of historical misrepresentation, some consideration of specific historical inaccuracies highlights a series of critical omissions that undermine the purported aims of the film. That is, vital facts ignored by *Suburbicon* undermine its intent to respond to Trump's election rhetoric in an age of Black Lives Matter. For instance, the police in Suburbicon respond aggressively to the white mob, beating them back from the Mayerses' house with Billy clubs. The police in Levittown, often inhabitants of that very suburb, were complicit with the mob, allowing them to congregate and act with impunity, terrorizing a family with three children, one only a month old at the time. Under their supposed 24-hour guard, several crosses were burned on sympathizers' lawns and racist epithets were painted on houses.[39] The KKK had fully intervened in this program of harassment, and community members even leased a house close to the Myers' property in order to meet and continue their assault with noise and light. The police, as well as other levels of city administration, did nothing to stop this as the violence and protests persisted for weeks, not a single night as in the film.[40]

Suburbicon certainly downplayed the extent and severity of the racist violence. It also implied various things about the Mayers/Myers that were troubling. In failing to particularize Mr. and Mrs. Mayers as individuals with personal histories, experiences, and motivations, *Suburbicon* allowed certain important facts to be (literally) whitewashed. For instance, Mrs. Myers may well have been a model housewife according to 1950s gendered norms and may indeed have spent time hanging laundry, reminding her children to do their homework, shopping for groceries (as we see her do in the film), but she was also enrolled as a Master's student in social work at NYU and active in local politics in her community. Daisy Myers worked as a loan officer who determined eligibility for low-income families. In this job, she saw first-hand the conditions in which Black families lived: no electricity, no running water, outhouses, etc.[41] She was shaped by this reality, one not her own growing up. But it became her own during the 1950s as she and her husband spent years dealing with racist practices that denied them entry into the homes they could easily afford. And while *Suburbicon* suggests Mr. and Mrs. Myers were simply upstanding citizens looking for a better life for themselves and their children in the suburbs—which was true—they were also deeply committed to civil rights causes.

Indeed, the film treats the rumor that their arrival was a communist plot, expressed in *Suburbicon* through footage of one of the racist neighbors interviewed for *Crisis in Levittown*, as just that: a scandalous rumor. However, their move *was* orchestrated by a local neighborhood organization intent on desegregating the community in the interest of democracy and the Myers did consider the importance of integration and the risks they would assume in an era where horrific crimes were being perpetrated against Black people. The Myers' move was organized primarily by Bea and Lew Wechsler, long-time activists with Communist roots and continued socialist sympathies. And all concerned were well-aware of how integration itself was often framed as a communist plot, thanks to the likes of Joseph McCarthy, a public promotor of the Levitts.[42] In fact, by the time the Myers were preparing to move in, Levittown itself had long been a site of contestation around desegregation. The Levitts were known for flouting a Supreme Court ruling prohibiting segregation in housing and openly assured their white clients that they would always refuse to sell to Black families.[43] At the same time that white veterans camped overnight for the opportunity to buy into Levittown, civil rights activists staged sit-ins at the suburb's sales office to highlight the developer's racist practices.[44] The Myers knew precisely what it meant to move to Levittown and carefully weighed the personal risk against the importance of actively attempting to desegregate this postwar American suburb.

By ignoring, if not actively trying to deny, the Myers' history of political activism and their calculated reason for moving into an all-white community, *Suburbicon* ignores their agency as civil rights actors and the leftist inclinations of key civil rights actions and alliances. It also maintains the Mayerses' status as generic "Black bodies" represented simply in order to register violence and white response, rather than as individuals with deep moral convictions, relationships with communities of support and activism, and thus broader social movements. It ignores the risks taken by the Myers and others, suggesting progress was sparked by changes of heart in white people rather than the concerted efforts of civil rights activists.

Insufficiency and error in historical representation matters tremendously here, for *Suburbicon* offers not a generalized representation of postwar racism but a very specific historical event and one that, as of this writing, has not yet been subject to cinematic representation in its own right.[45] As such, Clooney's film situates itself as one of the originary touchstones of the event. A cursory review of the various cinematic Fifties types shows that, for the most part, first or early representations of this construct become entrenched as reference points for subsequent ones. They set the (visual and narrative) terms, establishing the tropes and themes that others feel obliged to acknowledge in order to signal their response to that same construction. Films about historical periods and events bear this burden as they necessarily enter into dynamic and evolving discussions (visual, auditory, textual) of the past on offer. While such images surely change over time, shedding their sentimental inflection for a critical one, specific elements of a trope often remain consistent. Specifically, difficulties in representing white supremacy in the history of suburban development was written out of Leave It to Beaver Fifties representations so definitively that recent titles still struggle to navigate their imbrication. Indeed, if anything, *Suburbicon* seems to (unintentionally) reveal something of the irreconcilability of cinematically produced Leave It to Beaver worlds and the white supremacy in which they are grounded. This is not to suggest that racism hasn't been at issue in films recreating postwar suburban neighborhoods as their settings. However, most attempts are deeply insufficient in this regard. *Pleasantville*, *Edward Scissorhands* (1990), the first season of *Mad Men* (set in 1959), all acknowledge racism and segregation, but do so either metaphorically, without a single person of color in the film, or by using Black actors as receptors of racist abuse. That is, they exist to manifest the existence of racism, but little else. The agency, emotions, subjectivities, and desires of Black characters remain undeveloped.

Suburbicon thus seems to allegorize a shift away from postmodern practices with respect to the representation of history toward if not metamodern ones outright, then at least some of the tendencies that constitute a metamodern sensibility, specifically sincerity. That is, *Suburbicon* allegorizes this transition within a single film, thanks to the crime caper narrative written a few decades ago and Clooney's decision to graft onto this an actual historical event during a time when the 1950s became, once again, resurrected in political rhetoric. The film thus represents two ways of engaging the 1950s: through irreverent parody and sincerity, however flawed the result. The Coen brother's crime caper works well set in a Fifties structured by mediated illusions, performative characterizations of housewives and organization men in gray flannel suits, props and tail-finned cars too new and shiny not to self-consciously signify a culture of display, newness, futurity, and middle-class ostentation. This satirical take on a Leave It to Beaver world instantiates *Suburbicon* in a long line of films that *play* with history through a myriad set of intertextual references, ones that resurrect well-worn remnants of our media history. Whereas this approach challenges our capacity to ever know history and the 1950s, in particular, the Mayerses' narrative is and needs to be seen as historical truth. Emotions expressed in response to the events that constitute this dimension of the film are inexorably authentic, whether the self-righteous racism of the violent white supremacists beating on drums and singing "Dixieland" or the fear and stoicism of the Mayerses. Here, for Clooney, postmodern irreverence has no place. It is part of the history of American suburbanization too long ignored in cinema and one in need of resurrection in 2016 (and since) given its return in many decidedly unironic ways.

As such, the film seems to oscillate between the Fifties and the 1950s in its attempt to plot two narrative strands into a single film. While the postmodern historiographic practices that challenge our capacity to know and access history introduces a criticality of vital importance to thinking through cinematic engagements with the past, the metamodern structures that privilege sincerity and aim for truth matter more when historical events that have long gone insufficiently acknowledged, or entirely unacknowledged, are at issue. But the irreconcilability of the postmodern and metamodern (or Fifties and 1950s) in *Suburbicon* in particular is worth addressing from yet another perspective, because it also exposes the failures of the film to show precisely how a history of Leave It to Beaver representations of suburbia have dealt ineptly and insufficiently with race: both whiteness and Black history. As Nathan Holmes argues, *Suburbicon*, like other films invested in critiquing the racist history of American suburbs, "mystifies the suburban history it attempts to represent."[46] It does so by ignoring critical historical realities surrounding the Myers' move, as noted above and by "psychologizing whiteness," framing racism as an individual moral failing rather than something that is also systemic and collective.[47] Moreover, *Suburbicon*, like other suburb films, fails to show how such spaces also *produced* notions of whiteness. Drawing on the work of Barbara and Karen Fields, Diane Harris, and David Roediger, Holmes explains how certain films ignore the ways which "diverse groups of Americans who moved to the suburbs in the postwar era, many of whom were recent immigrants, didn't necessarily think of themselves as white until they were interpellated as such by federal policies and real estate practices."[48]

Holmes and other contributors to Merrill Schleier's important collection, *Race and the Suburbs in American Film*, show in precise terms the extent to which the complexity of actual American suburbs has been acknowledged or elided by cinema, including how even Levittowns became sites of activism and collectivity. *Suburbicon*, for Holmes, is an example of such elision, testament to how even purportedly critical interventions into postwar suburbia perpetuates historical inaccuracies. Jordan Peele's *Get Out* (2017), however, is often heralded as an example that does effectively consider more nuanced constructions of whiteness and machinations of white supremacy. The film opens with Andre (LaKeith Stanfield) lost in a white suburb late at night. As he walks nervously down the sidewalk, a car begins to follow him. He changes direction and so too does the car. His instincts are right and eventually he is attacked and kidnapped. With this prelude, Peele sought to "subvert the idea of the perfect white suburb," a subversion that continues throughout the film by way of several incisive references. For instance, the "Behold the Coagula" video that Chris (Daniel Kaluuya) is forced to watch—i.e., the short film that explains the brain transplantation method—concludes with the Armitage family standing in front of their house, waving to the camera in what reads like a parody of a postwar domestic sitcom title sequence. Peele suggests too that the character Georgina (Betty Gabriel), the Armitage's Black maid who is really Grandma Armitage, is based not just in principle, but in characterization, on the Stepford Wives. Her mannerisms and language read as from the 1950s; she doesn't understand the terms "snitch" or "rat you out" and offers "tattle tale" in an effort to decipher what Chris is saying to her. Her hair and some of her clothes have a Fifties vibe about them. As Chris observes, Georgina and Walter (who is really Grandfather Armitage) act "like all of them missed the movement." However brief, these moments that allude to the Fifties and mobilize a history of postwar suburbs do much to highlight how white supremacy is entwined with the histories of such spaces. Moreover, the film itself allegorizes the very problem with *Suburbicon* and other films that use the black "body." As Peele explains: "Your will is taken and your body is used; this is a modern form of slavery." He continues to explain that there are different reasons why the white characters want a black body, "but the commonality is that you are being valued for your skin, and your culture and what you bring that enhances our lives, but you're not being valued as a soul, that is equally as human being."[49] Indeed this encapsulates Hollywood's history of using black "bodies" without acknowledging individual "souls."

This particular charge of exploitation was also leveled at a television anthology series, but one helmed by Black artists: *Them*. Created by Little Marvin and executive produced by Lena Waithe, *Them* is a ten-part series on Amazon Prime that unfolds over a ten-day period in 1953. Like *Get Out* and *Lovecraft Country* (2020), it blends supernatural horror with the horrors of postwar racist violence in America, particularly in new suburban developments, to represent the experience of the Emory family as they move to the then all-white neighborhood of East Compton (Figure 3.4). This move is precipitated by Henry Emory's (Ashley Thomas) new job and greeted with hesitation by Livia "Lucky" Emory (Deborah Ayorinde). *Them* heavily relies on horror film conventions, alluding visually to a range of films and practices, from *The Shining* (1980) to Saul Bass–style opening credits. But unlike *Get Out* and *Lovecraft Country*, or other recent productions that engage histories of white supremacist violence through various genres, *Them* polarized the

Figure 3.4 Gracie (Melody Hurd) and Livia "Lucky" Emory (Deborah Ayorinde) in *Them* (2021)

Black reviewing and viewing community because of the graphic brutality of its violence. Whereas reviewers for *Ebony* and *Essence* praised the series for revealing difficult historical truths, others found the series complicit in white supremacy.[50]

For Angelica Jade Bastién, *Them* is "one of the most anti-Black pieces of pop culture," a series that trades only in "virulent imagery" and stands as evidence of how "people of color sometimes participate in their own degradation."[51] Bastién itemizes the show's relentless barrage of racist language, racist imagery (e.g., various racist caricatures including the Tap Dance Man based on blackface minstrel performances), racist practices (e.g., segregation, redlining, realty scams) and violence directed at racialized people (e.g., rape, torture, physical assaults, the murder of an infant). Bastién asks for whom this show is meant, for *Them* "doesn't wholly consider just how damaging such language and imagery is not only for the psyche of the characters involved, but for the Black people in the audience who understand it on a visceral, intimate level."[52] In addition to these assaults mined from American history, *Them* also terrorizes its protagonists with supernatural forces through figures that manifest each characters' fears. However, these supernatural entities have historical roots too, originating from events that transpired in the geographical place they inhabit, specifically the brutal torture of two escaped slaves by an insular religious community during the Civil War era. This earlier history, the subject of Episode 9 ("Covenant II: Welcome to Eidolon"), is shot entirely in black and white, suggesting a cartographic and aesthetic palimpsest, an accumulation of histories and their representation.[53]

Them makes wholly explicit the racist violence perpetrated by white people against Black families integrating white suburbs. It mobilizes precisely the kind of Leave It to Beaver imagery that audiences have become accustomed to: perfectly manicured lawns, pastel bungalows, milkmen on delivery, candy-colored cars parked in driveways, husbands watering lawns, wives entertaining in aprons, etc. These images are part of what Holmes calls a "familiar gesture of suburban iconoclasm" that "sustain what has become a common sense idea, that the suburbs are a zone of artifice and inauthenticity."[54] But unlike most other films that appeal to allegory, metaphor, or euphemistic intimation to engage the violent history of suburban integration, *Them* seeks to foreground in unflinching terms the violence that Black pioneers did experience, in the southern states they left as well as the regions of the United States to which they moved.[55] Little Marvin defends the brutality of the violence depicted by explaining that he "wanted a scene that would rip through the screen, grab the viewer by the jugular and force them to contend with a history of violence against Black bodies in this country." Horror was the vehicle that Little Martin thought was best equipped to enable viewers to "actually feel the impact" of the history represented, that is, segregation era narratives that "were often very staid."[56] In this way *Them* effectively critiques not only nostalgic visions of the Leave It to Beaver Fifties, but the inadequacy of the ostensibly critical, or "iconoclastic" ones as well.

Them may be focused on chronicling a specific history of the 1950s, but in a series of gestures that reflect the process of percolation, it reaches both back (through flashbacks) and forward (through allusions to the culture of subsequent decades and events that transpired during the show's production). The idea for the show was sparked by Little Marvin's experience during Trump's presidency, specifically a series of events that aligned the racist violence of postwar America with the continuation of racist violence in the twenty-first century, including the resurgence of visibility of white supremacist groups bolstered by the public support of numerous politicians. For him, 2021 was a "scary place to be," with "people who want to take the country back to a time they consider great," while other "folks . . . are fighting for progress."[57] In this context, he was also "waking up every day and seeing cellphone videos of Black people being terrorized in some ways, either by threats from police, surveillance or something else."[58] This prompted Little Marvin to excavate the history of this terror, one that "goes all the way back to the founding of our country." Indeed, as he edited the series during the summer of 2020, the murder of George Floyd and others "absolutely validated the need for it." He continues: "I was also thinking about the American Dream. There's nothing more emblematic of that than owning one's home. There's great pride in that, particularly for Black people. But as you know, it's been anything but a dream. It's been a nightmare for Black folks."[59] What *Them* makes explicit in ways that *Suburbicon* fails to, is how this nightmare was a product of more than just individual and collective racism. *Them* certainly "psychologizes whiteness" in the case of Betty (Allison Pill), a sociopathic Stepford wife (or proto-Karen, as she is commonly called) intent on tormenting the Emorys; Betty's father, who had an incestuous relationship with her; and George (Ryan Kwanten), the seemingly benign milkman who eventually kidnaps and murders Betty. But it also creates space to attend to the individual, community, institutional, and government machinations that collectively orchestrated tactics meant to exploit Black homebuyers.

In an interview with D'Shonda Brown, Little Marvin explained that he "set out to make a show that felt like a show about the '50s that was shot in the 1970s."[60] As such, he signals both the origins of the Fifties nostalgia economy which *Them* does much to severely upend as well as a critical period of Black activism in the United States. And whereas visually, *Them* self-consciously appeals to devices found in 1970s horror films like *The Exorcist* (1973), musically, it involves "everyone from Diana Ross to Roberta Flack, to Nina Simone, to Sarah Vaughan."[61] That is, it mobilizes assorted musical genres from the 1950s through to the 1980s and, with them, the performers who themselves have been iconic voices in the civil rights movement. As such, *Them* engenders a sense of historical continuity through its myriad interventions into past practices and events, past visual and music culture. In this way it contributes to a corpus of Black films that complicate even the most iconoclastic visions of the postwar era, from the generically similar *Lovecraft Country* to other titles like *Fences* (2016) and *Hal King* (2021), films considered in the chapters that follow and that represent, aesthetically speaking, highly divergent ways of fracturing cinematic representations of the 1950s.

Notes

1. David Kushner, *Levittown: Two Families, One Tycoon, and the Fight for Civil Rights in American's Legendary Suburb* (New York: Walker and Company, 2009), xii.
2. I attend to how television accomplished this in *Screening Nostalgia*.
3. Bill Levitt in Kushner, *Levittown*, xiv.
4. There was no shortage of reporting on the 2020 presidential election and its aftermath that invoked *Leave It to Beaver* as well, from local newspapers in New Jersey, to major publications in Chicago, to *The Guardian*. Much of this coverage was sparked by Trump's appeal to "the suburban housewives of America," though commentators were quick to point out the demographic diversity of US suburbs today. Lauren Gambino, "Donald Trump Stokes Racial Fears with Appeal to White Suburban Voters, *Guardian*, July 29, 2021. https://www.theguardian.com/us-news/2020/jul/29/donald-trump-white-suburban-voters-rule-rollback.
5. Thom Hartmann, "The new GOP 'Southern Strategy': Civil War or *Leave It to Beaver*?" *Salon*, November 19, 2021. https://www.salon.com/2021/11/19/the-new-southern-strategy-civil-or-leave-it-to-beaver_partner/.
6. Andrea Vesentini, "Sheltering Time: The Containment of Everyday Life in Nuclear-Shelter Film Narratives," *Material Culture* 47.2 (Fall 2015): 42.

7. As Lawrence J. Siskind puts it, the Maisels "are living proof that while you can take the Jew out of the shtetl, you cannot take the shtetl out of the Jew." *Times of Israel*, January 7, 2019. https://blogs.timesofisrael.com/the-two-houses-of-the-marvelous-mrs-maisel/.
8. Eleonora Ravizza, "The Politics of Melodrama: Nostalgia, Performance, and Gender Roles in Revolutionary Road," in *Poetics of Politics: Textuality and Social Relevance in Contemporary American Literature and Culture*, ed. Sebastian M. Herrmann et al. (Heidelberg: Winter, 2015), 63–80.
9. Pablo Gómez Muñoz, "Displacing Conformity: Postwar US Suburbia in 2000s Cinema and Television," in *Making Sense of Popular Culture*, ed. María del Mar Ramón-Torrijos and Eduardo de Gregorio-Godeo (Newcastle Upon Tyne: Cambridge Scholars, 2017), 80.
10. Richard Yates, *Revolutionary Road* (New York: Little, Brown and Co., 1961), 126.
11. Ibid., 296.
12. Ibid., 5. These same observations are repeated later in the novel. In the "Log Cabin" bar parking lot, "slick, chin-high tops of the cars made an undulating surface that stretched away into the darkness in all directions; beneath it stood endless shadowy ranks of fenders and fins, of intricately bulbous bumpers and grills alive with numberless points of reflected neon" (265). And, again, the cars are "ice-cream colored" while the neighborhood looks like a "toyland of white and pastel houses" (339).
13. Sam Mendes and Justin Haythe, "Director's Commentary," *Revolutionary Road*, DVD, directed by Sam Mendes (Dreamworks, 2008).
14. That said, the start of the film, set in 1948, is very much dependent on a Hollywood vision of the 1940s, a predominantly brown/sepia palette.
15. Ravizza, "The Politics of Melodrama," 70.
16. Degrees of performativity permeate both the novel and the film. For instance, Sklar cites Yates's description of the similarities that Frank notices between Maureen Grube's (his affair) and April's voices, specifically "a quality of play-acting, of slightly false intensity, a way of seeming to speak less to him than to some romantic abstraction." Robert Sklar, "*Revolutionary Road*," *Cineaste* 34.2 (Spring 2009): n.p. http://www.jstor.org/stable/41690770. Likewise, Angela McRobbie cites the small central cast of the film as something reminiscent of a stage play while C. Richardson employs Judith Butler's concept of performativity on several registers as an analytical tool to consider the film. See Angela McRobbie, "Feminism, the Family and the New 'Mediated' Maternalism," *New Formations* 80–81 (Winter 2013): 122; and C. Richardson, "The Empty Self in Revolutionary Road or: How I Learned to Stop Worrying and Love the Blonde," *European Journal of American Culture* 29.1 (2010): 5–18.
17. Mendes, "Director's Commentary."
18. Mark Nicholls, "Sam Mendes' *Revolutionary Road* and the Talent to Bemuse," *Quarterly Review of Film and Video* 29.4 (2012): 333.
19. Andrew Slade, "'You Are the Most Beautiful Creature': The Ethics of Masculinity in *Revolutionary Road*," *Quarterly Review of Film and Video* 34.7 (2017): 674.
20. Ibid.
21. See Sklar, "*Revolutionary Road*," n.pag.

22. See Tammy Oler, "Re-Imagining *Revolutionary Road*," *Bitchmedia*, December 30, 2008. https://www.bitchmedia.org/post/re-imagining-revolutionary-road.
23. McRobbie, "Feminism," 124.
24. Stephen Rowley, "Buffeted by Culture: Urban Planners, Notional Places, and Narratives of Fakery," *Planning Theory and Practice* 19.4 (2018): 637.
25. Clooney and Heslov kept the name of the first Black family to move into a house in Levittown, Pennsylvania, but changed the spelling from Myers to Mayers.
26. George Clooney and Grant Heslov, "Director's Commentary," *Suburbicon* (Black Bear Pictures et al., 2017).
27. This was perhaps prescient, given the extent to which the Charlottesville neo-Nazi rally looked an awful lot like Clooney's scenes. Of course, the rally itself was likely in part determined by its participants' consumption of historical and mediated images of such rallies in the past.
28. Clooney, "Director's Commentary."
29. Wesley Morris did the math: "None of the scenes with the Mayerses go on for more than 90 seconds; most last less than 15. And all are intended as a moral counterpoint to the darkening frivolity going on at the Lodges.'" Wesley Morris, "George Clooney's Awkward White Guilt in *Suburbicon*," *New York Times*, November 3, 2017. https://www.nytimes.com/2017/11/03/movies/george-clooney-suburbicon-racism.html.
30. Manohla Dargis, "Glib Laughs and Race Hate in *Suburbicon*," *New York Times*, October 26, 2017. https://www.nytimes.com/2017/10/26/movies/suburbicon-review-george-clooney-matt-damon-julianne-moore.html.
31. Morris, "George Clooney's Awkward White Guilt."
32. The historical roots of this rhetoric are subject to withering critique in Barry Jenkin's *The Underground Railroad* (2021) in Episode 2, "Chapter 2: South Carolina."
33. This feels somewhat disingenuous here and requires us to believe that eleven-year-olds aren't likely to have already internalized the racism of their parents (i.e., Rose speaks of a possible decline in property values with the arrival of the Mayerses and though Margaret initially encourages Nicky to play with Andy, later in the film, she seems to feel tremendous satisfaction for heeding her boss's instructions to charge Mrs. Mayers $20 for milk.).
34. Although, I'd venture to say that part of this nostalgia may be for a 1990s period of self-reflexive postmodern Fifties representations.
35. Clooney, "Director's Commentary."
36. According to Clooney, much time was devoted to the design of the house. He considered it a character in its own right ("Director's Commentary").
37. Although I cannot confirm either way, the film does not appear to use Daisy Myer's own memoir of the event, *Sticks 'n Stones*, published in 2005.
38. It does so sometimes in odd and unexplained tangential ways. For instance, the Myer's allies, the Wechslers, had a son named Nicky, who befriended the Myers children. Also, baseball plays a role in this event, insofar as Jackie Robinson, a key figure in the civil rights movement, meets the Wechsler's and gives Nicky a signed ball, expressing his appreciation to the family for their allyship.
39. Kushner, *Levittown*, 109.

40. Ibid., passim.
41. Ibid., 51.
42. Ibid., 45.
43. Ibid., xiv.
44. Ibid., 46.
45. Mahogany Productions launched a public funding campaign in 2018 to secure the funds to start the process of bringing Daisy Myers's 2006 memoir *Sticks 'n Stones: The Myers Family in Levittown* (York County Heritage Trust, 2005)to the screen, but failed to reach its target, canceling the project.
46. Nathan Holmes, "The Limits and Possibilities of Suburban Iconoclasm: *Suburbicon* and *99 Homes*," in *Race and the Suburbs in American Film*, ed. Merrill Schleier (Albany: SUNY, 2021), 241.
47. Ibid., 245.
48. Ibid., 240. Holmes draws specifically on Barbara and Karen Fields's notion of "racecraft" as defined in Barbara J. Fields and Karen E. Fields, *Racecraft: The Soul of Inequality in American Life* (London: Verso, 2014) as well as Dianne Harris, *Little White Houses: How the Postwar Home Constructed Race in America* (Minneapolis: University of Minnesota Press, 2013) and David Roediger, *Working toward Whiteness: How America's Immigrants Became White* (New York: Basic Books, 2005).
49. Jordan Peele quoted in Mary Cantoral, "Rising Up from the Sunken Place: Representation as Resistance in *Get Out*," *Medium*, February 18, 2021. https://medium.com/@marycantoral/rising-up-from-the-sunken-place-cd0ce57bfdc7.
50. See for instance, Kevin L. Clark, "Creators Little Marvin and Lena Waithe Get Us Right with *Them*," *Ebony*, April 5, 2021. https://www.ebony.com/entertainment/creators-little-marvin-and-lena-waithe-get-us-right-with-them/.
51. Angelica Jade Bastién, "*Them* Is Pure Degradation Porn," *Vulture*, April 14, 2021. https://www.vulture.com/article/review-them-amazon-series.html.
52. Ibid. This was the structuring question posed by Sonia Saraiya and Cassie da Costa in their conversation reviewing the series for *Vanity Fair*, an assessment that found a good deal of faults of the kind highlighted by Bastién. See "Who Is the Racism Horror Anthology 'Them' Really For?" *Vanity Fair* April 2021. https://www.vanityfair.com/hollywood/2021/04/them-amazon-little-marvin-lena-waithe.
53. For Elizabeth A. Patton, this is also the structuring approach for *Get Out*. She argues that Peele's film "acts as a spatial palimpsest that uses collective memory to reveal the deep and masked layers of racism in places that have historically emerged from ideologies of white supremacy, especially the suburbs. "Geographies of Racism: American Suburbs as Palimpsest Spaces in *Get Out* (2017)," in *Race and the Suburbs in American Film*, ed. Merrill Schleier (Albany: SUNY, 2021): 219.
54. Holmes, "The Limits and Possibilities," 239.
55. Episode 3, "Holy Ghost," of *Lovecraft Country* takes a very similar approach in this regard, integrating horror and history (also in a palimpsestic way) to reveal how white neighbors intimidated and assaulted Black pioneers, in this case Leti (Jurnee Smollet) and those who lived in her large Victorian boarding house. However, whereas

Lovecraft Country provides a cathartic ending, offering multiple avenues of revenge, *Them* does not, suggesting the historical continuity of such aggressions.

56. Little Marvin quoted in Austin Considine, "In *Them*, a Black Family Is Haunted by Real-Life Monsters," *New York Times*, April 8, 2021. https://www.nytimes.com/2021/04/08/arts/television/them-amazon-series.html.
57. Little Marvin quoted in Greg Braxton, "Does Amazon Prime's *Them* Take Its Racist Violence Too Far?" *LA Times*, April 9, 2021. https://www.latimes.com/entertainment-arts/tv/story/2021-04-09/amazon-them-covenant-little-marvin-lena-waithe-violence.
58. Ibid.
59. Ibid.
60. D'Shonda Brown, "*Them* Covenant Creator Little Marvin Talks Dismantling the American Dream," *Essence*, April 7, 2021. https://www.essence.com/entertainment/little-marvin-them/.
61. Ibid.

4
The Jukebox Fifties

The Jukebox Fifties is primarily concerned with the experiences of the 3.4 (white) children of the Leave It to Beaver Fifties as teenagers.[1] These are the adolescents who listened to rock n' roll, congregated at drive-ins and soda shops, and sometimes "suffered" from the somewhat newish social malaise, juvenile delinquency. To a certain extent, they rejected the ideologies of their parents and the "conformity" of the Leave It to Beaver suburbs, those purportedly insular realms cultivated in an effort to shield children from the challenges, vicissitudes, and politics of life.[2] Generically speaking, this narrative tendency can be located in melodramas, B-movies, romances, musicals, and the more specific subgenre of juvenile delinquency films.

Rebel without a Cause (1955) is a particularly apt example for it not only establishes suburban domesticity as something inherently flawed (though it does so in some troubling ways) and productive of social norms to be rejected but also helps configure a vision of masculinity that we can track across the decades and up to the eventual (re)convergence of the Jukebox and Leave It to Beaver Fifties in the world of rockabilly. Spearheading this refutation of domesticity is Jim Stark (James Dean), who, along with Marlon Brando's *The Wild One* (1953), came to represent the model for future generations' revivals of the "greaser" in style, if not fully in subjectivity.[3] But while suburban dysfunction is central to *Rebel without a Cause*, this element is all but expunged in Jukebox Fifties constructions during the 1970s and since, where parents and home—suburban or otherwise—are almost entirely absent, leaving narrative space for the exploits of youth, exclusively. This is certainly the case in one of the inaugural examples of the Jukebox Fifties, *Grease* (1978), discussed here for both its contributions to shaping this construct as well as its legacy, evident not only in faithful remakes but also in numerous films and cultural practices informed by it.[4] Thus, in this chapter I track how the "greaser" as a primarily working-class identity construct, continues life not just through various cinematic roles but also within rockabilly culture, itself of recent interest to documentarians and photographers like Jennifer

Greenburg. This work is noted before turning to my second cinematic case study, April Mullen's *Badsville* (2017).

In the Spring of 2017 I walked into my classroom, sat down, and scanned the room to see who had arrived. I promptly did a double-take, having registered something oddly familiar, but nevertheless out of place or, rather, out of time. One of my students was dressed and coiffed like Sandy (Olivia Newton-John) after her transformation into a greaser girl for "You're the One That I Want." It was, after all, presentation day, an opportunity for students to share with peers their final projects. My assignment required them to select any cultural object (artwork, film, novel, video game, etc.) that represents a past era or event, analyze the context in which it was produced, and assess how it engages or produces its historical subject. This particular student, part of the first-year cohort, selected *Grease* and opted to focus on its construction of the 1950s. But I soon realized she wasn't alone. Yet another student, though not fully costumed, was just as committed a fan as she.

Both students did an excellent job investigating how *Grease* constructed its late-1950s setting. They unearthed sources that itemized how postwar America was brought to life on screen through props, fashion, music, social practices, people, cars, sites, and media. They noted instances when the 1970s makes itself felt and attended to some of the pitfalls of historical representation. They rightfully acknowledged the extent to which the past on display was mythic and nostalgic and how it evaded many of the harsh realities of the decade. As such, they were attuned to both the force with which *Grease* entranced its audiences, securing legions of loyal fans, and where and how it failed in historical and representational terms by erasing people of color, perpetuating deeply troubling ethnic stereotypes, and delegitimizing the experiences of other marginalized constituencies. They were also particularly attuned to the film's use of popular music, its diegetic force and legacy. Still, I found their investment in *Grease* quite surprising. That is, until I discovered the extent of its continued popularity: as a high school play; through many direct and indirect references in kindred productions like *Glee* (2009–15) and *High School Musical* (2006), both favorites among this generation; the ratings success of *Grease Live!* (2016); and the fact that the YouTube clip of "You're the One That I Want" had over 262,000,000 views in 2018 and over 437,000,000 in 2021 . . . and counting.[5] *Grease: Rise of the Pink Ladies*, a prequel set in 1954 destined for television, has just begun principal photography as of this writing.

I opted to classify the type of Fifties represented by *Grease* and its progeny "The Jukebox Fifties" because, as an iconic object of twentieth-century material culture, the jukebox carries with it certain resonances that are particularly apt at orienting the analysis that follows here. A coin-operated technology that plays recorded music, its origins date back to the late nineteenth century and Thomas Alva Edison's phonograph. The mid-1930s to the end of the 1940s constituted its heyday, one marked by the repeal of Prohibition, World War II, and dramatic changes in the broadcast media and music industries. By 1950 it was entering a period of decline, and by 1960 it was poised on the brink of obscurity.[6] Nevertheless, it retains a privileged place as a period marker in film and television productions that represent the 1950s. It is featured prominently in the opening credit sequence for *Happy Days* (1974– 84), reproduced as a stylized case for the DVD of *American Graffiti* (1973), and foregrounded narratively in a key scene in *Pleasantville* (1998) as a harbinger of free thinking. By virtue of its function and continued associations, the jukebox remains aligned with three key and interrelated things: the construction and performance of youth identities, popular music, and public sites of (primarily youth) socialization. And these three things, to varying degrees, constitute the core of films belonging to the Jukebox Fifties.[7]

Although *Grease* announces its setting in 1959 in no uncertain terms, there was debate, right at the outset, among reviewers over the time period represented and the nature of the film's relationship to the 1950s. Whereas for some, the postwar period resonates strongly and meaningfully throughout, for others, like Charles Champlin, it is a film grounded almost exclusively in the 1970s. He writes:

> This was the '50s? This sleazy and cynical piece of work? You've got to be kidding. I was there, and only the tail-fins look familiar. I didn't see "Grease" on stage, but on testimony of this strident, cluttered, uninvolving and unattractive movie, it is the '50s—maybe the last innocent decade allowed to us—played back through a grotesquely distorting '70s consciousness.[8]

Still others recognize the imprint of the 1960s throughout. As Oliver Gruner suggests, "[a]lthough ostensibly set in 1959, *Grease* blurred the boundaries between the 1950s and the early 1960s" through its cameos from Beach Party film stars.[9] Other nuanced assessments also point to how the film's present structures and filters the late-1950s worlds and practices that it revives.[10] For instance, Vera Dika attends to the film's "time confusion" and mixing of "past and present, blurring boundaries."[11] Even initial reviews hinted at this, with one claiming that "the text as a whole trembles uncertainly in its grasp of the 'fifties.'"[12]

The ways in which *Grease* incorporates multiple pasts in its periodization of the late 1950s recalls, once again, Michel Serres's account of this process and his insistence on recognizing the multitemporality of historical eras. Indeed, here again his thoughts on percolation are especially pertinent for analyzing how, in *Grease*, youth identities, popular music, and sites of youth socialization are deeply punctured and determined by an array of pasts. It also permits us to examine the signifying work that these intertextual references perform in the context of *Grease* and to consider how their inclusion intervenes in our understanding of historical representation, mediation, and the circulation of cultural memory. Indeed, the kind of nascent postmodernism here is worth considering for how later films like *Badsville* lean more toward a set of metamodern sensibilities.

Grease is ostensibly about the exploits of youth. It offers vignettes of fairly typical teenage antics that define high school lives and afterschool activities. A good deal of attention has already been paid to how some of the nodal points that constitute the subjectivities of the key characters serve as an indictment of 1950s social mores, a nod to the legacy of 1960s social movements, or way to filter the past through the film's late-1970s present. For instance, Rizzo's (Stockard Channing) agency and expression of sexuality and the T-Bird's "white ethnic" and working-class background have been astutely analyzed in these respects.[13] While I acknowledge such moments of agency, I want to focus on how the youth are defined in relation to their parents' generation and defined by the media landscape they inhabit. That is, I want to see how various pasts percolate through people in a way that shapes the identity of the core cast. To do so, I will start with the film's casting of the parental generation and then explore how star images are mobilized to define the "teenage" generation.

With very few exceptions, the entire older generation of *Grease* is populated by celebrities of the 1950s: Eve Arden (Principal McGee), Dody Goodman (Blanche), Joan Blondell (Vi), Edd Byrnes (Vince Fontaine), Sid Caeser (Coach Calhoun), and Alice Ghostley (Mrs. Murdoch). Their star images, so deeply enmeshed in 1950s popular culture, arguably motivated their casting more so than age alone. Many of them enjoyed careers stretching back to the 1940s and even 1930s, but for late-1970s audiences, they are recognizable from 1950s television, film, and radio and, in the case of Eve Arden, all three.

Tom Symmons, building on the work of Vivian Sobchack, argues for how such overdetermined and intertextual star images function in historical films by transcending the figures they represent and "exceed[ing] the particularity of the past with the universal values and meaning their image embodies."[14] In *Grease*, they are not playing known historical characters, but in many ways themselves. Their meanings are, in part, sourced by the texts and contexts in which they appeared and their value determined by what they all share: status as media figures of the 1950s. Through them percolate a range of past roles, genres, television programs, and films. As much as these casting choices offer the pleasures of familiarity, nostalgia, and fandom, their real significance lies in the implications that such casting has for the youth in *Grease*: if the older generation of characters is defined first and foremost by their status as media celebrities, then the youth are not as much the progeny of people as they are of media culture.

This is all but confirmed by the absence of actual parents in *Grease* and by the cultural references through which the film introduces its core characters in the 1977 final shooting script. Most aspects of these introductions never made the cut, but they nevertheless give us insight into how each role was defined through other star images or cinematic personalities. As Randal Kleiser puts it in the director's commentary, "a lot of the casting was based on icons of the '50s." Sandy was supposed to first appear in a "Rose Marie Reid swimsuit," lying on a beach as "Love Is a Many Splendored Thing" plays on the radio.[15] The song, of course, remains in the film, providing a soundtrack to other cinematic references. Although Sandy does not appear in a swimsuit, the specificity of this wardrobe decision earlier on in the production process reveals an attempt to channel Beach Party films and the Hollywood stars, like Marilyn Monroe and Jane Russell, who made it famous. After finishing work for the day at a hamburger stand, Danny (John Travolta) was to retrieve his clothes from a locker, inside of which hangs a portrait of James Dean, one of the Hollywood star images after which he crafts his own. The reference to James Dean survives in the film, but through an entirely different mechanism. The type of jacket that Danny wears on the beach is a replica (though in a different color) of the one worn by Dean in *Rebel without a Cause*.

According to the screenplay, the Pink Ladies and T-Birds do not announce themselves as ready-made conduits to past stars and characters. Instead, they are seen in the process of constructing their Hollywood-inspired personas, giving us insight into their respective morning routines and the steps necessary to achieve their particular looks. Kenickie (Jeff Conaway) was to leave a massive grease stain on his pillow after waking up, Frenchy (Didi Conn) to wear a "flamboyant wig," and Doody (Barry Pearl) to appear snuggled up with his namesake, a Howdy Doody puppet. We were supposed to see Sonny put grease on his comb, Marty (Dinah Manoff) stuff her bra, and Rizzo remove her torpedo rollers in an effort to look like "a cross between Ava Gardner and Annette Funicello."[16] Following these fairly specific instances of modeling involving the core cast, the screenplay then calls for more general references to postwar grooming practices and sartorial options: Brylcreem and beehives, crinolines and greaser jackets.

Ultimately, however, the finished film instead introduced its core characters through an animated sequence, one that retained a few of these references, but embedded them in a much more expansive landscape of postwar social, political, and cultural citations. Nevertheless, the use of star images from the 1950s to define the film's protagonists continues throughout. For example, in the shooting script, Frenchy tells Marty she can make her look like Grace Kelly, Rizzo takes a "Betty Davis drag" off her cigarette, Rizzo calling Kenickie "Pinky Lee," Frenchy wishes for a guardian angel "like Debbie Reynolds had in Tammy," and Danny, in an effort to woo Sandy, is dressed as "Pat Boone, perma-pressed slacks and all."[17] According to the screenplay, the film was to end the way it began, by filtering characters both primary and background through star constructs: "Students are dressed as different 50's images. Two girls are dressed as the Dancing Old Gold Cigarette Packs. There are Davy Crocketts, Marilyn Monroes, Marlon Brandos, Toni Twins, Frankensteins and Draculas galore, Elvis Presleys and one girl gotten up as a nun on roller skates. Marty is dressed as a WAC [Women's Army Corps]."[18]

These images are both real and not real, to varying degrees cinematic constructions and products of celebrity culture, but also defined by the experiences of living, breathing people. That personal history, sometimes mired in scandal and marred by trauma, is difficult to write out, especially now in the age of Me Too. Take Sandy, for instance. Olivia Newton-John's star image as a popular musical artist is very much present throughout. But *Grease* also takes great pains to define her through Sandra Dee, visually, musically, and narratively. However, then as now, Sandra Dee is understood both through her iconic roles and her turbulent life. She stands as testament to a particular construct of femininity and to how laws, expectations, and social mores can constrict, victimize, and then perpetually revictimize. She is a cipher to various horrid realities that are complexly and inextricably entwined with the 1950s "good girl."[19]

Danny is an equally complicated construction. Through him emerge the trappings of greaser style as popularized by Elvis and James Dean. But he also channels himself. That is, John Travolta evokes a number of other star texts as much as he does his own recently cultivated one. Commentators writing at the time of the film's release already noted some of the sources of his complexity. For them, Travolta embodied a "doubleness in the historical meaning of his image: the greasy hair, the singing, evoke Presley but the bony face (Presley was chubbily feminine) and the bunched-shouldered heel-toe walk recall Fred Astaire (and the smile perhaps Gene Kelly?)."[20] He thus channeled two distinct postwar performative traditions and two constructs of masculinity, each mediated by the cinematic genres with which they have become deeply aligned: beach party films in Presley's case and classical film musicals in Astaire and Kelly's. And further embedded in each of these are multiple musical histories, for rock and roll and Hollywood musicals can be omnivorous in their appetite for disparate musical genres and sounds. Of course, *Grease* itself does much to revive both traditions through other means including choreography, narrative strategies, and ways of integrating musical numbers into the fabric of the film. John Travolta meshes these well-entrenched star images (along with their histories) with his own nascent one. With the help of a few iconic dance gestures, performance of white-ethnic working-class masculinity, and especially that pink shirt, he cements the connection to *Saturday Night Fever* (1977). In doing so, his star image also contributes to the system of visual and aural anchors that secure *Grease* to its present, ensuring we read the late-1950s world of the film through a late-1970s perspective.

Olivia Newton-John and John Travolta are stars of the 1970s and thus very much of *Grease*'s time. The fact that many of the film's postwar references they enact and embody are played for parody also helps keep our consciousness anchored in the present. So too does the unreality of their ages, which effectively unmoors them from any teenage world. In fact, Stockard Channing and Michael Tucci were even teenagers in 1959. As Travis Malone suggests, the advanced age of the cast was often at issue and just as often defended on the grounds that older actors could bring a "sexual confidence lacking in any age-appropriate casting."[21] But this particular disjunction also suggests an adult perspective on the past and thus a more contemporary lens on the social mores of the 1950s. As Brickman argues, "[t]he film may bring us back to the end of the 1950s, but the particular politics of the 1970s unquestionably shape both its main characters and their expressed desires in the film."[22] She builds on this claim later, in a way that grounds her argument about the subversive nature of the film (one located in its queerness and female-centered focus) by revealing that the multiple references to closeted gay stars (Troy Donahue, Rock Hudson, and Sal Mineo) in Rizzo's "Look at Me I'm Sandra Dee" are speaking directly to a post-Stonewall audience.[23] For Brickman, the identities enacted by *Grease*'s characters foreground the performativity of gender in a way that "denaturalizes [it], heteronormative exigencies, and the entire moral polemic of 1950s parent culture."[24] Although I am convinced by Brickman's compelling evidence for a number of individual instances in which this happens, as a whole, *Grease* leaves me with less of an overall impression of its critical capacity to denaturalize. I would also amend that "parent culture" itself might sometimes be the source of such critical challenges. For while the actual (invisible) parents are indeed likely to be carriers of moral polemic, as the progeny of media culture, *Grease*'s characters have a rather different DNA, one in which we might find blueprints for reading how and through what (mediated) means identities can be crafted.

Producing a film version of the musical *Grease* was a shrewd business decision. It benefited greatly from the popularity of the stage version's long theatrical run and ready-made soundtrack.[25] In fact, this formula also underpinned the economic logic of jukeboxes, which played chart toppers but were not responsible for their initial success. As Kerry Segrave explains, jukebox operators didn't "gamble on music hits," but instead "waited until a tune had become thoroughly popularized on the radio or elsewhere before placing it on their machines."[26] It was thus a technology that amplified and reinforced the appeal of popular music. It did so in the narrower sense of the term, cementing the fame of popular music artists whose songs reflected the full range of rock and roll sounds, ones inspired to different degrees by swing, blues, and jazz. But it also did so in a broader sense, proliferating music from many genres that was popular—familiar, recognizable, and loved—from across several decades. For both senses of "popular" music, the jukebox's history resonates with *Grease* and the vision of the Fifties it generates. For as much as the film is known as a rock and roll musical (and all the layers and practices of appropriation this admits into the fray), its references to the world of music extend much wider culturally and deeper historically.

Grease's integration of music is complex and heterogeneous and a key way in which the Fifties is both channeled and juxtaposed against other eras and their media: radio, television, and cinema. Aural histories are mobilized here as well as some of the visual traditions that attend the multitemporal sonic landscape of the film. This multitemporality is enhanced not only by the myriad pasts on offer through sound, but by future expectations too, for the resulting soundtrack—and especially the new numbers composed specifically for the film—point the way forward to coming hits. However, my concern here is with how popular music is mobilized in *Grease*, how the film engages the technologies that structure our experience of music and the spaces in which we encounter it.

Grease's first aural juxtaposition hints at the range of musical forms and traditions that percolate throughout the film and which are responsible for infusing it with its multitemporality. The song, "Grease," written by Barry Gibb to accompany the credit sequence, is very much a product of the 1970s. Its disco sounds and reflective lyrics accompany a series of references that flit by in an attempt to recall the 1950s or, rather, construct the Fifties. As noted above, this sequence is animated, a decision likely made for expediency's sake, but one that nevertheless cements the mediated nature of the past on offer here. Representation remains at issue in the very next shot, a cinematic pastiche—the beach scene from *A Summer Place* (1959)—set against the popular song "Love Is a Many Splendored Thing." Just as *Grease* promises to turn its eponymous title track into a hit, this second song was also made popular by its cinematic context, for it contains few aural suggestions of the era's more energetic rock and roll. Its classical riffs and sweeping crescendos point back to much earlier musical traditions, though ones anchored in cinema. There is thus a jarring disjunction between the first two instances of music that we hear, a sign of *Grease*'s self-conscious positioning of its viewers as removed from the temporal setting of the film and thus in a position to evaluate its melodramatic source material with cynicism. But there is also a firm alliance between the two sets of images that accompany these songs, for both are suggestive of representational practices and mediation itself.

Grease manages to abide by a fairly consistent formula for determining how actual recorded music of the 1950s is incorporated into the film as opposed to how original music is integrated into the narrative flow. Popular music from the 1950s is channeled almost exclusively through other media. Recognizable songs by well-known artists of the period are heard on the radio, television, and the jukebox at the Frosty Palace. The screenplay offers explicit instructions to this effect that were more or less followed by the film. "A 50s song plays on the radio [television or jukebox]" appears on many occasions throughout.[27] Sometimes, a specific song is indicated, like Ricky Nelson's "Poor Little Fool." The historical 1950s is thus mediated, our access to the aural past only possible through its recordings and distribution through broadcast technologies. Of course, music is made to be reproduced, both through exact copies and subsequent performances that leave room for degrees of reinterpretation.

Despite *Grease*'s adherence to this formula for integrating popular music, there is an important moment when actual 1950s songs are performed live. During the National Bandstand sequence, the fictional band, Johnny Casino and the Gamblers, play quintessential 1950s songs like "Hound Dog" and "Blue Moon." However, pastiche structures this instant too, for the fictional band is played by Sha Na Na, a 1970s retro/nostalgia group made famous for their 1950s covers and thus prevalence in a Fifties nostalgia economy.[28] In *Grease*, they are in essence playing themselves. As such, a degree of mediation continues here, and it does so through an appeal to the nostalgia culture that gave rise to appetites for films and theatrical productions like *Grease* in the first place. This mediation is then reinforced by the black-and-white television footage that Frosty Palace guests watch of the dance competition. In other words, we watch Vi and others watch Johnny Casino and the Gamblers on television perform the 1950s songs they would have performed as Sha Na Na in the 1970s.

The musical numbers performed by the principal characters in *Grease* do not even have much of a 1950s sound. As John Bush Jones notes, "[t]he songs weren't actual '50s songs but pastiche sounds of the songs sung by the girl-groups, guy-groups and hip-swiveling solo-performing heart-throbs in the golden age of rock and roll."[29] The distinctive 1970s sonic veneer distinguishes *Grease* from other 1978 releases also invested in the music of the 1950s: *The Buddy Holly Story* and *American Hot Wax*. Through the film's soundtrack we hear an aural lineage, 1950s sounds that inform *Grease*'s present but are not constitutive of it. These past sounds survive in new and adapted ways in the 1970s, helping chart a number of evolutionary trajectories and possibilities for integration. Sometimes the present impresses itself through the music, as in "You're the One That I Want" and "Summer Nights." At other times it does so almost exclusively through lyrics, for instance the more sexually explicit lines in "Tell Me More." Sex was of course at issue in 1950s rock and roll, as a structuring force and in no uncertain or ambiguous terms. But there is a parodic if not hyperbolic element to *Grease*'s sexual innuendos, ones achieved by dance moves (e.g., "Hand Jive") or that, progressively, enable a queer reading (e.g., "Greased Lightnin'"). *Grease* also gives us lyrics even *more* thinly veiled than those written by 1950s musical acts, some of which rest squarely and regressively in the domain of rape culture ("did she put up a fight?").

The variety of musical numbers in *Grease* channel the past in different ways. As choreographer Patricia Birch explains in the director's commentary, there are "Paramount," "semi-Paramount," and "in-script" numbers. For Birch, "Paramount" describes highly theatrical, precisely choreographed, often surreal musical numbers of the studio-era variety, ones that feel and look fully removed from the reality of the diegetic world. There are two examples: "Beauty School Dropout" and "Greased Lightnin'." In both instances, the setting—the Frosty Palace and shop class, respectively—are replaced by nondescript white backgrounds against which theatrically costumed actors and props organize into lavish spectacle. As Brickman explains, there is a distinct "anachronism of presenting old fashioned, studio-era musical numbers in a 1970s blockbuster film."[30] This anachronism is activated by what the screenplay calls "Busby Berkeley production numbers" to deliver the two most 1950s sounding songs in the film.[31] For example, "Beauty School Dropout" is sung by teen idol Frankie Avalon, but the postwar heteronormative culture channeled by Avalon is undercut when "the image of patriarchal dominance, the male idol, is exposed as part of the mechanics of this system, an inauthentic spectacle—all sparkles and cruel mastery—while the female subject is centered as a more authentic, sympathetic, and knowing audience."[32] In "Greased Lightnin'," the anachronism is sustained by aligning another "Paramount" or "Busby Berkeley" treatment of a resolutely 1950s song with overtly homoerotic choreography.[33] These anachronisms thus open up the possibility for critical readings of *Grease* in terms of gender and sexuality and for reflection on the ways in which multiple cinematic pasts are mobilized, carry meaning, and swirl in a constellation of visual and aural alignments that perpetually make and remake the past.

Sounds and gestures, along with markers of identity rooted in various star images, help constitute *Grease*'s multitemporality, alternately celebrated and ridiculed for its simplistic postmodern intertextuality. But it is important to remember that all of these things unfold within—and are contextualized by—space. And, in *Grease*, these spaces are generative of the film's construction of the Jukebox Fifties.

The Jukebox is a large, expensive object designed for *public* space. Although the wealthy may have been privileged enough to own one, they were not destined for homes. Instead, they were rented or bought by operators to generate additional revenue for cafes, diners, restaurants, ice cream parlors, snack bars, taverns, and cocktail lounges.³⁴ As R.G. Norman, advertising manager for Wurlitzer believed, a good site for a jukebox had to be one that was popular with young people and preferably had a space for dancing.³⁵ This aptly describes the Frosty Palace, the quintessential postwar diner and site of much social interaction between the youth in *Grease*. The jukebox, standing literally and figuratively at the center of this themed diner, provides a 1950s soundtrack to the action that transpires here, from dancing to dates to teenage drama.

As *Grease* unfolds, it becomes evident that what defines the space of the Frosty Palace also defines the nature of space throughout almost the entire film (Figure 4.1). Virtually every scene takes place in a public site where youth congregate and interact against a backdrop of music: a drive-in movie theater, the beach, lovers' lane, the fairground, various streets, and the high school. At Rydell High we see the action unfold in classrooms, hallways, the gym, the athletic field, and the courtyard. The only exception is the scene set in Frenchy's bedroom. But even here the site is not utilized in a way that foregrounds its domestic, private nature. Instead, it too is framed as a site of teenage socialization involving the Pink Ladies as they bring Sandy into their fray. It is a space of performance and one in which references to the external world abound through posters, photos, television, and the lyrics for "Look at Me I'm Sandra Dee."

In this way *Grease* eschews the spaces that structure the Leave It to Beaver Fifties, ones infused with domesticity and aligned with family dynamics like the kitchen and living room. Such domestic sites play a key role in articulating not just ideological positions that seek to support a return to patriarchal

Figure 4.1 The "Frosty Palace" diner in *Grease* (1978)

family structures but also ones that advocate for their deconstruction. The kitchen or living room can be subject to very different cinematographic treatment depending on the approach of the film. Jukebox Fifties films also differentiate themselves from the Cold War Fifties, where court rooms and sites of political significance tend to contain the action. But again, these sites are just as likely to be exalted as representative of law and order or the nation as they are to be condemned as advancing troubling ideological principles. A similar claim can be made for the construction of spaces in the Jukebox Fifties, for not all offerings in this category are apt to celebrate public social sites as places that shape benign teenage antics.

The spaces historically aligned with the jukebox resonate here in a way that helps isolate how a specific cinematic construction of the Fifties is (partly) founded on the mobilization of social sites. However, there are two scenes that feature the jukebox itself in situ in rather interesting ways. One involves the start of the reconciliation process between Sandy and Danny. Sandy excuses herself from her date, Tom Chisum (Lorenzo Lamas), to select "new music" on the Frosty Palace's jukebox, a pretense for passing by Danny's table. Despite being right next to the jukebox, Danny takes a circuitous route, one interrupted by Patty Simcox (Susan Buckner), to initiate his apology to Sandy. During this conversation, Danny is center-frame, with Sandy to the right and the jukebox to the left (Figure 4.2). The jukebox is thus blocked as a third character and, just like Danny and Sandy it, too, speaks. First it speaks to popular musical history, for it plays Ritchie Valen's "La Bamba," a period accurate release that would have received much play during 1959. After a clink of coins, "It's Raining on Prom Night" begins. Now it speaks

Figure 4.2 Danny (John Travolta), Sandy (Olivia Newton-John), and a Jukebox in *Grease* (1978)

to *Grease*'s own theatrical history, for this was a song written for the stage version that never made it into the film. It also speaks to the future, for both songs are about dancing, foreshadowing the next stage in Danny and Sandy's reconciliation—pairing up for the dance competition. Sandy leaves this conversation first and, after she exits the frame, the camera shifts to give both Danny and the jukebox equal weight. Even if we managed to overlook the presence of the jukebox during Sandy and Danny's dialogue, it announces itself now as a key participant in the scene and a key character in the space of the Frosty Palace.

The jukebox also plays a somewhat poetic role in the transition from the Frosty Palace scene involving the Pink Ladies and T-Birds to "Beauty School Dropout." After Frenchy imagines—and then readily dismisses—a series of possible careers in her conversation with Vi, she kneels on a booth bench, facing the back of the jukebox. As in the shot with Danny, the jukebox is blocked like a character, occupying the left half of the frame while Frenchy inhabits the right. Vi is positioned centrally behind them but as the light starts to dim, only Frenchy and the chrome arc on the top of the jukebox remain illuminated. The camera then zooms in on Frenchy, cutting the jukebox—and source of music for the previous ten minutes of the film—out of the scene. She slowly turns away from the jukebox as the spotlight on her starts to glimmer, anticipating the surreal strobe effect that introduces Frankie Avalon's "Paramount" number. The sounds and images associated with the jukebox and the diner fade away, holding its last sliver of light, as a parody of film musical spectacle (quite literally) takes the stage. The space of the diner is replaced by a space of performance, where costume and choreography are foregrounded. But of course, in *Grease*, every space is one of performance and it is so on many levels: with respect to the various musical numbers; in terms of the star images mimicked in the articulation of characters' identities; and through the mediated performances we see (on televisions and movie screens) and hear (on radios and jukeboxes).

After decades of cinematic and televisual representations, the jukebox is now aligned in the cultural imagination with youth identities, popular music, public sites of socialization, and, despite its much longer history, the Fifties. These resonances help illuminate what is of chief concern in *Grease* and responsible for its complex multitemporality. They structure the defining investments of this film, but also serve as an effective template for analyzing others that, to varying degrees and in different ratios, concern themselves with variants or subtypes of teenagers, rock and roll, and diners—the ingredients that constitute the Jukebox Fifties. I want to turn now to the legacy of one particular construct at the heart of *Grease*, one that unites this triumvirate of features: the (male) greaser. I will start with its origins—more complex than typically acknowledged—but focus on the implications of its continued circulation across our cultural landscape and impact on conceptions of the Fifties generally and Jukebox Fifties, specifically. That is, I want to trace the pathways taken by the greaser cinematically, musically, socially, and photographically to show how some of its current iterations help us see both the critical potential and profound failings of Danny as one of its progenitors.

The greaser, an icon of postwar rebellion, found its most popular expression for subsequent generations' attempts at revival in Marlon Brando's John Strabler in *The Wild One*, James Dean's Jim Stark in *Rebel without a Cause*, and Elvis Presley. But while each of these sported a similar look and antiauthoritarian stance, there are differences in their respective enactments of masculinity, especially in terms of the degree of vulnerability they exhibit. The greaser also has some very British roots, ones that determined its initial figuration but also its subsequent revival. For instance, the DA (Duck's Ass) haircut sported by greasers was invented in 1954 by Mr. Rose, an English East End hairdresser.[36] Likewise the term "greaser" itself, was first applied to "a fifties teddy boy with his hair slicked back with Brylcreem or a similar product."[37] Even the rockabilly revival of the 1970s—which positioned the greaser at its center—originated in Britain.[38] Indeed now, the greaser (and rockabilly more broadly) is a global phenomenon, with devoted fans far beyond the Anglo-American world.[39]

The rockabilly revival of the 1970s was complemented by a number of films invested in greaser culture, and often for the sake of confronting visions of the Leave It to Beaver Fifties mobilized as part of the burgeoning Fifties nostalgia economy. As such it played a role in engineering facets of the "suburban iconoclasm" that now suffuses this construct. For instance, the 1970s witnessed the release of *Badlands* (1973), *The Lords of Flatbush* (1974), and *The Wanderers* (1979). The 1980s saw titles such as *The Loveless* (1981), *The Outsiders* (1983), and *The Heavenly Kid* (1985). The 1990s were punctuated with their own rather particular visions of greasers, as in *Cry Baby* (1990) and *Roadracers* (1994). The greaser's presence continues to be felt and evolve into the 2000s with fictional and documentary films as well as low-budget and mainstream offerings: *Rebel Beat: The Story of L.A. Rockabilly* (2007), *Deuce of Spades* (2011), *The Ghastly Love of Johnny X* (2012), *It's a Rockabilly World* (2016), and *Badsville* (2017).

Comparing Danny to Wink (Ian McLaren) in April Mullen's *Badsville* is instructive for showing one evolutionary trajectory taken by this identity construct. *Badsville* appears to be set in the present, but an alternate one heavily impinged upon by numerous other periods. It feels like a heterochronic amalgam of different registers of time, once again recalling Serres's idea of percolation, but in a very self-conscious way. The film seems to signal through glaring anachronisms when the practices and habits of other eras—some ostensibly real, some distinctly cinematic—pierce through. For instance, *Badsville* is suffused with brutal violence of a degree not seen in 1950s films, between rival gangs with 1950s-inspired names, the Kings and Aces. This violence extends to conflicts between best friends, Wink and Benny (Benjamin Barrett), leaving them both dead in the end. And yet, despite the contemporary feel of expertly choreographed and bloody altercations, Benny regularly calls Wink "Daddy-o," without even a hint of irony. Such 1950s slang, which sounds ridiculously wholesome and thus wholly out of place in this violent world, is likely what inspired *Los Angeles Times* critic, Gary Goldstein, to suggest that the film's "unidentified time setting often evokes the 1950s."[40] It certainly does through language ("cool cats" is another oft heard example), but also through other visual means. Wink himself is a quintessential greaser with slicked back hair, tight rolled up jeans, and a gang jacket that reads "Badsville Kings" on the back. He even has a small football jacket version, one he presumably wore as a child. Wink—and all others—smoke continuously, a rarity in contemporary cinema. I'm hard pressed to find a single scene where a character doesn't light up or appear without a cigarette dangling from their mouth. In cinematic greaser fashion, the gangs are also divided along ethnic lines, recalling *Westside Story*'s (1961) Jets and Sharks, itself subject to a 2021 remake by Steven Spielberg. However, there is one key exception. The Kings are all Latinx, except for Wink, who is white, while the Aces are all white with a high school football team vibe about them.

The Fifties also persist through characterizations. The Ace's ringleader, Cutter (Paul James Jordan), is weak in the eyes of his father, himself once a gang member. Cutter is also still under his father's control in a way only believable in a 1950s cinematic context. Here, especially, periods collide, for although Cutter looks like a typical (too old) 1950s teenager, the narrative positions his father as a gang member whose heyday was likely the 1950s even though, technically, he is much too young for that to be possible. Mr. Gavin (Robert Knepper) still sports a haircut that suggests as much. Moreover, he disciplines his son with a belt for not being "man enough," something very much in keeping with the film's exposure of toxic masculinity.

Of course, Cutter could also belong to that moment of a 1970s revival of the 1950s, spurred on by *Grease* and the broader nostalgia economy of the time. There are several visual clues that point to this possibility. For instance, most of the film's vehicles are 1970s muscle cars, with the exception of a 1950s pick-up truck that looks about twenty years old (Figure 4.3). Likewise, the furniture inside Wink's house and Sammy's trailer also looks dated to this period. However, none of it appears new. Instead, it is ragged, stained, and worn, indicating the dire economic circumstances in which virtually all characters find themselves. Only Helen's (Chelsea Rendon) family home, though small and decidedly working class, is well kept. But here too the drapes and furniture recall the 1970s.

The gang members of both the Kings and Aces are attired in slightly edgier versions of Fifties greaser and football culture fashions, respectively. Suzy's (Tamara Duarte) clothing, however, recalls 1970s B-movies. She wears cut-off shorts (Daisy Dukes) and a 1970s-style graphic T-shirt underneath a tight leather vest, the latter a nod to exploitation genres of the 1970s. In fact, all costumes in *Badsville* have evolved through their circulation across time and various cinematic contexts, accruing the resonances of the films and genres with which they are aligned. This recycling extends beyond sartorial signifiers to narrative fragments invested in the greaser's origins as well: Wink's plan to escape includes Suzy and Sammy (Greg Kasyan), a ten-year-old boy whose mother is a heroin addict. In so doing, they recreate a more desperate and downtrodden version of the alternate family structure assumed by Jim, Judy,

Figure 4.3 Wink (Ian McClaren), Benny (Benjamin Barrett), and Georgie (Rene Rosado) in *Badsville* (2017)

and Plato in *Rebel without a Cause*. Their plan ends in tragedy with Wink's death, but Suzy and Sammy do manage to escape.

Films that mobilize many of the standard greaser tropes often follow *Grease*'s lead in their adherence to the Jukebox Fifties by foregrounding 1950s popular music and the practices and sites of youth socialization (e.g., *The Wanderers*). *Badsville*, however, departs in certain marked ways. While the film focuses on youth and their social practices (i.e., bowling, congregating at bars, driving around, and shooting cans), parents are also recurring characters. They are filmed within and thus aligned with home, but in no instance are they or these spaces sources of comfort. Sammy's mother is only fully conscious when begging Benny for more heroin. Cutter's father is a ruthless sociopathic tyrant who tries to shape him in his own image. Wink's mother may be adored by him as his fellow gang members, but dies at the very start of the film, precipitating his effort to escape Badsville.

Music is central to *Badsville*, providing the soundtrack for instances of youth socialization and, like much else in the film, belongs to two distinct times. The majority of the songs belong to underground garage blues punk or garage punk noise, forms that cannibalize past genres but substantially rework them. The result is closely aligned with rockabilly, itself of two eras— past and present. *Badsville*'s soundtrack includes several original songs written and performed by AJ Gallardo. These exude an amateur quality that fits well with the aesthetic roughness of the film. Other songs are performed by The Meekers (aptly described as putting The Osmonds through a blender), Lucifer in the Sky with Diamonds, and the Immortal Lee County Killers, a blues-punk band deeply informed by the members' vast historical knowledge of the blues.[41] The soundtrack is thus structured by an aggressive retooling of older sounds, a reworking of postwar musical tendencies and traditions. And while the sonic textures of the soundtrack help place the film in the present, the aggression with which The Osmonds, for example, are reimagined, correlates with how masculinity itself, for greasers, is reconfigured in *Badsville*.

In cinema, the male greaser, from Danny to Wink and a number of iterations in between, becomes increasingly embroiled with worlds of violence, toxic masculinity, despair, and economic disenfranchisement. The menace written out of Danny is reintroduced in films like *Badsville*, where the specter of Danny functions as little more than an inauthentic foil. However, the benign Danny does persist as a model in television for "good greasers," especially in youth-oriented productions like *Glee* and *High School Musical* or star images from Luke Perry to Drake Bell.[42] It even reappears in *The Identical*, a cinematic outlier in many respects that attempts to imagine what happened if Elvis Presley's twin brother lived and was adopted. However, the twins, Ryan Wade and Drexel Helmsley (both played by Elvis impersonator Blake Rayne) coexist alongside Elvis and without ever commenting on their resemblance to one another. This film retools Danny in the other direction, presenting an unreflexively nostalgic vision of a 1950s popular music and youth scene that was marketed by churches and other conservative organizations as "faith friendly."[43] While reviews for this film made *Suburbicon* seem like a critical triumph, its particular sanitized vision of the Jukebox Fifties aligned with a conservative, politically charged "kinder, gentler" vision of the postwar past. And, however routinely and summarily rejected *The Identical* was by most critics, it did find an audience in those who felt it accurately detailed when America was once "great."

The greaser also permeates social practices well beyond cinema and television. For instance, Danny is a model for drag king identities. For k. bradford, this is because of how Travolta embodies a theatrical masculinity that queered itself through the process of performance, a theatricality highlighted by the care and relish with which Danny (and Tony from *Saturday Night Fever*) get "done up."[44] Danny and Tony also provide the source material for bradford's own drag king alter ego, Johnny T. Transforming into greaser Johnny T is an imperative for bradford personally, but also politically. As they argue, "[m]aking our deviant desires public is a fundamental operating principle of queer and trans movements and communities.... This is our revolutionary work: we put our bodies on the line to enact queer and trans visibility and to forge new social spaces and relations in a rigid, role-bound society."[45] Danny's queer sensibility, articulated through dance and gesture, has inspired critical reassessments of the film but also reflection on the value of his performance for queer youth who were, as Michael Borgstrom observes, "just coming to terms with their own sense of social difference, particularly within the sexually liberated culture of the 1970s."[46] By satirizing masculinity and serving up "identity as irony," *Grease* disrupted—and continues to disrupt—marginalizing social conventions.[47]

A queer sensibility also infuses roller derby, an offshoot of rockabilly culture through its fashion, the music of half-time shows, and the adoption of theatrical identities, including many from greaser culture and *Grease* itself. Names of skaters include Maulin' Brando, Elvis REFley, Grease Frightenin', Rumblin' Rizzo, and at least ten variants of Bettie Page (e.g., Bettie RamPage).

Roller derby has become a staple attraction at rockabilly festivals, and bouts between the Pink Ladies and T-Birds have been staged from the United States to New Zealand. It is a full-contact women's sport, and one often celebrated for its trans-inclusivity and regular participation in LGBTQIA+ initiatives. As such the ways in which *Grease*, greaser identities, and the music of rockabilly work through roller derby recall the critical possibilities around sexuality and gender that more recent commentators, like Brickman, have located in the film through Rizzo's agency and Sandy's self-determination.[48]

But the queer sensibility and agency embodied by roller derby is often deeply at odds with other facets of rockabilly culture, a key site of continued dominance for greasers, some very much on display at the same rockabilly festivals. Some subscribers appeal to more than the aesthetic trappings of a male greaser identity and seek to revive the (patriarchal) masculinity associated with its postwar antecedents, including strict gender hierarchies and divisions of labor in the home. Stay-at-home wives are expected to be subservient, supportive, and always visually on display in a relationship defined by noxious heteronormative dynamics. And it is here where, once again, the Leave It to Beaver Fifties come into contact with the Jukebox Fifties. For as much as rockabilly and the greasers that populate it are invested in music and hotrods, some are also invested in transforming their homes and domestic life into a midcentury American Dream.

But this contact between a Leave It to Beaver type of domesticity and the greaser world of the Jukebox Fifties where (youth) style and music are paramount, is effected in ways that extend beyond a simple purposeful re-enactment of gender inequality. As Kimberly Adele Kattari's field research demonstrates, for both rockabilly and psychobilly, there are many different ends to which the "worked-over language" of the 1950s (to borrow Dika's phrase) can be used.[49] Kattari observes that "[t]here are LGBT individuals as well as people with homophobic ideologies. Some women idealize the 1950s vision of domesticity while others have no interest in being a housewife. Some women prefer the feminized pin-up fashion style while others dress as the men do, in cuffed jeans, t-shirts and flattop quiffs."[50] In terms of fashion, inspirations are as likely to found in postwar domestic sitcoms as they are in burlesque culture and, in some instances, a blend of the two.

Beyond social relations, the intersection of the Leave It to Beaver and Jukebox Fifties reveals other interesting (ideological) retoolings, one aptly captured in Jennifer Greenburg's photodocumentary project, *The Rockabillies* (Figure 4.4). Completed over the course of a decade, Greenburg's

Figure 4.4 Jennifer Greenburg, *The K-Wals*, Itasca, Illinois, 2004

photography of the everyday life of this subculture was sparked by hers and her friends' investment in the styles and social practices of 1950s America. This subculture is comprised of people, typically white and lower-middle income, who adopt not just the fashions and leisure pursuits of greaser culture, but orient their domestic lives and spaces in ways that resemble a Leave It to Beaver set. Rockabilly greasers, often heavily tattooed and thus resembling Wink more than Danny, or Rizzo more than the Sandy (initially), are as likely to prize a hot rod as they are a pink tail-finned Cadillac. They are as prone to listening to 1950s rock and roll as they are punk-infused adaptations of these earlier sounds.

Somewhat ironically, Greenburg's project was instigated by her nostalgia for the world of her grandparents in the 1950s, a nostalgia sparked by feelings of defeat and hopelessness in a post-9/11 world that celebrated "mediocrity and religious fundamentalism" and in which an appointed president (George W. Bush) waged a "xenophobic 'war on terror.'"[51] Indeed for many of Greenburg's fellow travelers, they not only sought to revive the styles of 1950s greaser culture, but also marry young, move to the suburbs, and have children.⁵² They sought to turn "away from the horrors of contemporary American culture to focus on family, friends, music and vintage Americana."⁵³ As such both the rockabilly subculture and the conservative political establishment were turning to the same object, though to somewhat different ends. For while there may well have been an alignment in terms of retrograde assumptions about gender roles within the domestic sphere, rockabilly and Republicans share very little.

There are two further differences of note between rockabilly's investment in a Leave It to Beaver Fifties and the Republicans' activation of this image, even though both initially turned to this past era at roughly the same time: the 1980s. The first involves divergent approaches to commodity culture and planned obsolescence—the purported civic duty to spend for the sake of prosperity and keep commodity culture churning out annual replacements of rather expensive goods, ones that continue to be fully functional and thus not in need of replacement. Whereas wasteful practices of consumer capitalism continue to be vaunted by many Republicans as a patriotic act, the very objects that defined this ethos during the 1950s are now treasured and repaired to extend their longevity. There is a widespread DIY ethos that runs through the domestic arm of the rockabilly scene where pink toasters, avocado green refrigerators, and tail-finned cars are sought out in antiques markets and meticulously conserved. As Audrey Michelle Mast puts it, "[t]he emerging youth-oriented consumerism of yesteryear is today's booming antiques market."⁵⁴ Even a cursory glance at Greenburg's images highlights this facet of rockabilly domesticity, one in which participants selected where and with which objects they wished to pose.⁵⁵

The second key difference between a rockabilly and Republican approach to America's postwar past is the degree of self-reflexivity that guides a rockabilly investment in the 1950s and an acknowledgement (by some proponents) of its models as fictions. As Greenburg explains, "the rockabillies have idealized the lifestyle present in the idealized advertisements and Hollywood films of the 1950s. *Life* and *Look* magazines serve, to most rockabillies, as a record of the way the perfect life must have looked in the 1950s and, more importantly, as a blueprint of the way they want their lives to be now." However, rockabilly adherents recognize these sources and images as little more than fantasy, though it is "the fantasy that rockabillies want."⁵⁶

But rockabilly's amalgamation of a Jukebox and Leave It to Beaver Fifties takes us down another much more disturbing path too. Some subscribers take the "billy" (from "hillbilly") to celebrate the segregated south as part of a disturbing neoconfederate and white supremacist agenda. As Dick Hebdige explains, rockabilly points in two directions, one of which is "back and down to the embarrassing atavistic origin—to the holler and the still, to Daniel Boone and Davy Crockett, the confederacy, mass illiteracy, the slave states, Civil War, the literal origin of the nation, to lynching, rape and racial murder, back and down to the ultra-charged, hyper-patrolled binaries of race and sexual difference in the South."[57] On its way down this particular path, rockabilly pierces through Grease, reaffirming the film's whiteness and perhaps drawing attention to how this whiteness is constructed in relation to gender. Black people are all but erased in Grease, the exception being Dennis Greene of Sha Na Na. Here, Greene only appears as a performer for a white audience, thus replicating the deeply troubling dynamics of segregated spaces and performance practices that subjected people of color to a white gaze. The blinding whiteness of Grease is something Grease Live! made some attempts to rectify by casting Keke Palmer as Marty, Wendell Pierce as Coach Calhoun, Boyz II Men as Teen Angel, and a diverse cast of background actors and dancers.[58] However, what remains erased from both iterations is any acknowledgment of the civil rights struggles that marked the 1950s, the racism that Sha Na Na or Marty, for instance, would have been subjected to, and the ways in which the spaces inhabited by the characters—those public social sites like diners—would have been segregated in 1959.

The greaser, with its many iterations and mediations, is part of the legacy of the Jukebox Fifties. So too is Grease. Grease warrants detailed consideration here (despite its 1970s origins) because of its cult status, a status that affects its circulation, legacy, and cultural impact. It is a film continually rescreened, rereleased, and reimagined through various platforms, practices, and media. As such, it persists into the twenty-first century in both its original and various modified forms and thus in ways other films may not. Grease is a multifaceted work, rife with internal differentiations and ones that point to various media practices and moments in time. The film's image of the Fifties has been formed from intertextual references that both predate and postdate the 1950s, from 1930s classical musical forms to the sounds and star images of the 1970s. This visual and aural amalgam produced an array of critical responses with very little agreement about the nature of Grease, its genre, value, approach to the past, and even temporal setting. For commentators reflecting on the film now, these inconsistences and the film's omnivorous approach to culture have provided opportunities to read critical possibilities into its characters, music, and lyrics.[59] It has sparked analysis of constructs of white postwar masculinity and the cultural recalibration of such constructs in the forms of Wink and Johnny T, to name but two divergent iterations. But its troubling failings are also instructive for how certain gendered and racialized subjectivities are vanquished by the film and the cinematic visions and subcultures it has since spawned, often despite recent efforts to contend with such elisions (e.g., *Grease Live*). As such, ensconced within the Jukebox Fifties is a series of histories of ideologically constituted subjects and willful erasures surrounding youth and music culture in particular. These are not only instructive for grappling with representations of the past, the Fifties and its myriad afterlives, but also how its tropes and forms continue to replicate in ways that expand both conceptions of the Fifties and the various ends to which its fractures might be harnessed.

Notes

1. The fertility rate in the United States during the 1950s hovered around 3.4%, and not 2.4%, a British statistic from the 1970s that has since evolved into a common expression, one often aligned with the Leave It to Beaver Fifties.
2. Of course much of this is false, including the purported (political) innocence of childhood during the 1950s. As Victoria M. Grieves argues, the popular culture and leisure pursuits carefully curated for children in postwar America interpellated them as politicized subjects with a key role to play in the ideological battles of the Cold War. See *Little Cold Warriors: American Childhood in the 1950s* (New York: Oxford University Press, 2018).
3. In other words, despite the historical significance of Latinx and "white ethnic" greasers, it is the star image of Dean (and Brando) that have been adopted and heralded as originary by contemporary greaser communities.
4. *Grease* began life as a successful play in 1971; for a thorough account of its development as such, see Scott Warfield, "From Chicago to Broadway: The Origins of Grease," in *Grease Is the Word: Exploring a Cultural Phenomenon*, ed. Oliver Gruner and Peter Krämer (London: Anthem Press, 2020), 23–40. For a detailed production history of the film, see Alexander G. Ross, "'We Were Just Trying to Entertain': *Grease* in Production," in *Grease Is the Word: Exploring a Cultural Phenomenon*, ed. Oliver Gruner and Peter Krämer (London: Anthem Press, 2020), 41–58.
5. *Grease* appears in the top ten list of most popular high school musical productions staged in the United States and Canada from 1938 to 2004. Raymond Knapp, Mitchel Morris, and Stacy Wolf, *The Oxford Handbook of the American Musical* (New York: Oxford University Press, 2011), 400.
6. See Kerry Segrave, *Jukeboxes: An American Social History* (Jefferson, NC: McFarland 2002).

7. As with other Fifties types, there are a number of films or parts of films—from coming-of-age dramas to biopics to more quintessentially "Jukebox Musicals"—that fit the bill to different degrees. A sampling includes the following: *American Graffiti* (1973), *Buddy Holly Story* (1978), *American Hot Wax* (1978), *Cry Baby* (1990), *Diner* (1982), *Back to the Future* (1985), *La Bamba* (1987), *Going All the Way* (1997), *Liberty Heights* (1999), and others.
8. Charles Champlin, "50s as Seen through *Grease*," *Los Angeles Times*, June 16, 1978, 130.
9. Oliver Gruner, *Screening the Sixties: Hollywood Cinema and the Politics of Memory* (London: Palgrave Macmillan, 2016), 102.
10. There are several ways in which this presentness is achieved. For instance, Travis Malone locates it in the film's production values: "While the sounds of the 1950s setting were familiar to late 1970s audiences, the technology employed in the film's production gave the film a present-ness that conflicted with and subsequently erased any historical reference." Travis Malone, "Utopia, Nostalgia, *Grease*: How a Film Can Create a Stage Legacy," *Theatre Annual* 63 (2010): 46.
11. Vera Dika, *Recycled Culture in Contemporary Art and Film* (Cambridge: Cambridge University Press, 2003), 123.
12. SEFT Manchester Discussion Group, "*Grease*: The Wobbly Hot-Dog of the Seventies," *Framework* (Spring 1979): 39.
13. See, for instance, Dika, *Recycled Culture*, 124–42, and Barbara Jane Brickman, *Grease: Gender, Nostalgia, and Youth Consumption in the Blockbuster Era* (New York: Routledge, 2017), loc. 1277.
14. Tom Symmons, *The New Hollywood Historical Film, 1967–78* (London: Palgrave Macmillan, 2016), 9.
15. Bronte Woodard, *Grease*, Shooting Script, June 9, 1977, 1.
16. Ibid., 4–5.
17. Ibid., 41, 47, 114.
18. Ibid., 113.
19. For a thorough account that attends to the complexity of the star legacy of Sandra Dee, see Dwyer, *Back to the Fifties*, 169–77.
20. SEFT, "Wobbly Hot-Dog," 39.
21. Malone, "Utopian, Nostalgia, *Grease*," 47.
22. Brickman, *Grease*, loc. 296.
23. This is first noted by Scott Miller, *Sex, Drugs, Rock and Roll, and Musicals* (Hanover, NH: University Press of New England, 2011), 52. See also, Brickman, *Grease*, loc 1264.
24. Brickman, *Grease*, loc. 1337.
25. Justin Wyatt, *High Concept: Movies and Marketing in Hollywood* (Austin: University of Texas Press, 1994), 20.
26. Segrave, *Jukeboxes*, 50.
27. Woodard, *Grease*, 1, 47, 49, 57, 70.
28. See Daniel Marcus, *Happy Days and Wonder Years: The Fifties and Sixties in Contemporary Cultural Politics* (New Brunswick, NJ: Rutgers University Press, 2004),

12; Dwyer, *Back to the Fifties*, 49–50; Dika, *Recycled Culture*, 125–26; and Elizabeth E. Guffey, *Retro: The Culture of Revival* (London: Reaktion, 2006), 98–99.
29. John Bush Jones, *Our Musicals, Ourselves: A Social History of the American Musical Theater* (Hanover, NH: University Press of New England 2003), 312.
30. Brickman, *Grease*, loc. 1460.
31. Woodard, *Grease*, 7.
32. Brickman, *Grease*, loc. 1570.
33. This isn't to suggest that 1950s musicals didn't contain homoerotic choreography, but that "Greased Lightnin'" may be considered a different caliber. My thanks to the anonymous reviewer who reminded me of the "Ain't There Anyone Here for Love?" number from *Gentlemen Prefer Blondes* (1953).
34. Segrave, *Jukeboxes*, 229.
35. Ibid., 68.
36. Jenni Veitch Olson, "'We Go Together': Nostalgia, Gender, Class, and the London Reception of *Grease*: A New '50s Rock 'n' Roll Musical," *American Music Research Center Journal*, January 1, 2004, 84.
37. Ibid., 84.
38. According to Roy Brewer, the term "rockabilly," which refers to music produced between 1954 and 1958, "was first printed in June 1956 by a trade magazine but generally was not used by the performers themselves until the rockabilly revival." Roy Brewer, "The Use of Habanera Rhythm in Rockabilly Music," *American Music* 17.3 (Autumn 1999): 301.
39. See, for example, Michael Furmanovsky, "American Country Music in Japan: A Lost Piece in the Popular Music History Puzzle," *Popular Music and Society* 31.3 (2008): 357–72.
40. Gary Goldstein, "Escape is the Challenge in Gritty Crime Drama *Badsville*," *Los Angeles Times*, November 30, 2017. https://www.latimes.com/entertainment/movies/la-et-mn-capsule-badsville-review-20171130-story.html.
41. Jackson Ellis, "Interview: Chet Weise of Immortal Lee County Killers," Features/Interviews. *Verbicide*, March 4, 2005. https://www.verbicidemagazine.com/2005/03/04/interview-chet-weise-of-immortal-lee-county-killers/.
42. In fact, "best greaser film" lists that dare to include *Grease* are summarily criticized for including a musical. Greg Falone of California offered the first comment on one such list with the remark: "Why the fuck is *Grease* on this list?" There are some exceptions, including a research participant who unashamedly acknowledged *Grease*'s influence on his psychobilly greaser persona. Kimberly Adele Kattari, "Psychobilly: Imagining and Realizing a 'Culture of Survival' in Mutant Rockabilly" (PhD Diss, University of Texas at Austin, 2011), 292.
43. Rebecca Ford, "'The Identical' Faith-Friendly Marketing Campaign: Churches, NASCAR and the Emmys," *Hollywood Reporter*, September 5, 2014. https://www.hollywoodreporter.com/news/identical-faith-friendly-marketing-campaign-730539.
44. k. bradford, "Grease Cowboy Fever; Or, the Making of Johnny T," *Journal of Homosexuality* 43.3–4 (2003): 22.

45. Ibid., 28.
46. Michael Borgstrom, "Suburban Queer: Reading *Grease*," *Journal of Homosexuality* 58.2 (2011): 153.
47. Borgstrom, "Suburban Queer," 159.
48. Full disclosure: I write this paragraph as now-retired Grisly Blaire of Forest City Roller Derby.
49. Dika, *Recycled Culture*, 142.
50. Kattari, *Psychobilly*, 222.
51. Jennifer Greenburg, *The Rockabillies* (Chicago: Center for American Places, 2010), xi.
52. Greenburg, *The Rockabillies*, xii.
53. Ibid.
54. Audrey Michelle Mast in Greenburg, *The Rockabillies*, 77.
55. Ibid., 80. And these images are further mediated by a 1950s aesthetic veneer through "poses that tend to evoke the same mid-century feature magazine photography that is the rockabillies' source material" (80).
56. Greenburg, *The Rockabillies*, xiv.
57. Dick Hebdige, "Becoming Animal: Race, Terror and the American Roots," *Parallax* 13.1 (January 2007): 104.
58. However, *Grease Live!* essentially "de-queered" the original film, removing virtually all instances of homoeroticism and thus the possibility for a queer reading. For example, "Greased Lightnin'" now features a cast of female dancers who pair up with the male dancers to force a heteronormative reading of the number.
59. See, for instance, Oliver Gruner and Peter Krämer, eds., *Grease Is the Word: Exploring a Cultural Phenomenon* (London: Anthem Press, 2020).

5
The Cold War Fifties

The Cold War, with all its proxy conflicts and ideological battles, has been the subject of a range of cultural representation since its inception at the end of World War II. From archival footage to photographs, best-selling novels to historical tomes, documentaries to dramas, screen to stage, political fervor of all flavors has inspired a wide range of image and textual productions taking aim at the various events that constitute this long-running conflict and its legacies. However, in cinematic terms, there is some unevenness with regard to how the history of the Cold War's initial phase is represented. While cinematic engagement can be divided into three main subcategories—The Korean War Fifties, The McCarthyite Fifties, and The Atomic Fifties—variation within these groups is significant and instructive for considering not just *what* constitutes the Cold War, but also how its facets inform broader conceptions of the postwar era.

In what follows, I will look at twenty-first-century case studies from these three subcategories to examine the extent to which the Fifties are conceptualized through Cold War events and how these events align with other postwar historical currents. As such, I consider films produced during a period of what historians have named a New Cold War, one that extends certain older enmities, though now often aligned with somewhat modified ideological positions.[1] That is, I will consider how the first phase of the Cold War, starting with the Truman Doctrine and ending in the Bay of Pigs—and thus the period from 1947 to 1962—has found expression on film during the 2000s. Specifically I begin with The Korean War Fifties and *Hal King* (2021), as well as "Meet Me in Daegu," an episode of *Lovecraft Country* (2020) with similar investments. I then explore the McCarthyite Fifties through a brief introduction to *Trumbo* (2015) and somewhat more sustained focus on *Good Night, and Good Luck* (2005). *Hidden Figures* (2016), a film invested in the Atomic Fifties, will conclude this chapter.

The Korean War Fifties

The Korean War Fifties is noteworthy because it offers us some of the first examples of representations of the 1950s, just beyond the decade's end. There are about a dozen films, including *All the Young Men* (1960) and *The Hook* (1963) that attempt to grapple with the experience of the war.[2] It is noteworthy that some of the very first representations of the 1950s (futuristic visions aside!) should concern a hot battle in the Cold War and one that, technically, continues still to this day. Like the Vietnam War, the Korean War represented a series of failures from an American perspective. No ground was gained in either geographical or ideological terms, and no victory or end officially declared. Millions of lives—both civilian and military—were lost, and American service members were imprisoned in record numbers.[3] American interest in the Korean War has been minimal, and primarily found only in academic realms. Film and television documentaries do attend to the conflict at various anniversary junctures, but dramatic treatments remain limited.

In the past two decades, South Korean studios have produced an increasing number of accounts of this conflict and in ways that often align with shifting conceptions of its relationship with North Korea. For instance, as Kristen Sun shows, the Sunshine Policy era of the late 1990s and 2000s, when reunification was perceived to be "on the cusp of reality," generated a set of films that imagined collaboration and friendship between South Korea and North Korea, thereby ultimately rewriting the "enemy."[4] By doing so, they reconfigured the opposition between anticommunism and communism to one between Koreans and foreign forces or the Korean War itself, resulting in a change "to the very epistemological logic" of the conflict.[5] Films like *Welcome to Dongmakgol* (2005) and *2009 Lost Memories* (2002) even seek to "forget" the Korean War, the former by setting the action in a village that didn't realize a conflict was taking place and the latter by imagining an alternate future in which Japanese colonization never ended (and thus the war never began). As such *2009 Lost Memories* provides an interesting model for thinking through how representations of the past might be ruptured entirely by replacing memory with speculative futures. Nevertheless, it remains engaged with memory, for it is the memories, histories, and representations of the events elided that help determine the meaning and significance of what is offered in its place.[6]

More recent South Korean films, including proposed releases to coincide with the seventieth anniversary of the start and end of the (active) war in

2021 and 2023 respectively, fit squarely within an action-adventure blockbuster model. Consider, for instance, director John H. Lee's battle-focused titles *71: Into the Fire* (2010) and *Operation Chromite* (2016). The latter, dubbed for English-speaking audiences, features Lee Jung-Jae as protagonist Jan Hak-Soo and Liam Neeson as General Douglas McArthur. The film celebrates the efforts of Jan Hak Soo and his squad of infiltrators who pave the way for the Battle of Incheon. This film frames the conflict by appealing to the aesthetic conventions of Hollywood World War II films, though edits street battle sequences in ways reminiscent of contemporary South Korean action cinema. With a desaturated palette of greens and browns as well as the use of harsh lighting that foregrounds the details of violence enacted on bodies, it recalls, for instance, *Saving Private Ryan* (1998) and *The Thin Red Line* (1998). As such, Lee's strategy creates an interesting triangulation between the 1940s, 1950s, and the present of the film's production. What is more, narratively, *Operate Chromite* suggests a definitive victory by framing the battle of Incheon as the beginning of the end for the North when, technically, no such end or victory was ever achieved. The division between North and South along the 38th parallel shifted during the conflict but became re-entrenched by the end of fighting. Initially called a "police action," the Korean War was suspended by armistice, rather than a peace treaty, one that continues to hold to this day. Whereas scholars have named a New Cold War to describe the nature of relations between the United States and Russia, in many respects the Korean peninsula remains embedded in the dynamics of the old one.

Though beyond the geographical scope of this project, I wanted to start with these examples of South Korean cinema to note the visual and narrative ways in which this conflict has been subject to cinematic invigoration, thus generating additional models for complicating the representation of historical subjects. What is more, these films testify to the very different processes, temporalities, and expressions of memory for a conflict that involved several state actors as well as millions of civilians and military personnel. For while the Korean War remains largely "forgotten," in the United States, as the common moniker suggests, it is being actively remembered cinematically and through other public forms of commemoration in South Korea.[7] There too it was for a time repressed and often for political reasons that mirrored shifts in the agendas of various leaderships. However, since the turn of the twenty-first century, monuments and films have sought to reinscribe the conflict into a national consciousness. For instance, while South Korea produced only a handful of films about the conflict before 1990, since 2000 over a dozen have been released. Christopher H. K. Lee, for instance, has spearheaded a number of productions—dramatic and documentary—on the Korean War, the most recent of which is *Lost Bastards* (as of this writing still in preproduction).

The reverse is true in the United States, with the majority of titles released during the 1950s and 1960s and only a handful since 1970, with *MASH* (1970) and its televisual (re)iteration, *M*A*S*H* (1972–83) arguably the most popular. However, this comedy-drama about the exploits of staff in a mobile field hospital was effectively more about Vietnam and the Cold War generally than the Korean conflict specifically. Titles since tended to feature the Korean War as one event among others as in the biopic *MacArthur* (1977) or *For the Boys* (1991) about USO entertainers from World War II to Vietnam.[8] Various twenty-first-century offerings use the Korean War as the backdrop for narratives privileging other concerns as in *Indignation* (2016) or as part of a parodic lampooning of the war genre, generally, as in *Retreat!* (2016). Other nations too have released films detailing their involvement, including the Turkish film *Ayla: Daughter of War* (2017).

The question of why the Korean War remains forgotten in an American cultural context is a pertinent one that historians continue to attempt to answer. With the conflict's seventieth anniversary in 2021 some journalists took up the question once again. For instance, historian Owen Miller explains the conflict's continued omission from public commemoration initiatives by citing its eclipse by the two more prominent conflicts that bookend it (i.e., World War II and Vietnam), different generational attitudes toward military service, and the distinct "media eras" during which each of these conflicts unfolded.[9] Miller also cites a degree of "deliberate amnesia" among American veterans, itself a product of multiple factors, including the conflict's extreme brutality and targeting of civilians, lack of definitive or successful conclusion for the United States, and the fact that veterans had to petition for adequate pay, benefits, and recognition since its initial classification as a "police action" restricted their compensation.

Judith Keene offers another compelling explanation for the Korean War's cinematic elisions, one that accounts for the role of visual culture in generating certain tropes that anchor, in shorthand, the meaning of the conflict and the role of the soldier combatant. Keene argues that the Korean War does not suffer from lack of a definitive iconic image, as some have claimed. Instead, it is the nature of that image and what it represented in a Cold War context that contributed to a lack of celebration of this war. Keene writes: "Just as World War One conjures up a muddied soldier in the trenches, and a khaki-clad and helmeted GI in a jeep epitomizes World War Two, the Korean War evokes the figure of a prisoner of war: emaciated, defeated and—when mediated through Cold War fears—likely to be untrustworthy, and possibly even brainwashed to be a communist sympathiser."[10] This suspicion may explain why many veterans have refused to speak about the conflict or advocate for its commemoration. The Korean War resulted in over 10,000 American POWs, an extraordinary number that not only underscored a sense of failure, but meant that an exorbitant number of returning service members were subjected to repeated interrogation and continued suspicion.[11] This particular fear did find expression on film in one of the best-known titles to deal with the conflict or, more specifically, its aftermath in the context of American anticommunism: *The Manchurian Candidate* (1962). Based on Richard Condon's 1959 novel of the same name and directed by John Frankenheimer, the film stars Laurence Harvey as a brainwashed Korean War veteran programmed to assassinate a presidential nominee.

However, this question of "why" the conflict has been forgotten requires some amendment with the caveat "by whom?" For while mainstream white Hollywood has indeed paid little attention to the Korean War, two noteworthy independent productions spearheaded by Black creators have addressed, in rather disparate ways, the experience and consequences of the 600,000 African American soldiers who fought in this battle, a number double that which served in Vietnam: *Hal King* (2021) and *Lovecraft Country* (2020).

Created by Steve Wallace (a classical and popular music composer), choreographed by Diane McIntyre, and directed by Myron Davis, *Hal King* (2021) is an R&B opera set during the early 1950s. Loosely based on Shakespeare's *King Henry IV* and *Henry V*, it imports some of the familial dynamics and thematic investments of its source material. It also adopts (and adapts) a few of Shakespeare's characters' names (e.g., Scroop, Doll Tearsheet, Halfstaff) as well as the somewhat indeterminate perspective on war that marks these plays. The conflict at the center of *Hal King* is the Korean War, with nearly twenty minutes of the film (its second act) taking place on the battlefield. This is entwined with a key narrative concern, namely Hal King's (Tyrik Ballard) growing political consciousness, sparked by his experience in Korea and his conversations with poet and activist Kat French (Sharae Moultrie). Kat and Hal are the children of rival politicians, Leroy

French (Tony McLendon) and Henry King (Eric Roberson). French and King are both vying for the position of alderman in the fictional midwestern American Black town of Alaya, each promoting different visions for their community's future. While Leroy petitions for white investors, assimilation, and a focus on generating wealth or, as Kat observes "bowing and bending to the whites," Henry privileges grassroots community initiatives and a "new revolution." As such, *Hal King* also explores some of the ideological positions that differentiated (some) civil rights activists from Black power proponents. The complex relationship of Black power to civil rights in the postwar era is articulated through Kat, who often evaluates the shortcomings of Leroy's position and benefits of Henry's approach. She explains that Henry "spoke from a place of building within/not disempowering our people by running to the man/His platform was the New Revolution/He wants to boycott abusive institutions." Thus, the film tracks a lineage from the Korean War to Black power through the 1950s and 1960s, presenting a trajectory and set of imbrications often overlooked in film and other media. The Korean War Fifties as visually and narratively constructed in *Hal King* does much to fracture, both aesthetically and politically, the Cold War Fifties.

Hal King is an opera in terms of its structure but also in the sense that all dialogue is sung, even brief one-word exchanges between characters. It adopts operatic strategies, including recitative of both the secco and accompanied varieties, that is, the musical delivery of dialogue in a way that approximates spoken language.[12] Musical motifs also abound and are variously dedicated to love, jealously, destiny, surrender, and "the new revolution."[13] Characters are granted short, recurring motifs, as is common across opera and cinema. Moreover, as Wallace clarifies, the etymological origins of the term "opera," suggesting a practice that integrates all types of art within a single "great work," informs the film's incorporation of myriad art forms, genres, and styles. More specifically, he acknowledges Richard Wagner's conception of the Gesamtkunstwerk as a structuring idea for uniting the assorted elements of *Hal King* into a total production and, in particular a Gesamtkunstwerk "for today within Black culture."[14] Wallace is also intent on generating new relationships between opera and "the people," by bringing together Black cultural forms (Hip Hop, R&B, soul, etc.) with classical European art. This strategy was pioneered for cinema by Steve Townsend's *Carmen: A Hip Hopera* (2001), featuring Beyoncé, a production itself influenced by *Carmen Jones* (1954) and *Porgy and Bess* (1959).[15] It was also a structuring principle for the theater play *I Dream: A Rhythm and Blues Opera* (2010) about Martin

Luther King Jr. This practice of mobilizing contemporary Black music in an opera format also effectively brings past and present into collision.

In *Hal King*, this collision is accomplished in numerous ways, including musically with a harpsichord melody, but one clearly generated by an electronic keyboard. It is also produced by employing a classical musical structure as the foundation for an R&B song. Indeed, according Wallace, this practice extends beyond music, for his aim is to blend "both classic and modern styles on all levels of art, with music, poetry, costumes, acting, dance and film."[16] He does so to connect high-brow forms with popular culture in ways that generate new insights into the possibilities for art, and to expose what each, on its own, might be lacking. But this strategy also produces a degree of historical indeterminacy that is particularly effective at fracturing dominant visions of the Fifties in relation to Black history and culture. I want to spend some time considering how this historical indeterminacy is achieved through costume, music, and dance and the effect this has on a representation of the Cold War Fifties with the Korean War at its heart.

Hal King is an independent film featuring mostly new-to-cinema performers and produced with a limited budget.[17] As such there are certain elements of its production design that appear, at first glance, somewhat lacking. For reviewer Alan Ng, the "low-budget quality of the entire production is hard to overlook." While he acknowledges the passion of the actors' performances, he laments the absence of live musicians, the film's minimalist sets, low-definition, and frequent use of hand-held cameras."[18] Ng's assessment of the film makes it sound like *Hal King* might contribute to traditions of "imperfect cinema," Julio García Espinosa's term for works that challenge the ideological effects of high Hollywood gloss with a refusal to replicate its looks (and thereby its politics).[19] While there is a rejection of Hollywood tendencies with regard to representations of the Fifties, ones that generate political and ideological challenges, it is not through imperfections of the kind that Espinosa discusses. *Hal King* aims for as high production quality as possible given the cameras and budget available. Lighting is carefully considered, in particular with respect to how Black skin is filmed, and sound editing was meticulous, with Wallace and others approaching the soundtrack as one would a musical track. However, the sets are noticeably sparse and oddly populated in a way that suggests a specific politics of refusal to engage a vision of the Fifties beholden to material things.

As such, Ng isn't entirely wrong. Some scenes do bear the hallmarks of a limited budget, technical means, and filmmaking experience. Nevertheless, there is much that *Hal King* accomplishes as a result of its look and purposefully anachronistic approach to costume and production design. For instance, some sequences emulate the liveness of theater and opera, thus bringing more directly into the fray the generic allusions that inform how we ought to engage with the story. Certainly many spaces are framed and filmed cinematically. Cameras follow individuals as they move through a night club or capture in shot/reverse-shot configurations dialogue between characters. However, these moments are intercut with other scenes, often of extended duration, that present diegetic space as a potential stage (e.g., the community center, the barracks). In these instances, a few scattered and visually unassuming props (e.g., nondescript folding chairs) leave room for choreographed dances and vocal performances to unfold, for the camera to capture bodies moving through space. Bodies and their movements are thus privileged and not components to be visually integrated into patternings suggested by elaborate production design. A nod to more minimalist contemporary theater design rather than classical Hollywood musicals, this strategy does much to focus attention on the performance, and the ways in which gestures, vocals, and musical accompaniment contain layers of complexity through their myriad references. By stripping away set design components that, in other (period) genres, tend to subsume bodies into visual schemes, the focus remains on how subtle variations in costume, hair and make-up, and movements allude to the interplay of diverse historical moments. In other words, there are things to be gained by what initially reads as a low-budget DIY mise-en-scene, and I want to consider the implications of a few of these. Specifically, I want to focus on the remarkable temporal dissonances generated by a film set during the early 1950s, but one that makes little effort to hide more recent models of cars, wardrobe choices that integrate styles of the last seven decades, or musical numbers that sample a range of genres and sound-recording technologies.

The period setting of *Hal King* is virtually impossible to identify definitively for the first thirty-six minutes of the film. Indeed, despite the eventual reveal of the Korean War as an index of its timeframe, Wallace insists that he "never intended for *Hal King* to be in one specific time period." He wanted it "mostly to be 50s-ish, with touches of things from other eras."[20] While it is clear that the narrative does not unfold during the twenty-first century, the various choices regarding costumes and hair and make-up alone allude to the full range of Black style during the second half of the twentieth century. There are distinctly 1950s markers including fedoras, bowties, and suits of a particular cut, but also fashions from the 1960s onward. This is as evident in Madame Quickly's club, featuring a range of open mic performers whose styles move from the 1950s to 1970s, as it is in the community center, where multigenerational audiences assemble, dressed in fashions of the 1950s, but also 1980s and 1990s. Likewise, a variety of hairstyles, from the 1940s to the present, are evident in every ensemble scene. The political significance of Black hair, its place in both disciplinary and revolutionary practices, is underscored throughout *Hal King*. For instance, Kat's hair styles shift between a short Afro and coiffed updo while other women feature shaved heads, braids, and straightened hair.[21] Men too exhibit various styles from short fades to long braids. Late in the film, a dance sequence that features arguably more 1950s styles of clothing than any other and a color palette with highlights of yellow, turquoise, and green, also offers the widest historical range of hairstyles. In this way multiple pasts and presents collide. The signifying power of clothing and hair, in both historical and political terms, is harnessed here in order to underpin the film's overall concern with Black historical lineages and linkages.

In some instances, very specific historical moments—as opposed to generic periods—are harnessed. For example, when Kat first arrives at Madame Quickly's club, she sports a black leather jacket and black and white striped shirt and her hair is worn in a short Afro. Madame Quickly (Tarrey Torae), on the other hand, who shares the frame with Kat, wears a stylized updo with feathers, pearl necklace and bracelet, boa, satin gloves, and extensive makeup. That is, she signals the 1950s. Black leather jackets were not commonly worn by women in the 1950s, but were and remain potent symbols of the Black power movement and Black Panthers, specifically. As Kat's performance confirms, she indeed is destined for an important role in Black nationalist movements of the 1960s and 1970s.[22] Her "poem" begins by asking "Say daddy-O, what's your cause?" and launches into a critique of the leisure pursuits of those attending her performance, chastising them for not having "joined the fight." Initially, the crowd does not react kindly to her admonition that they are "wasting [their] power to fight" and "wasting [their] rights." By the end of her song, however, they are literally in sync with her, echoing her words and united in their gestures. The patrons of Madam Quickly's club offer further juxtapositions between 1950s styles and later (and even earlier) ones. On women we see full floral skirts, jersey dresses, and pants as well as stylized bouffants, blonde extensions, berets, and feathered fascinators. For men, the historical range is even broader, with fedoras, suits and turtlenecks, ripped jeans, open poet shirts that recall medieval stylings, and colorful satin vests of Renaissance vintage (Figure 5.1). In this regard, something of Shakespearean theater makes itself felt.

All this adds to the sense of historical indeterminacy that defines the first act of the film. Some scenes ostensibly confirm its midcentury setting with a vintage car, but then undermine any temporal certainty with a range of other period markers (including cars from the 1970s onward). Finally, thirty-six minutes into the film, we receive confirmation of a definitive setting. At this point, an intertitle announces "Coloreds drafted into the Korean War," overlaid with sepia-tinted war footage. This is the both the first time we see text and the first (and only) instance that a deliberately archaic aesthetic is deployed. What follows is a montage of short sequences that oscillate between archival footage, typically black and white or sepia, and highly choreographed training sessions featuring Hal and other key characters. A stylized dissolve involving translucent paint splotches meant to approximate blood splatter separates war footage presenting Black soldiers fighting in Korea (the only archival footage in the film) from the film's training sequences. These sequences, which take place in a nondescript forest setting that stands in for Korea, become ever more contemporary as the actors' gestures evolve from approximations of army drills (i.e., marching, shooting, etc.) to hip hop dance choreography. Further shifts between moving and still images, and thus between media allusions, characterize the latter part of this

Figure 5.1 Hal King's (Tyrik Ballard) performance at Madame Quickly's club in *Hal King* (2021)

sequence. Finally, Hal King and his fellow soldiers are subjected, in postproduction, to a "celluloid" filter, complete with scratches, then stilled for photographic capture. A sepia filter is applied to this image, thus aligning them with the archival footage that dominated other components of this sequence.

While the following scene of camaraderie in a bivouac tent alludes to *M*A*S*H*, acknowledged by Wallace as source material, other components of this "second act" aimed for historical verisimilitude. In a departure from the aesthetic strategies of the rest of the film, all scenes set during the Korean War featured costumes and props specific to that time. Director Myron Davies explains that much effort was dedicated to finding uniforms, authentic guns, and other genuine props.[23] This *visual* verisimilitude, which helps align the plight of *Hal King*'s characters with the "real" soldiers featured earlier in archival footage, emphasizes the histories of Black men who participated in this conflict. Nevertheless, connections to later decades remain. As noted above, this is first accomplished through the incorporation of hip hop dance choreography. Later, during battle scenes, it is accomplished musically. As the surprise attack that leaves two key characters dead and injured unfolds, a kickbeat, specific to music of the early 2000s, enters the soundtrack. However, as Wallace explains, this particular beat originated with Clyde Stubblefield, the drummer for James Brown, and then circulated more broadly through its sampling in late twentieth-century century hip hop.[24] Thus, a musical historical lineage is signaled here in a way that underpins the visual historical lineage between Black soldiers in the early 1950s and those enlisted today. And in both instances, Wallace's lyrical critique makes this explicit. In the bivouac, Hal sings: "When the battle's done / Same thing that always happens / we disappear into the smoke / white folks get all the claim / nobody even asks our names." Later, in conversation with his father, Hal observes: "That army was good for one lesson / It made me recognize the ways of oppression / Even in the army, with a medal in my hand / I still ain't seen as more than a Black man."[25]

The Korean War scene confirms the period of the film, indeterminate until this point, and affirms its commitment to telling the history of Black experiences on the front lines and beyond. In *Hal King*, the Korean War does not function as a conduit into the broader international dynamics of the Cold War as it does in other Korean War-centered films, but instead sparks Hal's political consciousness. This consciousness, in turn, is framed as informing the broader development of the civil rights struggles of the 1950s, eventually leading to the specific investments at the heart of the Black Power Movement of the 1960s. In this way, it explores one of the connections between the Cold War, civil rights, and Black Power, deeply entwined forces, the relationship between which is often overlooked in film (e.g., *Hidden Figures*). That is, *Hal King* presents a vision of the early 1950s, and one of its defining conflicts, as a way to register its role in the development of a Black political consciousness.

Following the Korean War sequence, the historical indeterminacy of the film only increases, but in ways that signal various trajectories and continuities within Black history. Kat ends one of her poem/speeches with a raised fist, a gesture echoing the salute popularized by Tommie Smith and John Carlos during the 1968 Olympics and instantly copied by all those in the audience (Figure 5.2). The camera then zooms in on her fist alone, held in abeyance and removed from its surrounding context. In this way it is isolated for contemplation as a symbol. But as a gesture in a film that has already blended and collided various historical periods, here it seems to gesture both backward and forward in time, back to its origins in antifascist initiatives of the first half of the twentieth century and forward to Black nationalist movements of the 1960s and 1970s. As such, the film emplots this gesture in a longer and broader history of resistance, thereby suggesting the connections between early antifascist and civil rights movements.

Kat's fist is followed by a lengthy "duet" between Kat and Hal that signals the pronouncement of their love for one another. While the focus remains on the complex vocal overlays through which each character expresses their

Figure 5.2 Kat French (Sharae Moultrie) in *Hal King* (2021)

internal thoughts, costume and setting conspire to maintain our consciousness in the 1950s, 1960s, 1970s, and present simultaneously. Hal's bowtie and fedora speak to the postwar years, whereas Kat's hair and blouse indicate her alliance with the 1960s and 1970s. Moreover, the setting is one whose only period marker—cars—indicates the twenty-first century. A row of parked vehicles appears in the background as the camera tracks around the protagonists, themselves choreographed to circle various unassuming objects—lamp posts and benches—in a nod to postwar musicals. As such, while they embody past decades, the space they inhabit is very much of the present; Kat and Hal represent histories made manifest in the present. They render the space of the city heterochronic by haunting sites where a need for protest continues. At this moment, the "new revolution" of which they often speak could just as easily signal Black Lives Matter, itself in many respects tied to the Black Power Movement.

Although early on we see a close-up of a portion of a gleaming late 1940s car, tail-finned cars (the quintessential period marker of the Fifties) are conspicuously absent in *Hal King*. But this omission seems calculated as a conscious rejection of a white middle-class vision of the Fifties, one dominated by particular ideologies that centered certain consumerist products and practices. Cars do appear later, but as supports for "reading" Kat as belonging to the 1960s and 1970s. For instance, after being kidnapped by Scroop, she is held in a 1970s muscle car. Indeed, beyond a rejection of such objects, we also have a complete avoidance of white spaces or, rather, a privileging of Black spaces to establish the whiteness of locales entrenched as Fifties without consideration of who actually inhabited them. That is, *Hal King*'s actions take place in a community center, church, family homes, outside homes on front steps, in public spaces like parks and jazz clubs like Madame Quickly's. There are no drive-ins, diners, high schools, or sprawling suburban neighborhoods, no segregated spaces or ones marked by histories of racist violence and exclusion.

It becomes clear as the film progresses that aesthetic alignment with what other films have visually described as the 1950s and thus replication of more dominant visions of the Fifties is not a chief concern here. In fact, it works against them, foregrounding different priorities: music, community politics, Black nationalism. Sampling, intertextuality, and mixing genres and styles may seem like a postmodern strategy. However, *Hal King* is not postmodern in its temporal dissonances in the way *Walker* (1987) is, admitting anachronistic objects into a late nineteenth-century setting. Irony and parody are entirely absent here. As such it is a different kind of temporal play that is activated not for laughs, but for something else. This temporal indeterminacy, yet eventual confirmation of a 1950s and, specifically, Korean War setting, has several consequences. For one, it makes manifest the idea of historical percolation. It keeps our consciousness moving between multiple pasts and the present and thus activates a more complex temporal constellation than a (binary) dialectic between the "now" we inhabit and the early 1950s. For another, it challenges not only ways of visually describing the Fifties, but the primacy of the visual itself in carrying the burden of defining a period. That is, *Hal King* not only fractures the homogeneity of certain visions of the Fifties, but challenges how they—and perhaps history itself—might be cinematically generated and engaged.

Hal King represents the involvement of Black soldiers in the Korean war and the consequences of their experience on the battlefield and beyond. While for Hal, this involves the emergence of a political consciousness, for Atticus Freeman (Jonathan Majors) in *Lovecraft Country*, it confirms his hatred of war and afflicts him with post-traumatic stress disorder (PTSD). While in Korea, Atticus was ordered to commit atrocities in the name of a war against Communism. *Lovecraft Country*, developed by Misha Green and executive produced by Jordan Peele, J. J. Abrams, and others, is a ten-episode series set during the 1950s, with segments that represent moments earlier in the twentieth century (e.g., the 1921 Tulsa Massacre), defining events that sparked the civil rights movement (e.g., the lynching and murder of fourteen-year-old Emmett Till in 1955), and various (Afro)futures. Though less rigid than *WandaVision* (2021), each episode privileges a different genre or subgenre as its framework for blending historical fact with cinematic and literary fantasy. Aliens and monsters populate *Lovecraft Country*, a world beset by both racist violence and supernatural horror, appealing variously to pulp science fiction and action adventure cinema of the *Journey to the Center of the Earth* (1959)/*Indiana Jones* (1981–2023) variety. Based on Matt Ruff's 2016 novel, it names and then upends H.P. Lovecraft's racism in various ways by adopting and transforming his monsters in the service of antiracist critique. It targets the history of racist acts perpetrated by white individuals, collectives, and institutions across the Jim Crow South as well as the Midwest and Northeast.

The Korean War plays a fairly prominent role in the series as an explanatory backstory for Atticus, but also as the focus of episode six, "Meet Me in Daegu," during which we are introduced to a key recurring character, Ji-Ah

(Jamie Chung). Ji-Ah is a nursing student who tends to the war's wounded, but she is also a Kumiho, a nine-tailed fox spirit who absorbs the souls of men and, in the process, bears witness to their memories, including their crimes. Ji-Ah first encounters Atticus after she and the other nurses on her shift are rounded up by American soldiers (Figure 5.3). The soldiers, including Atticus, shoot the nurses one by one at point blank range until Young-Ja (Prisca Kim), Ji-Ah's best friend, confesses to being the communist spy they were attempting to identify. Ji-Ah first befriends Atticus with the plan to kill him, but realizes he—like she—may be prone to "monstrous" behavior (like torturing Young-Ja) but, due to numerous complex circumstances, isn't truly a monster. They begin a relationship that continues for the remainder of the series, with Ji-Ah visiting Atticus in Chicago and playing an instrumental role in the series finale. In this way—and through other means—the Korean War remains an ever-present force in the series, interweaving (as in *Hal King*) with a range of defining historical moments in the struggle for civil rights (e.g., Emmett Till, segregation, neighborhood integration, the *Negro Motorist Green Book*). Indeed, the very first scene in episode one visualizes Atticus's dream of engaging in trench warfare.[26]

"Meet Me in Daegu" is a reference to *Meet Me in St. Louis* (1944) to establish Ji-Ah's obsession with American cinema and her felt connection to the troubled Judy Garland. The entire episode is told from Ji-Ah's perspective

Figure 5.3 Nurses lined up for execution in "Meet Me in Daegu," *Lovecraft Country* (2020)

and thus from that of a young woman living through the conflict. Atticus does not appear until the midpoint of the episode and, even when he does, the narrative does not shift to privilege his view. Although we learn that he detests war, finds his own actions reprehensible, and recognizes that he is fighting for a country that "hates" him, the focus remains on Ji-Ah as a way to expose several other facets of the conflict. For instance, it alludes to the massacre of civilians, the torture and murder of communist spies, the reasons for "comfort women," and American propaganda efforts. It also foregrounds the experience of women constrained by postwar patriarchal norms and threatened by sexual and physical violence from men both foreign and domestic. Moreover, the vast majority of the dialogue is in Korean and the mythology referenced here—the Kumiho—is of east Asian origin. As such, the history presented of the Korean War is not one defined by the battlefield, but by its impact on civilian women and, as in *Hal King*, on Black soldiers.

The McCarthyite Fifties

The McCarthyite Fifties focuses on the trials and consequences of the House Un-American Activities Committee (HUAC), often in an effort to shed light on contemporary ideological conflicts. Such was the case for the 1970s cycle of films, for example, *The Way We Were* (1973), *Fear on Trial* (1975), *The Front* (1976), and *Tail Gunner Joe* (1977), that challenged that decade's Fifties nostalgia boom.[27] Another wave of interest in McCarthyism dates to the end of the Cold War, reflected in *The House on Carroll Street* (1988), *Guilty by Suspicion* (1991), and *Citizen Cohn* (1992). *Good Night, and Good Luck* (2005) and *Trumbo* (2015) are two twenty-first-century titles of historical fiction that take on McCarthyism in relation to media—news media in the case of the former and cinema in the case of the latter. A brief comparison of their respective approaches is instructive for how they differ, including how, aesthetically, they exemplify two distinct visual strategies for representing this facet of the 1950s. Specifically, I want to consider the implications of their respective modes of integrating archival footage and ostensible focus on historical figures in otherwise fictionalized narratives. What they share— and indeed what they structurally replicate from older titles invested in McCarthyism—is a privileging of individual political or media figures to tell the story of McCarthyism.[28] As such, they register anxieties about how to both critique the HUAC while advocating for a "correct" form of liberal-democratic individualism, one that veers neither too far to the right (as McCarthy's does) or too far to the left (and into Communist territory). As such, the McCarthyite Fifties remains a vehicle for recounting the actions of individuals at the expense of broader structural and institutional concerns.

With obvious links to a Hollywood Fifties (a potential subcategory in its own right as noted in Chapter 7), *Trumbo* charts writer Dalton Trumbo's experience from the late 1940s to the end of the 1950s while occupying a prominent place on the blacklist and, specifically, as a member of the Hollywood Ten. *Trumbo* is deeply invested in film history and, as such, we bear witness to the machinations of the film industry. Footage of well-known postwar releases is often sutured into the film to confirm its historicity: *Roman Holiday* (1953), *The Brave One* (1956), *Spartacus* (1960), and various Edward G. Robinson movies. Shifting between black and white and color, between actual and staged footage (featuring Dean O'Gorman as Kirk Douglas), these segments aim to seamlessly integrate documented history into the world of *Trumbo*. For instance, the film incorporates archival footage from actual film premieres, HUAC hearings, and even a 1961 newsclip of Kennedy noting his enjoyment of *Spartacus*. It thereby foregrounds historical instances of moments that bring Hollywood into collision with McCarthyism, refracting the latter through the former.

Trumbo is, in many respects, a biopic and pays a fair bit of attention to family dynamics. It does not engage with complex historical forces and events or the interconnections between the McCarthyite Fifties and Korea or McCarthyism and civil rights in any sort of nuanced way. Civil rights initiatives are alluded to through Trumbo's daughter's activism and only in the most cursory fashion. McCarthyism's link to other social and political forces manifests exclusively through the experiences of individuals linked to Hollywood. Something similar happens in *Good Night, and Good Luck*, except through the framework of news media or, more accurately, a nostalgic vision of it centered on Edward R. Murrow at CBS. Directed by George Clooney and produced by Participant Media, *Good Night, and Good Luck* follows a few days in the life of Edward R. Murrow (David Strathairn) as he, with the support of his news team, including Fred Friendly (Clooney) at CBS, decide to forge ahead with the Milo Radulovich story, one that helps bring into question the ethics and efficacy of the McCarthy witch hunts (Figure 5.4).[29] It is thus a tale of the undoing of McCarthyism and Murrow's role in

Figure 5.4 Joseph McCarthy and Edward R. Murrow (David Strathairn) in *Good Night, and Good Luck* (2005)

it. It is historical fiction that reviewers have taken to task for its omissions, including the acknowledgment of Murrow's own politics and the widespread inaction (if not support) among Democrats like Truman and the Kennedys that contributed to McCarthy's longevity and impact.[30]

For Alison Landsberg, *Good Night, and Good Luck* offers "a history intentionally meant to intervene in the present."[31] In other words, through various strategies, it generates a split consciousness between past and present, while celebrating the journalistic approach of Edward R. Murrow in the 1950s that, for George Clooney and Grant Heslov, represents the pinnacle of integrity. It affiliates the Cold War with the "War on Terror" in its own multiple hot and cold guises, as does *Trumbo* when Arlen Hird (Louis C. K.), a composite character representing various members of the Hollywood Ten, complains: "All they care about is this nice, new war of theirs. These guys love war, and this is a great one: scary, vague, expensive. Anybody for it, is a hero, anybody against it, a traitor." In both films, Cold War anticommunism is characterized in ways that generate alignments with twenty-first-century practices from the rhetoric of terrorism to strategies of surveillance and limitations on press and creative freedoms. Both films aim to make audiences acutely aware of how the repressions and paranoia of the past remain driving forces behind various right-wing crusades still today and how "history" itself can be mobilized through its archival forms to indict both past and present.

However, scholarship on the extent to which archival footage functions to generate or impede a critical consciousness is somewhat divided, especially regarding *Good Night, and Good Luck*. I want to take some time to consider this scholarship for the ways in which it highlights not just how the image of the Fifties may be fractured through visually distinct representational practices, but also how analyses of the films open up discursive terrain around more general strategies for engaging history.

Trumbo and *Good Night, and Good Luck* differ quite markedly in their aesthetic approach to the past. *Trumbo* trades in expected period-specific markers and color palettes that otherwise track with conventional cinematic practices of representing the late 1940s with muted earth tones and the 1950s with increasingly vibrant hues. *Good Night, and Good Luck*, on the other hand, opted for monochrome and a minimalism in action and set design, thus presenting a world that, for Landsberg, "resists the temptation to indulge the viewer with an abundance of visual pleasure." Nevertheless, as Landsberg qualifies, there are other seductions to be had from its fetishization of old technologies and the way in which the "camera lingers over hairstyles, clothing, glasses, and, of course smoking."[32] I would add to this the allure of the film's fine-grained black-and-white palette that betrays its intent on "seriousness" and the documentary-style camera that, through its abrupt and sometimes messy tracking, suggests truths to behold, especially emotional ones captured through furtive close-ups. Tight framings of faces, Murrow's in particular, often reveal slight yet potent shifts in expression, unseen by other characters but saturated with insight into the thoughts of the individuals on whose faces they register. For Murrow, these expressions reveal exasperation at having to participate in journalism that trades in spectacle (i.e., "Person to Person"), disapproval of corporate interference, and deep concern with McCarthyism's threat to press freedoms. Moreover, there is something of a contemporary feel to the speed with which the camera whips around the newsroom to catch such expressions and other moments. The clarity of the camera's ability to do so betrays a much higher film speed than what was available in the 1950s. As such, it toggles between placing us as an observer in the room (with the camera as our proxy) and alerting us to its mediated nature, rendering obvious that this is a (future) camera intruding on the past.

Good Night, and Good Luck's black-and-white aesthetic makes sense on several levels and to imagine the film in (Techni)color, would require us to introduce parody into a film that otherwise trades in sincerity. For instance, to view its Alcoa commercial—an authentic one—in color would be on one level historically inaccurate but would also give vibrancy to something that speaks to the fetishization of postwar commodities through a language of parody not at play in the film's overall approach to the past. By mirroring the aesthetics of a 1950s television newscast—though less in terms of resolution than its monochromatic nature—the film is also able to integrate archival footage (e.g., of McCarthy, Milo Radulovich) in a visually similar, though certainly not identical, scheme. And yet, for both Landsberg and Valerie Rohy, this archival footage functions less to lend historical authenticity to the film than it does to generate indeterminacy and critical distance in ways that provoke questions about representation and the relationship between past and present. Landsberg notes how protagonists and other supporting characters are often seen scrutinizing footage, an act that encourages viewers to do the same, thereby invoking a "skeptical gaze."[33] What is news and thus "present" to them is "historical record" to us. This gulf is made evident through the film's use of a fairly wide range of types of footage featuring celebrities, politicians, and commercials, though often integrated in ways that prompt questions about whether or not this footage was manufactured for the film. Thus, as Landsberg suggests, "the inclusion of archival footage, in perhaps a counterintuitive way, works against the illusion of immediacy, preventing the viewer from being lost in or absorbed by the narrative."[34]

According to Rohy, there are "at least four orders of visual reality" in *Good Night, and Good Luck*, defined by how archival materials are framed by the film.[35] The mobilization of these frames, often in mise-en-abyme configurations, leads Rohy to conclude that archival footage does not unproblematically signify "unambiguous authenticity."[36] Instead, it is harnessed in a way that mediates queerness, specifically through footage of Liberace and Roy Cohn, to service the "film's central argument—that American political progress between the 1950s and today has not matched the pace of the considerable advances in other realms, notably sexual freedoms."[37] However, Rohy rightly criticizes how the film generates its queer subtext by foregrounding "caricatured" figures as a counterpoint to the homosocial relationship between Edward R. Murrow and Fred Friendly, "exonerate[ing them] . . . of potential queerness" and, in doing so, positions the archival footage as a site not of history, but source of a pervasive fantasy.[38] As such, while both Landsberg and Rohy argue that the "historical" power typically granted to archival footage is undermined in *Good Night, and Good*

Luck, they then proceed to demonstrate two very different implications for doing so.

Good Night, and Good Luck and *Trumbo* are also products of the type of archival footage that survives McCarthyism: clips generated by news media and the HUAC hearings themselves. This type of footage centered individuals and their testimony by foregrounding accounts of witnessing and personal narratives detailing beliefs, actions, and allegiances. Cinematic McCarthyism replicates this through biopic-style approaches, even if specific films differ in the strategies used to activate extant footage. What most share, however, is a tendency to use an abundance of footage, arguably more than most other Fifties films. This is likely a consequence of availability and familiarity: clips now canonical in their own right after circulation through numerous media contexts and decades. Moreover, it is also a result of filmmakers' aims to engage not just with history, but to mobilize the history of McCarthyism specifically to indict fascist tendencies in the present(s) of the films' release, from the 1970s through to the twenty-first century. As such, tracking moments like Army lawyer Joseph Welch's exasperated question for McCarthy, "Have you no sense of decency?" across fields of fictional and documentary media reveals a journey that replicates the processes of percolation, of bubbling up through time and carrying along with it the resonances of its encounters along the way. That is to say, while the McCarthyite Fifties has remained fairly consistent in its approach, abiding by certain structural tendencies and strategies, the canonical clips mobilized in its service nevertheless accumulate the residues of their travels, infusing its twenty-first-century visions with myriad pasts and media.

The Atomic Fifties

The Atomic Fifties includes a body of films concerned primarily with science, technology, and space flight during the 1950s and early 1960s, and thus coincides with the first phase of the Cold War. Although representations of the race into space are often divorced from the weapons-testing regimes suggested by "atomic," I want to foreground this term as a reminder of the ideological and scientific entanglements between the development of nuclear weapons and space technologies, as well as their significance to the Cold War ideological glorification of American scientific might more broadly. What is more, the "atomic age," sometimes employed to denote the

1950s, is a periodizing term that highlights certain postwar design and stylistic tendencies, ones cinematographically foregrounded in representations of this period.

The "atomic," figured in scientific, political, and design terms, suffuses a range of genres invested in both history and fantasy. Atomic concerns structure narratives in both direct and allegorical ways to engage fears of science weaponized. As with other Fifties categories, films that fit the "atomic" purview are also good candidates for analysis elsewhere. For instance, as discussed in the next chapter, *The Reflecting Skin* (1990) is seen by some scholars as manifesting fears of the atom bomb. Likewise, as considered previously, *Blast from the Past* (1999) champions the perseverance of postwar suburban domesticity in the face of a perceived nuclear attack. Twenty-first-century titles also alternate between history and fiction, direct engagement and allegory, and in alignment with other events and processes that marked the 1950s: the biopic, *Rickover: The Birth of Nuclear Power* (2014) and *The Shape of Water* (2017). A number of films focused on the space race as part of the period's broader heralding of American scientific supremacy include *The Right Stuff* (1983), *October Sky* (1999), and *First Man* (2018). The focus here, however, is on *Hidden Figures* (2016), a film invested in the science and math that propelled the space race. Science interweaves with politics in this film in terms of American nationalism and civil rights. As such, it not only invokes questions about historicity but also provides a point of contact with *Hal King* through its situation of the civil rights movement in relation to the Cold War. Despite ample historical evidence of the imbrication of civil rights and the Cold War, cinema has tended it ignore their connections.[39] The ways in which *Hidden Figures* negotiates this relationship—and also the ways in which it fails to—are particularly instructive for thinking through connections between their twenty-first-century iterations: Black Lives Matter and the New Cold War, both of which are implicitly acknowledged by the film.

Hidden Figures tells the story of the integral role played by Black women in the NASA space program in the early 1960s, focusing specifically on Katherine Johnson (Taraji P. Henson), Dorothy Vaughn (Octavia Spencer), and Mary Jackson (Janelle Monáe). It makes use of a deliberately archaic film aesthetic by opening in 1926 on a world described through sepia tint meets two-strip Technicolor. As we shift to the film's present in 1961, the desaturated bluish-greens transform into the vibrant greens made possible by three-strip technology. This moment of self-reflexive mediation in turn ushers in a scene that establishes the present as a lens through which to consider what follows. The newly verdant rural landscape becomes the setting for a stressful encounter between the women—whose car has broken down—and a white police officer who, with Billy club in hand, interrogates them. The resulting tension pierces through the conventionally nostalgic image of the rural postwar past by bringing to mind the many recent instances of police brutality. Past and present collide here to remind us of the long history of this kind of violence. However, no sooner does a sense of impending racist (and gendered) violence infuse this otherwise nostalgic mise-en-scene does it dissipate. The white officer is rendered innocuous through his (unintentional) comic antics. For instance, he stares up at a bright blue sky looking for Sputnik. Upon realizing that these three Black women are helping fight the "Commies," he offers a police escort to get them to NASA as fast as possible. The script renders Katherine, Dorothy, and Mary complicit in the comedy of this implausible scenario with Mary exclaiming, with relish: "Three 'colored' women are chasing a white police officer down the highway in Hampton, Virginia, 1961. Ladies, that there is a God-ordained miracle!"

The menace of the historical and present-day reality of racist violence associated with police stops is wholly evacuated at this early juncture in the film, never to return. While "tension" is reintroduced at various points in scenes that seem to offer the cinematic equivalent of the journalistic euphemism "racial tension" that seeks to obscure the willful racist agency of white perpetrators, actual violence rarely is. The only exception is a mediated one presenting a television—and thus monochrome—newscast of the KKK fire bombing of the Freedom Rider's bus in May of 1961. As such, while *Hidden Figures* offers a revisionist history of the early years of the space race to center the contributions of Black women, it writes out of that history the omnipresent racist violence that constitute the experience of Black communities during this era.

Hidden Figures also writes out of its own history some of the agency of the Black women it focuses on as well as the community organizing, activism, and collectivism of the civil rights movement. For instance, Tiyi M. Morris notes the undue dramatic energy that swirls around several invented white savior moments, including Al Harrison's (Kevin Costner) desegregation of NASA's washrooms.[40] Assigning this victory to an invented white character is especially problematic, given Katharine Johnson's actual practice of simply ignoring directives to use the "colored bathrooms," an action that Morris rightly calls "a form of resistance" that ought to have been included in the film.[41] What is more, Morris identifies this practice of supplanting the efforts and acts of resistance among Black civil rights activists with the changes signed off on by white men in positions of power as a kind of "top down" way of recounting social and political developments in the 1960s. She sees this at work in a number of films, including *The Help* (2011) and *Lee Daniel's The Butler* (2013) that celebrate presidents or the US government as the instigators of progressive change while obfuscating the significance of Black women's activism.[42] *Women of the Movement* (2022–) an anthology series produced by Jay Z and Will Smith for broadcast on network television, aims to rectify this issue with its first installment focused on Mamie Till.[43]

Indeed, this collective nature of the movement as well as the left-leaning sensibilities of civil rights activists, sits uncomfortably with the individualist ethos underpinning American ideology during the Cold War. This is evident in *Hidden Figures*. It is Katharine's mathematical "exceptionalism," Kevin Costner's individual act of sledgehammering the bathroom sign, Mary's one-on-one conversation with a judge, an individual occupying a position of power, that are celebrated as catalysts of progress. Moreover, the civil rights movement and the Cold War were deeply imbricated in a number of complex ways during the 1950s at the height of McCarthyism and beyond that *Hidden Figures* ignores, reducing the space race to a purely scientific battle. From connections between activists and Communism—both real and manufactured—to Jim Crow laws and their legacies that were highlighted by the Soviet Union (and other liberal democracies) as evidence of American's moral failings as a nation, these two broad forces entwined throughout the postwar years.[44] Some conservatives even suggested that the civil rights movement was a communist plot.

These elisions are the consequence of a revisionist cinematic history that simply inserts a "forgotten" event or individual into an existing narrative framework.[45] That is, *Hidden Figures* adds Black women to the oft-told story of the space race, one that privileges the courage of the astronauts, dedication of the scientists, drive of the military, and support of a young president—*individuals* working hard in a contest of intellectual prowess. Likewise, the racism perpetrated against Katharine, Mary, and Dorothy is also, with a few exceptions, individual. Racist white characters like mathematician Paul Stafford (Jim Parsons) and supervisor Vivian Mitchell (Kirsten Dunst) are initially introduced through their actions that support segregation, but are given space to grow, however minimally. White characters who are portrayed as "not seeing color," but only science, itself a deeply problematic assertion, like Al Harrison or John Glenn (Glen Powell), are never implicated in the broader institutional structures or cultures that secure their positions of privilege. Moreover, the widespread effects of Jim Crow laws, still in effect in early 1960s Virginia as the film does make clear, are detached from the machinations of McCarthyism, hot wars used to test advances in weapons (and chemistry), and government agencies working to undermine the civil rights movement. In this way, *Hidden Figures* does little to challenge the cinematic view of the 1950s or visions of the civil rights movement that are both informed by, yet paradoxically extricated from, the ideological logic of the Cold War.

However, there is one way in which *Hidden Figures* does introduce some fractures into visions of the Cold War and that is, through its representations of the homes of the three protagonists and in a way that returns us not just to some of the origins of nostalgia, but to the tenets of metamodernism in relation to history. Specifically, whereas public spaces, including work, are beset with humiliations and injustices, the space of home is a source of nostalgia, in terms of mood and not just aesthetic modes. Home is not offered up as a mediated construct, but as a space of comfort, community, safety, and belonging (Figure 5.5). It is a space where both family and community congregate, a space of nurturing and sociality. Houses, despite their (class) differences, are sources of pride and their interiors bathed in warm light. For instance, Katherine's home is working class, something communicated through its size, furniture, and mismatched and abundant patterns. Mary's is distinctly middle class and saturated with "atomic age" design flourishes,

Figure 5.5 Dorothy Vaughn (Octavia Spencer), Mary Jackson (Janelle Monáe), and Katherine Johnson (Taraji P. Henson) in *Hidden Figures* (2016)

with modern tulip chairs, a sleek wooden dining set, paneling, and use of modernist patterns. However, both perform the very same function by providing a space for the types of experiences that feed an authentic nostalgia. For example, our first view inside Katherine's home takes place upon her return from work and reveals the loving relationship she has with her mother and three children. But in foregrounding this, the film doesn't privilege some regressive notion of feminine domesticity. Whether or not she should work is not a vexed question, or even an option, as it is in other postwar set dramas; she is challenged by and receives fulfillment from both her roles, as a mathematician and a mother.

For Katherine, home is not simply a space of family, or at least it isn't in any narrow sense that excludes the political realities in which familial relationships are necessarily imbricated. It plays out through Jim's (Mahershala Ali) visits whereby his actions counter any patriarchal practices ideologically ingrained in domestic space; he makes soup for Katherine to nurse her back to health and serves dinner to her family. The civil rights movement and the space race are also part of the experience of home life for both Katherine and Mary. Archival footage of key events is mediated by the television sets and radios around which family and friends congregate. They consume, process, and discuss the significance of everything from Sputnik to the words of Dr. Martin Luther King Jr. A card game at Mary's house between Katherine, Mary, and Dorothy provides the backdrop to a conversation about the continued segregation of Virginia schools. The radio program that scores the dancing at Dorothy's son's birthday party is interrupted by a news bulletin detailing the successful completion of Yuri Gagarin's first orbit in space. The scene then cuts to archival footage of this event. A family dinner at Katherine's house is followed by actual footage of Alan Shepard's launch while Katherine and Jim's engagement cuts abruptly to footage of the Mercury Atlas rocket preparations. A news report of the bomb attack on the Freedom Riders functions as a bridge between scenes set in Katherine's and Mary's homes. Despite Mary's pleas to turn off the television, her husband insists that everyone needs to see this. These moments and images flow in and through family dinners, parties, and other decidedly domestic events. The nostalgia-worthy moments of home life (birthdays, engagements, familial love, friendship) are entwined with both actual and staged footage of broader social and political forces at work.

Home has been tasked with an anchoring function, the locus of stability and comfort and an object worthy of longing. It has been reinscribed with the power to access histories—personal and public—and especially ones too often neglected. Home may be a refuge, but it isn't a retreat from the many historical events that constitute the world of the film. Katherine, Mary, and Dorothy are shaped by them and, in turn, shape history. But the space race is also a part of Black history in many ways beyond their specific contributions, something mainstream cinema has long overlooked. As such, history matters here, publicly and personally, and in ways that introduce several important complications. While certain aesthetic modes keep our consciousness in the film's present, they are not mobilized in order to deconstruct, demystify, or challenge history. The authenticity of the past represented matters as a contextualizing framework for the events that unfold therein. This is not to suggest that the framework itself, one that privileges a white, patriarchal, individualist, and nationalist American history, isn't ingrained with racist and sexist tendencies. Again, one of the film's greatest problems is how it ignores the complexities of the civil rights movement and the many facets that constitute the protagonists' subjectivities. However, *Hidden Figures* does allow us to contend with what is excluded by a postmodern treatment of the past that reduces all history to textualized remains. For instance, how do we celebrate the very real contributions made by Katherine to the space program if historical events are offered up as little more than ironic constructs? How do we represent the postwar histories of marginalized communities when the cinematic language typically used to describe that era has been colonized by regressive nostalgic agendas but, also, critical ones that originate from a white perspective on the world that can afford the various consequences of playing parodically with history? This is as important for validating—and feeling nostalgia for—the protagonists' intersections with "H"istory as it is their own personal ones. For to exclude Black women from the experience of nostalgia, as Janelle Wilson's studies have shown, denies the powerful, identity-forming and affirming value of nostalgia for home as a salve in the racist context of postwar America. Indeed, we may be unlikely to ever truly know history, or even agree on what constitutes such knowledge, but a metamodern approach suggests that sometimes the stakes are high enough that we are obligated to try.

But a metamodern approach also requires skepticism and the maintenance of a critical perspective. In this regard, it is worth concluding with a return *Lovecraft Country* that makes explicit something *Hidden Figures* leaves out of its engagement with the imbrication of civil rights and the space race as pursued during the first phase of the Cold War. Specifically,

Hidden Figures fails to address the ways in which the vast budgets allotted to projects benefiting scientific nationalism during the Atomic age meant a diversion of funds away from social sectors and initiatives that would and *should* have benefited marginalized populations and especially people of color. This reality is poignantly encapsulated in a brief moment in *Lovecraft Country* through the inclusion of Gil Scott Heron's 1970 spoken word poem, "Whitey's on the Moon." One verse in particular is worth quoting to conclude this chapter, for it resonates not only with the imbrication of postwar civil rights struggles and the Cold War, but the New Civil Rights and New Cold War of the twenty-first century, made especially evident during the Covid-19 pandemic. Notably this was also the period during which Richard Branson and Jeff Bezos spent billions on themselves to (barely) leave earth's orbit in their personal rocket ships in a hyperindividualized space race of 2021, while racialized workers forced to stay during a climate change–fueled monster tornado were killed at an Amazon sorting facility:

> I can't pay no doctor bill.
> (but Whitey's on the moon)
> Ten years from now I'll be payin' still.
> (while Whitey's on the moon)

Notes

1. See, for instance, Edward Lucas, *The New Cold War: Putin's Russia and the Threat to the West* (New York: Palgrave Macmillan, 2008), and Susan B. Glaser, "Trump, Putin, and the New Cold War," *Politico*, December 12, 2017. https://www.politico.eu/article/trump-putin-and-the-new-cold-war.
2. There were several releases producing during and in the immediate aftermath of the conflict itself, but the interest here is in representations of the 1950s from the vantage of a later present.
3. As Owen Miller explains: "In the post–World War II period, there were other countries that suffered horrifically violent processes of decolonization, and other nations that were dragged as proxies into the inter-imperialist rivalry of the Cold War. The Korean peninsula had the great misfortune to experience both of these afflictions at the same time." "How Korea Became a Forgotten War," *The Jacobin*, February 26, 2021. https://www.jacobinmag.com/2020/06/korean-war-seventieth-anniversary-north-korea-south.

THE COLD WAR FIFTIES 155

4. Kristen Sun, "'Breaking the Dam to Reunify Our Country': Alternate Histories of the Korean War in Contemporary South Korean Cinema," *International Journal of Korean History* 20.2 (August 2015): 115.
5. Ibid., 87.
6. A similar logic underpins the Amazon Prime series *Man in the High Castle* (2015–19), which envisions a world in which Axis powers won World War II and America is under split occupation by Nazi forces on the east coast and Japanese forces on the west. Here, however, the 1950s suburban world perfectly aligns with the Nazi vision of family life and domesticity.
7. I would also suggest that given the wide circulation and popularity of South Korean cinema, including titles meant for export (e.g., *Operation Chromite* with Liam Neeson), that these films also contribute to a fracturing of the (American) 1950s, especially given the extensive role that US troops played in the conflict.
8. For precise numbers and lists of titles, see Robert J. Lentz, *Korean War Filmography* (Jefferson, NC: McFarland, 2008), and David Slocum *Hollywood and War: The Film Reader* (New York: Routledge, 2006), and Paul M. Edwards, *A Guide to Films on The Korean War* (Westport, CT: Greenwood, 1997).
9. Owen Miller explains that the Vietnam War, as opposed to the Korean War, was the first real television war, as the medium was too much in its infancy to capture the latter conflict. "How Korea Became a Forgotten War."
10. Judith Keene, "War, Cinema, Prosthetic Memory and Popular Understanding: A Case Study of the Korean War," *Journal of Multidisciplinary International Studies* 7.1 (January 2010): 7.
11. Keene, "War, Cinema," 8.
12. Steve Wallace, "Hal Analysis, Episode II," September 13, 2021. https://www.youtube.com/watch?v=9zX-z16cLX8.
13. Ibid.
14. Ibid.
15. To return to the earlier point about "forgetting" the Korean War, *Carmen Jones* was released in 1954 and thus filmed in 1953 and thus likely during the Korean War, but set during World War II.
16. Steve Wallace, "A New Opera for a New Generation," *Hal King*. https://www.halkingthemovie.com/about.
17. The majority of actors hail from the music industry or musical theater.
18. Alan Ng, "Hal King," *Film Threat*, June 19, 2021 https://filmthreat.com/reviews/halking/2/.
19. See Julio García Espinosa, "For an Imperfect Cinema, Translated by Julianne Burton," *Jump Cut* 20 (1979): 24–26.
20. Steve Wallace, "Hal Analysis, Episode IV," October 11, 2021. https://www.youtube.com/watch?v=221yo6H3wQM.
21. Initially, Kat was supposed to wear a beret, but discussions during filming led to the decision to show her natural hair, a powerful testimony to her future in the next decade's movements. "Hal Analysis IV."

22. Wallace confirms this saying he envisioned Kat to grow up to be a Black Panther. "Hal Analysis IV."
23. Steve Wallace, "Hal Analysis, Episode III," September 27, 2021. https://www.youtube.com/watch?v=cDlmIxF-bhU.
24. Ibid. There are other beat tracks as well, sometimes pared down and unassuming, sometimes more heavily foregrounded to generate drama. But in each instance, it sounds like a beat track, a computerized sound, and thus signals an alliance with contemporary musical genres.
25. Another potent instance involves Hal's desire to get "Uncle Sam's claw out our backs / Once they send us out here, we're as good as attacked; honor to the whites, shit to the Blacks."
26. This is an interesting sequence that begins in black and white in an approximation of archival footage, but then introduces color through an explosion. Moments later the fantastical takes over with an alien invasion in full Technicolor.
27. There were titles during the 1950s, of course, that took up the McCarthyite cause: *Big Jim McClain* (1952) stars John Wayne as a House UnAmerican Activities Committee investigator searching for Communists in Hawaii.
28. This is an approach that deserves analysis in its own right. Films invested in critiquing McCarthyism through the agency of individual actors in modified biopic form seems an attempt to posit a correct individualism—but still individualism—as an antidote to both Communism and McCarthyism.
29. Participant media, the production company behind *Good Night, and Good Luck* is an interesting entity in light of this discussion, one that has been analyzed by Sherry B. Ortner. Founded by Jeff Skoll, the creator of eBay, its mandate as a "social enterprise" organization involves creating "social impact through films and to amplify such impact through its campaigns." However, as Ortner has shown, it often undercuts its own intentions to effect real change, in part due to its connections with the establishments (Hollywood, multinational corporations, etc.) it seeks to critique. Sherry B. Ortner, "Social Impact without Social Justice: Film and Politics in the Neoliberal Landscape," *American Ethnologist* 44.3 (2017): 529.
30. See, for instance, Michael Cox, "Good Night and Good Luck," *Millennium: Journal of International Studies* 35.2 (2006): 435–37. Cox writes: "the hardest part of all perhaps being that McCarthy himself was merely the most extreme expression of something much bigger, more insidious and quintessentially liberal democratic in origin: namely the Cold War National Security state with its loyalty tests, its House on Un-American Activities, and its crew-cut gumshoes from the FBI spying on the comings and goings of 'premature anti-fascists,' librarians with weird reading habits and union organisers with copies of Gus Hall's speeches in their back pockets" (436).
31. Alison Landsberg, *Engaging the Past: Mass Culture and the Production of Historical Knowledge* (New York: Columbia University Press, 2015), 55.
32. Ibid., 56.
33. Ibid., 56.
34. Ibid., 56.

35. Valerie Rohy, "See It Now: Queer History and Archival Fantasy," *Textual Practice* 33.9 (October 2019): 1637. Specifically, Rohy lists: "archival material shown framed by an on-set television monitor, projection room screen, or viewers in the CBS studio; new footage similarly framed; new footage shown unframed; and archival material shown unframed—unframed, that is, by anything other than the border of the screen on which we watch it" (1637).
36. Ibid.
37. Ibid., 1643.
38. Ibid., 1644.
39. For an account of how Hollywood approached and thereby constructed the civil rights movement generally since the 1980s—and typically in ways that center Southern white people—see Sharon Monteith, "The Movie-Made Movement: Civil Rights of Passage," in *Memory and Popular Film*, ed. Paul Grainge (Manchester: Manchester University Press, 2003), 120–43.
40. Tiyi M. Morris, "Unlearning Hollywood's Civil Rights Movement: A Scholar's Critique," *Journal of African American Studies* 22 (2018): 417–18.
41. Ibid., 417.
42. Ibid., 419.
43. The six episodes that constitute the first installment of this series are helmed by esteemed Black women directors: Julie Dash, Tina Mabry, Kasi Lemmons, and Gina Prince-Bythewood. As of this writing, only the first few episodes have aired.
44. For a detailed and rich discussion of this entanglement, see Mary L. Dudziak, *Cold War Civil Rights: Race and the Image of American Democracy* (Princeton, NJ: Princeton University Press, 2011).
45. "Forgotten" appears in quotations here to signal that while reviews of the film feed into its own promotional discourses about its aim to celebrate the achievements of Black women forgotten by history, there are of course many within the Black scientific community who did not "forget" Katharine Johnson. Likewise, in the broader landscape of American popular culture and popular history, their contributions were not so much forgotten as actively suppressed or ignored.

PART III
LIMINAL FRACTURES

6
The Retromediated Fifties
Film and Photography

This chapter is concerned with films that adopt (and adapt) the aesthetic veneer of media from the 1950s, trading in what Marc LaSueur calls deliberate archaism. As noted in the introduction, this involves replicating the look (resolution, tonal variety, color palette, etc.) of older media. Sepia, black and white, and three-strip Technicolor, for example, have become aesthetic signatures applied, now almost exclusively in postproduction, to films so that they appear to have been produced decades earlier. I see deliberate archaism and retromediation as nearly interchangeable terms. However, the latter admits more readily into the fray both a focus on "retro," a term adept at signaling a certain structure of feeling toward the past and a nod to remediation, a concept that privileges media, inciting interest in its forms.[1] Although I will use deliberate archaism at particular junctures to describe the aesthetic strategy adopted by some of the following case studies, "retromediated" works better as an adjective applied to the Fifties. It signals something that has been done to the Fifties, that is, a treatment to which the Fifties has been subjected, resulting in the generation of a certain type.

The films examined here as part of a retromediated Fifties are engaged with the mediation of historical periods and the role of film, television, and photography in shaping our conceptions of earlier moments. For instance, *Sylvie's Love* (2020) *is* a postwar Woman's Film, *Far from Heaven* (2002) refashions the look of Douglas Sirk's 1950s melodramas, *Pleasantville* (1998) recreates facets of 1950s domestic sitcoms, and *LA Confidential* (1997) plays with the looks of film noir. *WandaVision* (2021) based each episode on the aesthetic and narrative conventions of domestic sitcoms from different decades, starting with the 1950s and, specifically, *I Love Lucy* (1951–57), itself subject to filmic treatment in *Being the Ricardos* (2021). Episodes took cues from multiple domestic sitcoms across the latter half of the twentieth century including *The Dick van Dyck Show* (1961–66), *Bewitched* (1964–72), *I Dream of Jeannie* (1965–70), *The Brady Bunch* (1969–74), *Family Ties* (1982–89),

Full House (1987–95), *Modern Family* (2009–20), and more. However postmodern such intertextuality first seems, any sense of postmodern inflection was irrevocably wrested from *WandaVision* upon the revelation that these domestic sitcom worlds were magically manufactured by Wanda Maximoff (Elizabeth Olsen) in her tragic attempt to escape the trauma and unbearable grief of losing Vision (Paul Bettany). Thus, in a rather metamodern turn of events, her attempt to insert herself into the familial comforts of various sitcom worlds is framed as sincere and her investment in these realms wholly genuine. But with an injection of postmodern skepticism, these worlds are eventually (and literally) shattered, exposed as artificial constructions. This doesn't erode their meaningfulness or value as emotional salves for Wanda, but does reveal their inauthenticity and "underbelly" in the way *Pleasantville* or *The Truman Show* (1998) aimed to.

Retromediated Fifties visions invested in postwar domestic sitcoms also play an important role in complicating a Leave It to Beaver Fifties through their interventions into suburban family spheres. But this category also takes aim at Hollywood. In fact, a fair number of titles are concerned with the movie industry itself—its postwar successes and stresses—and adopt the look of past Hollywood film genres to this end. We might even propose a subtype of "Hollywood Fifties" films that adds to *LA Confidential* titles like *Hollywoodland* (2006), *Hail, Caesar!* (2016), *La La Land* (2016), and *Hollywood* (2020-≥–). Other lesser known and independent titles include *Frank and Ava* (2016), *The Queen of Spain* (2018), and *The Studio Club* (2014). Following a brief discussion of *Hail, Caesar!*, *La La Land*, and *Sylvie's Love* for the diverse ways in which they contribute to a Retromediated Fifties, I turn to *Carol* (2015), an example of retromediation that leaves film behind. Directed by Todd Haynes, *Carol* documents the developing love affair between the eponymous socialite and a shop girl, Therese, but does so through an aesthetic template borrowed from 1950s street photography.

Directed by Joel and Ethan Coen, *Hail, Caesar!* is a veritable compendium of film genres. It stars Josh Brolin as MGM's actual "fixer," Eddie Mannix, and George Clooney as Baird Whitlock, a clueless celebrity kidnapped by a comical band of Communist screenwriters. It also provides backstage views of the production of a range of films: westerns, biblical epics, musicals, and aquamusicals. Scenes featuring rehearsals or the filming of these movies are reminiscent of the postwar iteration of the genres they revive, though framed through a highly satirical lens. For instance, the Gene Kelly-esque song and dance number "No Dames!" featuring Channing Tatum and set in a sailor's bar called the "Swingin' Dinghy" is blatantly homoerotic. Scarlett Johanssen's gracefully choreographed Esther Williams–style aquamusical performance is immediately offset by her brash offscreen persona. "Lazy Ol' Moon," the western featuring star performer Hobie Doyle's (Alden Ehrenreich) impressive acrobatics and disastrous acting is pure farce, as is Baird Whitlock's, who is tasked with the title role as a Roman centurion in the eponymous biblical epic, "Hail, Caesar! A Tale of the Christ." We even bear witness to a ballroom drama by a famed European director (Ralph Fiennes) and his herculean task of preparing Hobie Doyle for a serious title role. Indeed, the primary narrative featuring Eddie Mannix takes on the arcs and look of film noir.

As with other instances of cinematic retromediations that deploy deliberate archaism as a visual tactic, *Hail, Caesar!* takes pains to replicate the aesthetic templates of the various genres it cites, doing so through use of old film stock and digital postproduction modifications. "Hail, Caesar: A Tale of the Christ" looks very much like 1950s biblical epic (Figure 6.1). As director of photography Roger Deakins explains, although this film within a film could not be shot with three-strip Technicolor, it was lit in a manner reminiscent of 1950s epics and generated the signature color palettes now associated with films like *Quo Vadis* and *Ben Hur*.[2] "Lazy Ol' Moon" looks like an early color western with a restricted palette and the now antiquated practice of adding blue to signal night. In the dance sequences that allude to three distinct varieties (e.g., aquatic, tap, and ballroom), the camera moves and frames the action in ways reminiscent of the productions it draws inspiration from.

Figure 6.1 "Hail Caesar: A Tale of the Christ" movie in *Hail, Caesar!* (2016)

A degree of "surface realism," to invoke the term Marc LeSueur pairs with deliberate archaism, was also generated through an investment in period props including old studio lights and cameras, a Moviola editing console, vintage and custom-tailored costumes, and even filming locations used by the types of productions cited by *Hail, Caesar!*, including Esther Williams's pool.[3] The film is rife with allusions to Hollywood history, many of them visual. While some invoke specific scenes (e.g., the beach house from *North by Northwest*) or characters ("Carlotta Valdez," Hobie's date and Carmen Miranda–inspired *Vertigo* namesake), others offered layered references. For example, as visual effects supervisor Dan Schrecker explains, the Coens employed a matte painting of Rome that resembled one used in *Quo Vadis* as the backdrop to a scene featuring George Clooney.[4] As such, this scene unites both past image and past process, evidently fake and of cinematic origin. Likewise, a scene featuring Jack Huston in a car was shot on green screen and then subject to postproduction interventions that made it look like a rear-screen projection, to underscore the parodic take on rear projection itself.[5]

Some scenes, according to Schrecker, present a gray area, straddling the retromediations at play in the film's references to past genres and the "real" story involving Eddie Mannix. Toward the end, as Channing Tatum defects and boards a Russian submarine, 1950s-type visual effects were indeed employed, but then digitally modified to "look seamless," to prompt audiences to question whether the action is part of the "real" Mannix narrative or simply another movie in production.[6] Indeed the injection of real historical figures like Mannix and Herbert Marcuse (John Bluthal) as well as star personas obviously modeled on actual past celebrities, does feed into the film's play with registers of artifice and representation. Baird Whitlock's kidnapping by Communist Hollywood writers (and Marcuse) certainly references the Red Scare and practices of blacklisting but plays all of this for laughs. For Doru Pop, *Hail, Caesar!* is thus an example of "multiplexed Marxism," and belongs to a group of recent films in which "communist ideology is truncated as a farcical object," evidence of a turn from cinema's engagement with the "Red Scare" during the immediate postwar years to "Red Laughter."[7] But as a work with all the trappings of parody, intertextuality, and self-reflexivity of a now itself antiquated postmodern variety, the "real" here has little role in acknowledging truths or generating a sense of sincerity. In this way, it is at odds with the more metamodern sensibility of *La La Land*, released the same year.

La La Land, directed by Damien Chazelle, charts Mia (Emma Stone) and Sebastian's (Ryan Gosling) unapologetic devotion to the art forms that structure their lives, acting and jazz, respectively. More accurately, they are deeply passionate about nostalgic visions of these creative pursuits, grounded in their views of classical Hollywood cinema and the work of Charlie Parker and Thelonius Monk. The authenticity of their investment is never questioned, even though it should be given how the racial dynamics of Sebastian's particular commitments play out in the film, including the erasure of jazz's many alignments with civil rights struggles. In other words, the characters' (and film's) nostalgia for the cinema and music of the past is genuine, meaningful, unaffected, and problematically offered up as unproblematic.

But nostalgia in *La La Land* is also signaled aesthetically. As such, the other privileged pole of metamodernism's pendulum is not irony, as it is for McDowell, but pastiche of a postmodern variety that surfaces in a number of disparate ways. The film is shot in Cinemascope and introduced and concluded with retro titles. It references its classical Hollywood musical source material at every turn. It plays with visual artifice through location shots that look like painted backdrops and matte paintings that move through the real space of a Hollywood backlot (Figure 6.2). It recalls the cinematography, color palettes, and framing of midcentury American cinema. As such, while *La La Land* is readily identifiable as a nostalgia film because of its aesthetic trappings, its structure of feeling—one where feeling itself is emphasized and guided along distinctly unironic emotional vectors—results in a rather different type of engagement with the past.

Figure 6.2 Mia (Emma Stone) and Sebastian (Ryan Gosling) in *La La Land* (2016)

And so too are the commodified collectibles of Hollywood and jazz history that populate *La La Land*'s domestic and public spaces. For instance, Mia and Sebastian's apartments are sites of encounter with cultural history and bastions of preservation for its paraphernalia. Posters of movie stars like Ingrid Bergman and memorabilia like Hoagie Carmichael's stool are prized possessions, deeply infused with meaning and emotion. They are set dressing, but repeatedly come in and out of narrative focus in ways that foreground their authenticity as conduits to history and instigators of personal and collective longing. For instance, Sebastian implores his sister not to sit on Carmichael's stool, one of the few objects that managed to make it out of his many unpacked moving boxes. These objects render otherwise generic apartments meaningful to their inhabitants. But these spaces, carefully populated with such props, are also subjected to deliberate archaism. However, the cinematographic strategies deployed here are not in the service of a flippant visual intertextuality, but to underscore the emotional truths of the space's inhabitants as authentic. That is, Mia's apartment, shared with roommates, abounds with primary colors that recall the vibrancy of Technicolor as a way to give weight to her Hollywood dreams. Later in the film, Sebastian's apartment is bathed in *Vertigo*'s (1958) signature greenish glow. As Mia steps into the garish light wearing a complementary lilac dress, generating a ghostly effect reminiscent of Kim Novak's, cinema history isn't evoked simply for the sake of homage, though that is part of it. Instead, the full emotional weight of Hitchcock's scene is harnessed here with the hope that the emotional reality of Judy/Madeline and Scottie's relationship inform Mia and Sebastian's own doomed union.

In this way, *La La Land* reveals a metamodern oscillation between certain postmodern aesthetic modes and modern reinvestments in sincerity, reconstruction, authenticity, and meaning. Parody and irony are not forces structuring the film's engagements with postwar material culture. Instead, there is a commitment to sharing important facets of the past that ought to be heralded or confronted, even yearned for nostalgically in some instances. As such, nostalgia is not just signaled aesthetically, as is often the case in postmodern representations of the postwar past, but emotionally through figurations of home that recall nostalgia's origins as a sentiment predicated on genuine longing. But what purpose does a continued postmodern aesthetic serve? For one thing, it reminds us of the present and the mediated lenses through which we consume the images and histories on offer. To return to Vermeulen and van der Akker, it also helps filter "modern" virtues through the lens of skepticism. In other words, we ought to see the ideals and possibilities inherent in objects of yearning, entrenched in important historical moments too long neglected, and ingrained in a genuine longing or nostalgia, but recognize the limitations that necessarily complicate our efforts to represent them.

Whereas *La La Land* activates in wholly unironic ways certain tendencies of classical Hollywood, *Sylvie's Love* completely inhabits its source. It *is* a postwar "Woman's Film" in every regard. Directed by Eugene Ashe and starring Tessa Thompson as the eponymous Sylvie, it tracks Sylvie's romance with Robert (Nnamdi Asomugha) from their initial meeting in 1957 through various personal and professional tribulations, including a period of separation and final reconciliation in the early 1960s. Like *La La Land*, the protagonists are motivated by career aspirations grounded in their passions for various art forms: Sylvie aims to be a television producer and Robert a jazz musician. Both find a degree of success with these pursuits, though public appreciation for Robert's incredible talents diminishes as the 1960s usher in other popular forms of music. During their period of separation, Sylvie endures a fairly standard though ultimately loveless marriage to Lacy Parker (Alano Miller), the son of a prominent physician. A successful businessman in his own right, Lacy keeps a scandalous secret for Sylvie, that the daughter they're raising is actually Robert's. Revealing this secret would bring shame upon their families, especially Sylvie's mother, the owner of an etiquette school for young women. The pace of editing, dialogue, emotional tenor, narrative trajectories, spectacular costumes, aesthetic textures, and cinematography replicate with precision 1950s melodramatic fare. The film was shot on various backlots using Super 16, a stock that Ashe felt best replicated the look of 35mm from that period.[8] Its deliberate archaism is thus distinctly cinematic and the result, as Aisha Harris explains, is a vision of "New York as 1950s-'60s Hollywood often imagined it; hardly dirty, hardly crowded, sleek and elegant. Dreamlike" (Figure 6.3).[9] In many regards *Sylvie's Love* exceeds *Far from Heaven*'s imitation of Sirkian cinema and certainly *La La Land*'s adoption of similar strategies, for Ashe's film inhibits much of the self-reflexivity—and thus presentness—that percolates to varying degrees in these other two films.

But what sets *Sylvie's Love* apart from its sources of cinematic inspiration is its centering of Black experience, especially Black romance and love of all kinds: for partners, family, art forms, places, pursuits, and self. As Ashe explains, he "wanted to make a film where Black people of the era don't exist through adversity, but through love."[10] He was inspired by old happy family

Figure 6.3 Sylvie (Tessa Thompson) in *Sylvie's Love* (2020)

photographs of the 1950s and aimed to reflect "the truth he found in those pictures; an alternate reality not frequently mirrored in cinema."[11] As such, the film is deeply nostalgic both in (aesthetic) mode and in mood and in a way that highlights the complex imbrication of these two forces as well as the critical possibilities of nostalgia itself. In fact, the creation of a nostalgia film was Ashe's stated intent, part of his approach to a period in American history typically aligned with showcasing Black trauma.[12] This is not to suggest that historical realities of the 1950s are elided or obfuscated. They are signaled intermittently through Sylvie's cousin's involvement various civil rights initiatives throughout the film. The world outside and political realities of the late 1950s encircle the film and emplot it historically. But the emotional force of the film emanates not from the racism experienced by the protagonists (as it does in *Them* [2021]), but from the rich lives Sylvie and Robert carve out for themselves and with each other, ones connected to space (Harlem), community, and art.

For Richard Brody, the film thus functions as a "living counterfactual history of Hollywood." It is the type of movie "that Hollywood should and could have been making at the time, a movie by a Black filmmaker about the lives of Black people facing the same conflicts of family, romance, and work as white people."[13] This, I think, is the source of a deep melancholy that also pervades *Sylvie's Love*, one arguably underscored by slight adjustments to the (Techni)color palette that features deeper saturated teal tones and golden yellows.[14] There is a profound sense of loss of what could have been: of the possibilities—cinematic and beyond—enabled by a canon of classical

Hollywood cinema enriched by the full incorporation of Black melodrama in this vein. Ashe found inspiration in the work of Sidney Poitier and specifically *Paris Blues* (1961), but laments the absence of lavish spectacle and attention paid to ordinary lives as evident in Rock Hudson/Doris Day type films.[15] But while *Sylvie's Love* may indeed be a "living counterfactual history of Hollywood," it also challenges institutional histories of Hollywood and practices of historical representation itself. It is a response to the focus on trauma and violence as defining of Black experience during the 1950s and, in this respect, reveals the critical ways in which retromediations intervene in history, introducing new fractures into the Fifties.

Whereas for *Sylvie's Love* family photographs inspired a narrative investment in Black love, told through a retromediated aesthetic utilizing Super 16 and the narrative and aesthetic conventions of postwar melodrama, *Carol* retromediates the aesthetics of street photography (also through Super 16) to tell a story of lesbian love. Based on Patricia Highsmith's 1952 romance *The Price of Salt*, Todd Haynes's *Carol* charts the evolving relationship between the young, aspiring photographer and working-class shopgirl, Therese (Rooney Mara), and middle-aged, upper-middle class housewife and mother, Carol (Cate Blanchette).[16] It also registers the attainment of Therese and Carol's agency as lesbian subjects under the social and legal forces steeped in the patriarchal and heteronormative structures of early 1950s America. By the film's end, one that suggests the rekindling of their romance after a time of difficult separation, Therese is a *New York Times* photographer while Carol, having announced at a custody hearing that she is no longer willing to "live against her grain," has moved out of her suburban New Jersey mansion to find employment and an apartment in New York City. Named the best LGBTQ + film of all time by the BFI, *Carol* received near unanimous critical praise from reviewers, a plethora of nominations and awards, and a fair bit of scholarly attention.

Scholarship on the film tends to follow one of two often interconnected tracks. The first meticulously excavates the significance of Haynes's characterization of Therese and Carol, detailing how the film constructs their respective subjectivities in the context of early 1950s America.[17] The second, acknowledging writer Phyllis Nagy's deft shift of Therese from a set designer to photographer acknowledges the centrality of photography both narratively and visually to the film. From a concern with the gaze as mediated and reflexive to *Carol*'s mobilization of the aesthetics of 1950s street photography, these analyses foreground the implications of the cinematographic strategies that are pivotal to the film's engagement with lesbian desire and histories.[18] However, whereas the critical literature that attends to photography does so by foregrounding the act of taking pictures, analyzing the effects of framing strategies, or noting the midcentury photographers who inspired Haynes's aesthetic, in what follows I want to consider the significance of *Carol*'s retromediation of 1950s street photography and the ways in which the film harnesses the strategies of this genre in order to both generate a metamodern sensibility and to complicate the Fifties.[19]

When asked about the origins of *Carol*'s look, Todd Haynes typically answers with a list of notable midcentury street photographers that sourced the aesthetic template of the film. Saul Leiter was particularly influential, as were Esther Bubley, Vivian Maier, Helen Levitt, Lisette Model, Berenice Abbott, and Ruth Orkin. Save Leiter, these photographers, who often straddled the worlds of street, art, and commercial photography, were thought to offer a "female gaze" on the subjects and spaces they captured. Their images formed the foundation of a collection of visual source materials supplied by Haynes to his production crew in the form of an "image book," one meant to inform the visual approach of the film.[20]

The questions posed to Haynes about the distinctly photographic foundation of *Carol*'s aesthetic often involve a comparison with *Far from Heaven* and its Sirkian—and thus cinematic—palette steeped in the trappings of artifice. *Carol*, in contrast, appears more "natural." However, as Haynes rightly reminds us, *Carol*'s naturalism is also inherently artificial and constructed, its "realism" generated by codes of representation shaped by the contexts and discourses that enveloped midcentury street photography. But while this deliberately archaic "realism" is harnessed self-reflexively in *Carol* as we shall soon explore, it is also appealed to for its intimation of truth. That is, *Carol* may lean toward a postmodern sensibility in its retromediations, but the ends to which its particular aesthetic archaisms are used tend toward a metamodern one. Indeed, as Alison Gibbons observes, a postmodern staple or strategy might remain a key part of a metamodern text but be mobilized for a different purpose.[21] Here, deliberate archaism may be the governing visual strategy of the film, but it is used in the service of a variety of ends, not least of which is an appeal to truths and sincerity, histories of both personal and cultural importance.

Carol's deliberate archaism is multifaceted, a visual replication of more than just the already complicated genre of street photography. The various dimensions of its aesthetic are worth unpacking in greater detail for they lie at the heart of not just how Haynes seeks to generate the affective force of the film but also how the film engages historically with the 1950s to complicate this decade's prevailing legacies. Director of photography Ed Lachmann shot *Carol* on Super 16mm in order to give it a grainy feel and to achieve a particular kind of deliberate archaism. As he explains, they "wanted to reference film stocks of a previous time period."[22] The digital imitation of old stock is certainly possible, but imperfect and unable to yield what Lachmann sees as the depth of film, something made possible by its capture of light on separate layers of emulsion.[23] Of Super 16mm he explains that its "grain structure and color separation were different than that of today's digital photography.... The grain structure in film, and its movement, is affected by exposure: finer grain in highlights, larger in low light. That can't be represented digitally, even if you add digital grain later." These grains become perceptible on the big screen and give the film what Lachmann describes as its "three dimensional sense of texture and . . . impressionist quality."[24] It also bestows on the film its underlying feeling of pastness. This grain hovers just beneath the surface of the image as a constant reminder that we are viewing the world represented through the lens of a past media form. As such, it prompts a self-consciousness about the act of viewing as well as the imbrication of past and present on both an aesthetic and social plane.

The film's color also contributes to *Carol*'s multifaceted engagement with history. Its distinctive hues were carefully manufactured through the use of various green and magenta gels and informed by the look of early Kodak Ektachrome color still film. As Lachmann explains, "[w]ith early Ektachrome, there wasn't a full range of color spectrum as is there is today. Ektachrome had a cooler rendition: the colors were less saturated and tended towards magentas, greens and cooler hues."[25] This palette determined the aesthetic of the color street photography of the practitioners Haynes looked to for inspiration. Theirs was a "soiled and muted" look that effectively generated a patina, a grit, one that, for Haynes, mirrored the grittiness of New York itself during the early 1950s: "It looks like a postwar city, New York City. It looks distressed, it looks dirty."[26] *Carol* thus combats the more dominant images of 1950s New York as something separated in time from its own immediate past. That is, it acknowledges something of the history of the space and the traces of the past that are all but erased in other cinematic portrayal of the (postwar) city.[27]

Moreover, these color gels did much to complicate the temperature of the film, enabling it to waver between warm and cool.[28] Such indeterminacy, often within a single frame, inflects the affective tenor of a scene and admits into the same (mental and physical) space, competing if not conflicting feelings in order to attend to the nuanced emotions felt by Carol and Therese as they navigate their world and relationship. It was this vision of New York that Haynes hoped to represent in *Carol* as a way to distinguish its reality from the vibrant and often garish Technicolor palettes of the later 1950s and thus, for example, the artifice of his Sirkian world in *Far from Heaven*. Indeed, there are several narrative clues to confirm that Carol and Therese's affair unfolds during the initial years of the 1950s. In an early scene, a PA announcement at Frankenberg's department store instructs shoppers to "be sure to take advantage of our congratulations Ike and Mamie Inaugural early bird special." Toward the end of the film, we see a television set in Harge's parents home broadcast a snippet of Eisenhower's inaugural address: "the world and we have passed the midway point of a century of continuing challenge." Significantly, color enters the picture in an altogether different way in the very next shot to underscore this shift from an early 1950s period of uncertainty to its next phase, one marked by (forced) optimism and conspicuous consumption. That is, we move from Eisenhower on a black-and-white television set in a traditional home to Therese painting all the walls in her apartment a robin's egg blue and thus one of the new colors signaling the emergence of a more vibrant—chromatically speaking—material world. This establishes the narrative's temporal frame as one bookended by Eisenhower's election toward the end of 1952 and his inauguration in early 1953. Indeed, Haynes wanted to capture what it felt like politically and socially at this particular point in time and, specifically, the period's "indeterminacy and insecurity and vulnerability."[29] Underscored by a direct reference to the House Un-American Activities Committee as well as multiple allusions to practices of surveillance, this 1950s is of a decidedly different order than a Leave It to Beaver Fifties and at a visual remove from the Technicolor visions that have tended to dominate cinematic deliberate archaisms invested in the Fifties.

The color palette that defines *Carol* may have been generated by cinematic technical acuity, but it finds its origins in still photography and, specifically, New York street photography. Indeed, some of the images and tendencies that constitute this genre find rather direct expression in Haynes's film. "I like your scribbles!" Therese shouts down at Richard (Jake Lacy) as the camera frames him from above, leaning against his bicycle and surrounded on all sides by children's sidewalk chalk drawings. A staple of Helen Levitt's photography of New York and the experience of an urban childhood, such gestures of naïve inscription also appear in Ruth Orkin's images, becoming even foregrounded in her film with Morris, *Lovers and Lollipops*. Here Haynes not only acknowledges a trope of postwar street photography but one that, like the others, does so as a way to engage transient inscriptions, indexicality, and representation itself. In *Carol*, these chalk drawings are indeed childish (presumably made by neighborhood children), but they can also read as early naïve indexical traces of creative gestures, ones that point to Therese's own nascent image-making endeavors.

Esther Bubley's *Elevated Train Platform with Gum Machines, New York City* c. 1951 features alternating vertical forms of yellow and red fixtures attached to a line of posts against the otherwise dark, almost monochromatic train platform. This is not only replicated by the patterning and color scheme of Therese's hat but also figures in various other street scenes in the film that feature yellow—and, later, yellow and red—taxis as well as splashes of what Patricia White calls *Carol*'s "Vincent Minelli red" against gloomy cityscapes.[30] It does more than this, for it also offers a template for *how* to include colors that reside outside the more muted palette that otherwise dominates the film, that "muted" and "soiled" look pursued by Haynes. In *Elevated Train Platform*, as in *Carol*, these splashes of more intense saturated color appear sparingly and are framed in a way that confirms that hue, rather than subject or action, determined the orientation of the camera's focus.[31]

The first two scenes in which Therese wears her hat generates a stark contrast between its vibrant stripes and the spaces she moves through: first, a bike ride on a dreary fall day through a park and, second, as part of sullen procession of Frankenberg workers lined up in the weak light of dawn, waiting to enter the store. In both instances, Therese's hat functions as the focal point within the frame, a beacon to follow as the camera navigates spaces of the city. The next time the hat appears, it does so through the dirty front window of Scotty's restaurant, where Therese waits for Carol to arrive for their first lunch date. Again, it offers the only instance of saturated color, aligning the scene with a fairly common visual trope of midcentury color photography.

The signifying force of the deep saturated red/golden-yellow pairing on Therese's hat grows as the film progresses, connecting Therese and Carol to the city that surrounds them and, increasingly, to each other. It can be read as one of the many instances in which the film offers "a subjective viewpoint of the amorous mind . . . when you read every sign and symbol of the other person."[32] Initially, this color signature aligns Therese with New York through its appearance on the red and yellow taxis that drift in and out of frame throughout the film. These cars appear in stark contrast to the other automobiles that populate the streets. In fact, it seems as though a concerted attempt was made to avoid any of the vibrantly colored cars often appealed to in 1950s-set films as privileged props tasked with signifying the Fifties. Carol's car is a muted beigey-gray, Abby's is dull gray, and Harge's is black. Other vehicles typically fall into this severely restricted color range as well, despite the fact that early 1950s cars did come in a variety of rather bright hues, including candy apple red, turquoise, and various two-tone arrangements.

As the film progresses, and Carol and Therese's relationship develops, this red/yellow paring starts to appear elsewhere. One scene is instructive in demonstrating how. An establishing crane shot of a city street features two red and yellow taxis parked in front of what we learn is Carol's lawyer's office. Carol enters the frame from the right, wearing a deep red A-line coat and hat. She stands out amid a sea of dark-colored suits worn by other pedestrians as she strides purposefully down the sidewalk. After a traumatic meeting with her lawyer, during which she learns that Harge intends to invoke a "morality clause" in his pursuit of sole custody of their daughter, she returns to the street. At first obscured by a dirty storefront window that all but erases the color of her coat, she steps into the light of day and the commotion of the street, down which a bright red truck drives and then stops to share the frame with her. She retreats again into a doorway that superimposes a reflection of the red truck over her, but also makes space in the frame for a window display of cameras set among red and golden-yellow suitcases (Figure 6.4). Therese

Figure 6.4 Carol (Cate Blanchett) standing in a doorway in *Carol* (2015)

is thus signified, if not embodied, here in two senses: through color and object. Although we do not bear witness to the transaction, we later learn that Carol has bought one of those cameras and suitcases for Therese. However, before Carol bestows this gift in dramatic fashion on Therese by pushing the yellow suitcase over the threshold to Therese's apartment with her foot (while wearing that magnificent red coat), the scene cuts to Therese, in a record shop, buying a present for Carol. As the camera centers on the record, we see that it has a bright red center label, rendered visible through a cutout in its golden yellow sleeve.

What starts out as a visual nod to the use of punctuated color in midcentury street photography grows in a signifying crescendo to signal the burgeoning of desire, commitment, and love between Therese and Carol. Following scenes sustain the chromatic connection: Carol talks to Rindy about brushing her hair in a way that cues us to notice the contrast between Carol's own luminous blonde hair offset by a small but bright red hat; both Carol and Therese are seen wearing and folding, respectively, bright red sweaters; and the décor of the Drake Hotel replicates this color scheme. Indeed, aside from the interplays of moss greens and magenta, the red/yellow-gold color signature is a key means through which *Carol* not only references the tropes and strategies of a past photographic practice, but mobilizes it to great narrative effect.

There is something more to be said about the implications of transposing from photography to film an aesthetic strategy evident in, for instance, Saul Leiter's images of single red umbrellas punctuating rainy streets or glowing electric signs engulfed by darkness. In some cases where color is harnessed as a compositional or even narrative focal point in this way, Lachmann's camera lingers for a time to concentrate our looking within a defined frame. In others, however, the camera's fluid movement tracks bodies as they navigate a range of interior and exterior locations. Such oscillations between images that read as self-consciously photographic and distinctively cinematic moments defined by continuous motion encourage a kind of phenomenological indeterminacy, one that wavers between photographic and cinematic ways of looking. That is, while some shots allude to a specific photographic history, to Cartier-Bresson's "decisive moments" that take time—generated by the camera's stillness—to unpack, others are characterized by uninterrupted flow, by fluid pans tracking a range of movements that enliven space and mark the passage of time.

These injections of color—sometimes frozen, sometimes animated—are also subject to a further manipulation borrowed from street photography, specifically one made use of by Bubley and Leiter. That is, they are subjected to filters in the form of weather and various reflective surfaces. Fog, rain, and snow all feature prominently in many of Bubley and Leiter's images of New York streets and in *Carol* as well. Lachmann's camera spends time surveying the slick texture and reflective allure of wet asphalt. When rain hits the windows of buildings and cars, screens form that filter and distort portraits of the protagonists, obscuring and transforming their expressions. Inspired by Leiter's liberal use of these opaque screens, Haynes too makes use of such obstacles between photographer/cinematographer and subject to generate awareness of the "act of looking" itself. As Haynes explains: "Creating barriers between us and the objects we are looking at reveals the predicament of looking and maybe at some level stokes desire because, when there is something in the way, you want to get around it."[33]

An early scene that captures Therese, lost in thought, through the rain-streaked window of a taxi has been well analyzed in terms of its effect on establishing our access to her state of mind, point of view, and developing subjectivity. Likewise, astute analyses have deconstructed the rather pivotal scene at the Christmas tree farm when Therese snaps photos of Carol unaware through curtains of snowflakes. For instance, Jennifer Barker convincingly shows how this moment is centered on a "gesture of pure potential." She explains: "It contains within it the 'hesitations' among and between subject (and object) positions in the photographic encounter, the 'grasping' of each by the other. It stages in a single instant, and in a way a printed photograph cannot replicate, the tumultuousness of the dynamic between Therese, Carol, and the camera."[34] But this scene is also noteworthy for its replication of Saul Leiter's snow-screened photography of New York including images like *Postmen* 1952 and *Untitled* 1952. In these photographs, the snow helps visualize the suspension of time as well as the image's depth of field. It attunes us to the space between the objects that populate the frame. In *Carol*, the potential of movement is released with the falling snow, the promise of movement is fulfilled. And yet this movement is about to be halted with the click of Therese's camera, a sequence transformed into an image that we see only later when a forlorn Therese revisits the developed prints that captured this moment. And, yet, however much we might understand this sequence through photography—the gesture and the image—it also provides a point of connection with Douglas Sirk's Christmas tree scene in *All That Heaven Allows*,

THE RETROMEDIATED FIFTIES 177

bringing yet another media form into this constellation of image-making practices.[35] For as much as a photographic deliberate archaism structures *Carol*, it also engages on various levels with cinema history too in its bid to reframe the Fifties.[36]

A similar dual focus on film and photography as representational practices is prompted by the scene featuring Abby and Carol in conversation in the latter's convertible after Carol's first lunch date with Therese. The women are filmed in the car directly from the side with a rear projection of early 1950s New York filling the background behind them (Figure 6.5). This back plane has a resolute stillness to it and looks slightly different than the foreground, a consequence of a shift in color palette and seemingly larger grain. The foreground itself is compositionally complex, composed not just of Abby and Carol in their gray car but also another lane of traffic in front of them. The only pop of color is Carol's salmon headscarf and Abby's moss green one, until a yellow taxi obscures our view of them, framing them for an instant through its window as the camera—at car window height—continues to track with Carol and Abby. That is, for a moment, we see them through the taxi's windows and just over its hood. Then in a reverse shot, one that foregrounds Abby in the driver's seat, we see the yellow car again, catching up to them. However, in this stop and go traffic, the camera remains—stopping and starting—with the two women. Another car appears in the foreground from this perspective, while a new view of the city, composed of sidewalks and storefronts, fills the background. This generates a different sense of space

Figure 6.5 Carol (Cate Blanchett) and Abby (Sarah Paulson) in *Carol* (2015)

than the more distant rear-projected view of the apartments that constitute old New York.

A few things cue us to read this moment as concerned with an encounter between film and photography, stillness and movement. First, Abby's car's movement feels distinctly artificial. It doesn't appear to have contact with the road, but floats, an effect presumably of camera movement rather than car movement. The quality of this movement is rather different than the movement of the car that jolts into view behind theirs. Second, the framing makes use of a fairly common trope in midcentury photography, recalling images of people in cars, including, notably, several by Vivian Maier. There are a few other photographic precedents to Haynes's approach here including the "filmic photographs" by Robert Frank, specifically "Leaving Blackfoot Idaho" (1956) from *The American*'s series.[37] These photographic sources hover at the margins of Haynes's scene, supplying an image memory and photographic history that infuses this moment with significance. But photography also hovers, ontologically (and literally) behind the action in this scene in the form of an image of New York. Here, both its stillness and pastness are significant and harnessed in the moment's generation of a complex interplay between photography and film.

Carol animates these weather elements as it does the frames. Inspired by Leiter, frames are foregrounded in several interior scenes featuring the protagonists, particularly in Therese's apartment and Carol's home. Todd Haynes explains that he was particularly drawn to Leiter's "tendencies toward refracting the frame, interrupting the frame, and abstracting the frame, but also the site-specific light conditions of being inside a café looking out on the snowy streets, or through a dusty bus window."[38] The action often takes place in doorways, narrow corridors, or behind walls that partially obscure the action. In fact, the actors, who sometimes take up very little space on screen, compete with the various sites described through multiple frames and planes. The space itself is thus privileged and, as in the postwar images that provide inspiration, we are made aware of the agency of place. Moreover, as Alison McKee notes, the film's multiple frames suggest "entrapment and constraint within the world of postwar patriarchal norms of sexuality and gender roles for men as well as women." She also notes the "rigid horizontal and vertical lines that break up space and divide characters from one another, echoing a sense of personal isolation within that same social world."[39] This is particularly evident in one of the last scenes of the film at a house party. Two windows offering vignettes of encounters between people at the party—Therese included—are separated by a vast expanse of darkness that occupies the center of the frame.

Carol's reliance on the visual strategies of street photography and, specifically, what Victoria Smith calls an "aestheticized naturalism" prompts viewers to become "attentive to spaces, objects, and framings, since that is how and where the characters and their desires are transmitted and revealed."[40] Space is critical to the film, taking, as Smith argues, the place of speech.[41] It is activated in multiple ways by camera movement, lighting, color, filters, and shifting frames that variously constrict and channel Carol and Therese through worlds urban and rural, interior and exterior, psychic and social. But *Carol* borrows more than street photography's aesthetic strategies. It also activates the inherent tendencies of the genre and in a way that initiates engagements with its key concerns. That is, the film channels the subject matter, social significance, and critical work accomplished by this genre of photography, all the while setting up the conditions to think about relations between media in the pursuit of historical representation. In doing so, *Carol* also opens up a trajectory into broader issues concerning the representation of history on film and, more specifically, representations of an already heavily mediated entity, the Fifties.

Street photography enjoys a history as long as photography itself, with many of the medium's first images focused on the street.[42] However, as with any genre, historical and social contexts determine the nature of its iterations and evolution as does its relationship with adjacent practices. For instance, its relationship with photojournalism, documentary photography, amateur tourist photography, and fine art photography has generated what Scott calls a "taxonomic quandary."[43] As a documentary practice, questions of truth and impact necessarily enter the fray, especially in cases where images of the street are offered as a series with accompanying text designed to "provide information about the nature of things and to confirm the authenticity of a written account."[44] These questions, central to both still photography and documentary film traditions, reveal the extent to which such representations have a hand in constructing the realities they purport to reflect.[45]

With a strong documentary impulse at its heart, street scenes evolved from exposing social injustice in the 1930s to a concern with documenting "new kinds of cultural spaces . . . encountered in everyday life" by the 1950s.[46] More recent decades have witnessed a growing investment in marginalized subjectivities, though the critical efficacy of street photography to frame engagements with sexuality, gender, and racialized identities has been challenged. For instance, Katherine A. Bussard explains the limits of documentary or "realist" traditions in exposing certain social conditions, suggesting that Brechtian strategies foregrounding construction and fabrication in photography have been preferred by historically marginalized practitioners.[47] In their study of lesbian photography, Tessa Boffin and Jean Fraser make a similar argument, observing that because sexuality itself is socially constructed, documentary realism may be an unsuitable format. Their arguments are particularly apt for thinking through the rather distinct approaches assumed by Haynes in *Far from Heaven* versus *Carol*, with the former informed by the self-conscious presentation of artifice through a Sirkian palette and the latter appealing to a kind of documentary realism. However, as we shall see, realism itself is often complicated in the history of the street photography that Haynes mines, as well as by how he mobilizes its aesthetic tendencies to construct the film's deliberate archaism. In what follows, I hope to identify *Carol*'s critical force and to (partially) locate it within its metamodern oscillations. That is, between its investment in emotional truths and social histories and its constructed representational language that announces its own origins as something (re)mediated. For this reason, it is instructive to first look in a little more detail at the histories of what some of the source images for *Carol* instigated in terms of discussions about realism and truth.

For some photographers, like Helen Levitt, the streets became "sites of resistance," places where "we see in settings of decrepitude flourishing street culture."[48] Her images, like Haynes's, suggest both "microdramas," self-contained narrative moments involving relationships between people in all their complexity, and also social realities beyond the frame.[49] In a similar vein, Esther Bubley's street photography exceeded the observational and realist impulses often aligned with the genre. Her images of working-class women acknowledged their desires and agency. As Jacqueline Ellis explains, Bubley eschewed the practice of representing working-class women as "metaphoric sites of passive endurance" as had been commonplace in 1930s photography, especially those now canonical images of the Depression, poverty, and labor for the Farm Security Administration. Instead, she subverted such depictions by foregrounding "individual self-identity, personal empowerment, and self-conscious desire in working-class women which was—and still is—confirmed and repressed by economic disadvantage and systematic marginalization from an American society defined from a middle-class point of view."[50]

Berenice Abbott, often touted as a straight or observational photographer (and another inspiration for Haynes), acknowledged the complexity of "realism." She deployed the term in highly varied and inconsistent ways, as though she was "working through what the word 'realism' could or might mean."[51] According to Terri Weissman, Abbott's experimentation with a purportedly realist approach in photography enabled her to challenge some of the precepts of documentary photography and devise a "type of production that was both communicatively oriented and aware of its own representational limits."[52] That is, Abbott generated, through her images, "a space of communicative interaction. A space—between the photographic print, the photographer, and the spectator—of engagement that is open-ended and that reveals the social contexts out of which photographs come into sight in the first place."[53] This assessment of Abbott's photographs resonates with Haynes' *Carol*, for here too the aim was to generate a representational space of possibility where subjectivities, acts of looking, points of view and acknowledgments of histories of image-making intersect in meaningful ways to critical effect. Haynes' "naturalism" is, as he admits, also artificial.[54] Thus, like realism, it is "an effect to be produced."[55]

As an effect, both naturalism and realism in this regard do much to effectively point to their own representational status and constructed nature. However, as Weissman discusses in relation to Abbott, this leads to broader questions about representational practices around traditionally marginalized subjectivities.[56] Although Boffin and Fraser privilege Brechtian distanciation over documentary realism for engaging lesbian subjectivity in photographic practice, Weissman introduces a more recent debate of relevance over claims to truth in film and photography, citing how "the documentary mode within *art* contexts has emphasized—even developed a certain dependence on—the image's relation to the real."[57] Specifically, the question is one of how to "represent visually those unrepresented politically" or, in other words, how to devise a "realist strategy" to render visible constituencies typically excluded.[58] That is, how to ethically and effectively mobilize photography as a practice encoded with truth. Indeed, this returns us to the pressing question formulated at the outset of this study in relation to metamodernism, one that acknowledges the importance of truth in histories traditionally overlooked. In other words, the claim that history *matters*.

As such, by harkening back to street photography and its strategies, aesthetics, and attendant discourses, *Carol* also harnesses a particularly strong force with which these photographs are encoded: truth. These images are read as authentic historical records, a tendency that elides the more troubling elements that constitute the myth of photographic truth. Along with the grittiness or coded "realness" of Super 16, they do much to imbue the historical moment of *Carol* with a degree of authenticity and facticity too. Unlike *Far from Heaven*, *Carol* is not about deconstructing the problematic postwar identities shaped by toxic masculinity or passive femininity, though these do remain part of the lining of the film. Instead, it is about validating a set of experiences, processes of self-discovery, the development of agency, and articulation of lesbian desires that have not been afforded much representation, cinematic or otherwise.[59] This is an important history to document and a very real part of an early-1950s world somewhat at odds with more conventional images of the Fifties. In this regard it shares much with *Sylvie's Love*.

Although Patricia White argues that Carol uses "aesthetics to question truth," I think this is only partially the case. For as much as questions of realism are complicated through its photographic allusions, the truths signaled by the indexicality of photography and the emotional truths made accessible by color are also part of the critical force of the film.[60] For Allain Daigle, "[n]ostalgia, as an aesthetic style that draws attention to the formal qualities of memory, hails the inherent artifice of its experience without invalidating those sensations."[61] In other words, nostalgia is invested with critical potential. Deployed as an aesthetic style, it can engage questions of representation and artifice while generating an affective response that is meaningful and sincere. A nice encapsulation of metamodernism itself, this way of understanding nostalgia in relation to queer histories is especially productive for unpacking how *Carol* engages an early 1950s history of queer subjectivity through representational practices that do the work of keeping representation—as a problematic—in view.

Notes

1. For a fuller discussion of the term "retromediation," see Christine Sprengler, "Modern Art and Mediated Histories: *Pleasantville, Mona Lisa Smile*, and *Far from Heaven*," in *The Past in Visual Culture: Essays on Memory, Nostalgia and the Media*, ed. Jilly Boyce Kay, Cat Mahoney, and Caitlin Shaw (Jefferson, NC: McFarland, 2016), 15–16.
2. Roger Deakins in Iain Marcks, "*Hail, Caesar!*: Roger Deakins, ASC, BSC, discusses re-creating classical Hollywood genres for the Coen brothers' latest comedy," *American Society of Cinematographers*, February 2016. https://theasc.com/ac_magazine/February2016/HailCaesar/page1.html.

3. Kristen Anderson, "Behind the Scenes of *Hail, Caesar!*: Perming Josh Brolin and Making Scarlett Johansson a Modern-Day Esther Williams," *Vogue*, February 8, 2016. https://www.vogue.com/article/hail-caesar-mary-zophres-costume-designer-coen-brothers.
4. Dan Schrecker quoted in Brian Bishop, "How the Coen Brothers Used New-School Effects to Create Old-School Hollywood in *Hail, Caesar!*" *The Verge*, February 8, 2016. https://www.theverge.com/2016/2/8/10926066/hail-caesar-coen-brothers-special-effects-dan-schrecker-interview.
5. Ibid.
6. Ibid.
7. Doru Pop, "Multiplexing Marx in Contemporary Cinema," in *Contemporary Cinema and Neoliberal Ideology*, ed. Ewa Mazierska and Lars Kristensen (London: Routledge, 2017), 153. As Pop explains, "the kidnapping turns from a violent act into a ludicrous event. Instead of being evil monsters or torturers, the 'Malibu Commies' live in an extravagant beach mansion, eat home-made sandwiches, serve tea and employ a serving maid, exposing their hypocrisy and the empty nature of their entire conceptual background" (159).
8. "*Sylvie's Love* Q&A with Tessa Thompson & More," SCAD Film Fest 2020, *Entertainment Weekly*, November 2, 2020. https://www.youtube.com/watch?v=AKE3xAprLQg.
9. Aisha Harris, "Let *Sylvie's Love* Wrap You in All Its Goodness," *NPR* (December 24, 2020). https://www.npr.org/2020/12/24/949429032/let-sylvies-love-wrap-you-in-all-its-goodness.
10. Eugene Ashe quoted in Tomris Laffly, "*Sylvie's Love*," *RogerEbert.com*, December 23, 2020. https://www.rogerebert.com/reviews/sylvies-love-movie-review-2020.
11. Ibid.
12. "Eugene Ashe Interview: *Sylvie's Love*," Screen Rant, December 24, 2020. https://www.youtube.com/watch?v=jgLcP4_gZXs.
13. Richard Brody, "Review: *Sylvie's Love* Revives the Art of the Classic Hollywood Romance," *New Yorker*, December 22, 2020. https://www.newyorker.com/culture/the-front-row/review-sylvies-love-revives-the-art-of-the-classic-hollywood-romance.
14. Despite these slight shifts in color, there remains a fundamental coherence to the palette as defined for the film. Color is mobilized in ways that enliven spaces and accentuate emotion, thus aligning *Sylvie's Love* with its postwar inspirations.
15. "*Sylvie's Love* Q&A."
16. Patricia Highsmith wrote *The Price of Salt* under the pseudonym Claire Morgan. The novel is often celebrated as the first lesbian pulp romance with a *happy* ending.
17. For a thorough consideration of questions of motherhood as well as a much needed and astute interrogation of the film's focus on white middle-class experience that obscures the historical realities and diversity of queer kinship in postwar America, see Jenny M. James, "Maternal Failures, Queer Futures: Reading *The Price of Salt* (1952) and *Carol* (2015) against Their Grain," *Gay and Lesbian Quarterly*, 24.2–3 (2016): 291–314.

18. See, for instance, Jennifer Barker's excellent analysis of the act of taking photographs—photographic gestures—in the film in "Sparks Fly: Mediated Gesture, Affect, and Mise-en-Scene in *Carol*," *Mediaesthetics: Journal of Poetics of Audiovisual Images* 2 (2017): n.pag. http://dx.doi.org/10.17169/mae.2017.66. For a discussion of the construction of a female gaze, see Gabrielle O'Brien, "Looking for a Way Out: Reimagining the Gaze in *Carol*," *Screen Education* 86 (June 2017): n.pag. link.gale.com/apps/doc/A560314933/AONE?u = anon~3b6f093c&sid = googleScholar&xid = 58fce07f.
19. As noted with respect to *Hail, Caesar!*, LeSueur's companion term to deliberate archaism, "surface realism," is something *Carol* certainly invests in too. As director of photography Edward Lachman explains: "In the sets where we did paint, we went back and looked at what the colors of the paints they had used back then. We didn't want to reference modern colors . . . . So much of this came through in how production designer Judy Becker painted and dressed locations, and costume designer Sandy Powell picked the colors for the wardrobe and accessorized the actors. Sandy only used colors, fabric and stitching from the era and I think that captures the feeling of reality." As such, there was a deep investment in visually depicting the period with accuracy. "Edward Lachman Shares His Secrets for Shooting Todd Haynes' *Carol*," *IndieWire*, December 3, 2015. https://www.indiewire.com/2015/12/edward-lachman-shares-his-secrets-for-shooting-todd-haynes-carol-48627/.
20. Ruth Orkin and Errol Morris's *Lovers and Lollipops* (1956), a film as much about New York as about photography itself, is also cited as an inspiration for *Carol*.
21. Allison Gibbons, "Metamodern Affect," in *Metamodernism: Historicity, Affect and Depth after Postmodernism*, ed. Robin van den Akker, Allison Gibbons, and Timotheus Vermeulen (London: Rowman and Littlefield, 2017), 85.
22. Ed Lachmann quoted in Iain Stasukevich, "A Mid-Century Affair," *American Cinematographer* 96.12 (2015): 55.
23. Ibid.
24. Lachmann is attuned to the affective power of aesthetics, revealed by his belief that "with *Carol* people would feel something different than if I had shot it digitally." "Edward Lachman Shares," n.pag.
25. Ibid.
26. Todd Haynes, "Director's Dialogue, 53rd New York Film Festival, Lincoln Center," November 15, 2015. https://www.youtube.com/watch?v=Wcyp5cSvBwg.
27. Consider, in this regard, the first season of *Mad Men* (2007–15) or *The Marvellous Mrs. Maisel* (2017–).
28. Haynes, "Director's Dialogue."
29. Ibid.
30. Patricia White, "Sketchy Lesbians: Carol as History and Fantasy," *Film Quarterly* 69.2 (2015): 13.
31. Indeed, this is also the case in several photographs by Saul Leiter, which feature preternaturally saturated reds and golden yellows as compositional focal points in otherwise monochromatic images.
32. Lachmann in Stasukevich, "A Mid-Century Affair," 55.

33. Todd Haynes, "*Carol* Q&A, Film Society at Lincoln Center," December 11, 2015. https://www.youtube.com/watch?v=tyXweg_yf1o. Ed Lachmann builds on this sentiment, explaining: "by seeing the characters partially obscured, we're attempting to express their dislocated and fragmented identities." Lachmann in Stasukevich, "A Mid-Century Affair," 55.
34. Barker, "Sparks Fly," n.pag.
35. For an examination of how Haynes reworks Sirk's Christmas tree scene, see Walter Metz, "Far from Toy Trains," *Film Criticism* 40.3 (2016): 1. He argues that "while simultaneously taking on the function of Ron, as Carol's younger lover, Therese also adopts the stance of Sirk himself. Therese films the scene of *Carol* at the tree stand, as Sirk did Cary at hers."
36. For instance, the structure of *Carol* is borrowed from David Lean's *Brief Encounter* (1945). However, as Margaret Sönser Breen suggests, another layer of signification may be at play here, for "*Carol*'s engagement with *Brief Encounter* thus inevitably calls forth and pays homage to the queer specter that is Noël Coward within the context of mid-century film and theater." "The Locations of Politics: Highsmith's *The Price of Salt*, Haynes' *Carol*, and American Post-War and Contemporary Cultural Landscapes," *Gramma: Journal of Theory and Criticism* 25 (2018): 22.
37. See Ann Sass, "Robert Frank and the Filmic Photograph," *History of Photography* 22.3 (1998): 247–53. Moreover, in terms of subject, we might also recall the much later photographic images of lesbian romance in a convertible by artist collective Gran Fury.
38. Haynes quoted in Nick Davis, "The Object of Desire: Todd Haynes Discusses *Carol* and the Satisfactions of Telling Women's Stories," *Film Comment* 51.6 (2015): 32
39. Alison L. McKee, "*The Price of Salt*, *Carol* and Queer Narrative Desire(s)," in *Patricia Highsmith on Screen*, ed. Wieland Schwanebeck and Douglas McFarland (London: Palgrave Macmillan, 2018): 153.
40. Victoria L. Smith, "The Heterotopias of Todd Haynes: Creating Space for Same Sex Desire in *Carol*," *Film Criticism* 42.1 (2018): n.pag. http://dx.doi.org/10.3998/fc.13761 232.0042.102.
41. Ibid.
42. The "street," according to Westerbeck and Meyerowitz, involves a range of public spaces, including ones prevalent in *Carol*: bars, restaurants, and parks. See Colin Westerbeck and Joel Meyerowitz, *Bystander: A History of Street Photography* (London: Lawrence King, 1994): 34–35.
43. Liz Wells, *Photography: A Critical Introduction* (London: Routledge, 2015): 117.
44. Ibid.
45. Ibid., 124.
46. Ibid., 117.
47. Katherine A. Bussard, *Unfamiliar Streets* (New Haven: Yale University Press, 2014), 1.
48. Alan Trachtenburg, "Seeing What You See: Photographs by Helen Levitt," *Rariton* 31.4 (2012): 4.
49. Ibid., 1.

50. Jacqueline Ellis, "Revolutionary Spaces: Photographs of Working-Class Women by Esther Bubley 1940–1943," *Feminist Review* 53 (Summer 1996): 74–94.
51. Terri Weissman, *The Realisms of Berenice Abbott: Documentary Photography and Political Action* (Los Angeles: University of California Press, 2011), 2.
52. Ibid., 3.
53. Ibid., 18.
54. Todd Haynes, "Q&A With Cast and Filmmakers," *Carol*, DVD (Killer Films, et. al, 2015).
55. Weissman, *The Realisms of Berenice Abbott*, 5.
56. The representation of marginalized subjectivities is further complicated in *Carol*, however, by its exclusions. As Breen explains: "For Haynes, however, the striking delineation of silent and subordinate black characters not only reflects his commitment to recording one key aspect of the racial politics of mid-century Hollywood but also functions as a marker of his awareness of the difficulties that attended the making of a lesbian film more than half century later. Indeed, the history of adapting the novel to the screen attests to how strategies of erasure leveled against women, people of color, and queers continue to shape decisions regarding which films are made and which then singled out and awarded prizes." Breen, "The Locations of Politics," 23.
57. Weissman, *The Realisms of Berenice Abbott*, 9.
58. Ibid.
59. Very few titles set in the 1950s are invested in lesbian desire and subjectivity. The British film *Tell It to the Bees* (2018) is a recent exception. Gay male desire and subjectivity is the focus in a limited number of films, including *A Single Man* (2009).
60. White, "Sketchy Lesbians," 10.
61. Allain Daigle. "Of Love and Longing: Queer Nostalgia in *Carol*," *Queer Studies in Media & Popular Culture* 2.2 (2017): 206. For an extended discussion of the possibilities of "queer nostalgia" and, specifically, the genuine creative visions produced at the intersection of nostalgia and queer visual culture, see Gilad Padva, *Queer Nostalgia in Cinema and Pop Culture* (London: Palgrave, 2014).

7

The Fifties Reframed

Borders and Boundaries

In 1962, Michael Harrington outlined in sociological terms the existence of an "other" America in his best-selling book. Taking aim at how widespread poverty was obfuscated by the proliferation of the American Fifties as an age of plenty and possibility, Harrington exposed the rampant spread of poverty, one experienced at an astronomical rate: statistics mined by Harrington revealed 40,000,000–50,000,000 Americans—one-quarter of the population—living below the poverty line during the 1950s.[1] He explains that while America "worried about itself" during the 1950s, its *publicly* shared "anxieties were products of abundance," suburban malaise and the perils of consumer society.[2] Hidden from view were the destitute realities of "unskilled workers, the migrant farmworkers, the aged, the minorities, and all the others who live in the economic underworld of American life."[3] Harrington believed that if people were simply made aware of these conditions, they would be mobilized to demand change. Sadly, as the preface to the new edition of Harrington's book makes clear, this was not to be the case.

This "other" America was fully excluded from the visual culture of the Fifties economy, though not entirely absent from cinematic representations during the 1950s or since. The concern here is with more recent returns to a vision of the Fifties at odds with its dominant Populuxe-infused, Leave It to Beaver strains. Although initially inspired by a desire to contend with this "otherness," I do not wish to retain this term for the relationality to a purported center that it suggests. However, I do want to preserve something of the spirit of Harrington's analysis, to show how cinema seeks to render visible realities and experiences often elided.[4] More specifically, I want to conceive of how borders and boundaries between different visions of the 1950s are instantiated cinematically and ultimately crossed, how searching beyond national and metaphorical borders as well as boundaries between genres and art forms, have inflected representations of the 1950s, generating new histories, insights, and cultural memories in the process. I want to preserve

Harrington's desire to foreground marginalized experiences, but also include representations of the period purposefully recalibrated by looking elsewhere. Put another way, I want to consider how the Fifties has been reframed in two ways: by moving the camera's lens to focus on subjects often excluded and by recalibrating the lens itself to see its subjects differently. For my primary case studies, this entails looking across the Atlantic to the United Kingdom and across the stage to live theater. But to start, I want to briefly consider two examples that foreshadow, in certain ways, the films at issue in this chapter, ones concerned with the "other" America as Harrington first imagined it and thus the experiences of the poverty-stricken masses.

Windswept wheatfields, dusty roads, rusting cars, dilapidated houses, litter strewn rural properties and outdated and tattered clothing constitute an image of primarily white postwar poverty in a number of releases during the 1990s. Drawing from earlier depression-era dustbowl photographical representations and foregrounding, narratively, the horrors of childhood, they exist in stark visual contrast to titles invested in Populuxe worlds either for nostalgic celebration or social critique. Whereas some, like *Bastard out of Carolina* (1996) document poverty and abuse through a realist lens, *The Reflecting Skin* (1990) appeals to horror and "fairy tale symbolism" to confront coming of age in an atomic age as part of a maligned underclass. These two films will serve as prologue and precursors to the later releases that open up the Fifties in various ways, namely *Fences* (2016) and *Brooklyn* (2015).

All of these films—and more that deserve mention—share a concern with boundaries: social, geographical, racialized, gendered, aesthetic, and generic. *Bastard out of Carolina* and *The Reflecting Skin*, for instance, engage class borders and do so through a wholesale eschewal of the visual and commodity culture of postwar America. While the odd conventional period marker is introduced in both films in order to confirm the era in question, it is often modified or recalibrated to upend its typical significatory power. *Brooklyn* and *Fences* are also concerned with class to varying degrees, but draw on them to then permeate multiple other boundaries: international and generic in the case of the former and intranational and art forms in the case of the latter. The effects of these gestures are varied. While both complicate the visual legacy of the Fifties, there is a marked difference in impact that such aesthetic interventions have on the ideological legacies engaged in each case.

Bastard out of Carolina, based on the harrowing autobiographical novel by Dorothy Allison and directed for television broadcast by Anjelica Huston, recounts the traumatic childhood of Ruth Anne "Bone" Boatwright (Jenna

Malone) in 1950s rural South Carolina. Borne to an unwed young mother and thus labeled a "bastard" by the state, Bone survives a litany of horrors: rape, physical abuse, and neglect, as well as victimization by the institutions (e.g., the family, the legal system) supposed to protect her. As Leigh Gilmore put it with respect to Bone's status in the novel, with "bastard" the narrative "conflates a sexual and economic judgment which is then imposed on the child as a legal identity."[5] For Bone, and indeed all women in the extended Boatwright family, lack of economic agency becomes entwined with an inability to wrest free from the constraints of gender, from the patriarchal power structures that replicate themselves across all manner of institutions.

The film opens with a well-known quote from James Baldwin's *No Name in the Street*, read by an adult Bone (Laura Dern) in voiceover: "People pay for what they do... and still more for what they allow themselves to become. And they pay for it simply; by the lives they lead." Applicable to nearly every character in the film, these words presage the many narrative turns that beset Bone with multiple traumas and categories of neglect. The adult Bone then recalls: "The day I was born started off bad and only got worse." What "got worse" was not just that day, but indeed her entire childhood. She utters these words as we witness an old rusty car careening down a rural road moments before it crashes. The impact ejects Bone's mother, Anney (Jennifer Jason Leigh), then nine months pregnant with Bone, through the front windshield. The aesthetic here—dusty and desaturated—provides the visual template for the entire film, one used to describe even the rare happy moments in the film. For instance, Bone's birth is celebrated by her extended family, laughing and smoking cigars as they peer through a hospital window at the newest Boatwright (Figure 7.1). In this scene costume is tasked with maintaining the film's washed out look with everyone present wearing outdated and tattered clothes in the same limited palette of pale blue, green, gray, and brown. In a reversal of the logic of (British) heritage film, as we will discuss shortly in relation to *Brooklyn*, an aesthetic of wretched bleakness collides with the otherwise genuine happiness of the moment depicted.

Reminders of the 1950s are scattered about this poverty-stricken world, otherwise dominated by clutter and refuse, objects broken, abject, and worn. While at work, Anney's hair, make-up, and uniform approach expectation of the look of a waitress in a 1950s diner. But this is a public site in town and thus in a space at both a physical and social remove from her home life. Likewise, clothing worn by other people serve as a reminder of a different postwar experience, one more closely aligned with dominant representations

Figure 7.1 The Boatwrights in *Bastard Out of Carolina* (1996)

of the period. But in *Bastard out of Carolina*, this vision of a more prosperous, middle-class Fifties is relegated visually and narratively to the margins, it is decidedly "other" to the lives and experiences privileged by the story. This is made manifest during Lyle's (Dermot Mulroney) funeral, Anney's "decent" husband to whom she was married for an almost comically short time. On one side of the casket stand the Boatwrights, wearing effectively the very same tattered clothes they did to Bone's birth. On the other side stand Lyle's family, clearly of a higher economic station, but likely not quite middle class as envisioned by postwar domestic sitcoms. They are dressed "appropriately," that is in black mourning clothes of a style that signals some awareness of 1950s fashions. Following the service, during which disapproving looks are exchanged between the families, Anney's sister Ruth (Glenne Headly) tells Lyle's family that they have no right to cast judgment. Even death fails to erode the class boundaries between these two families or afford any opportunity for connection through shared grief.[6]

Bastard out of Carolina suffered from a troubled broadcast and distribution history. Initially developed for TNT by Huston, it was rejected by the network for its depiction of child abuse and rape. Huston then attempted to secure its release as a theatrical film, but did not manage to find support until Showtime agreed to air it on television in 1996.[7] Later, in a decision that replicated its fate as a novel in various US school districts, Atlantic Canada banned its broadcast. While the content that initiated this ban is extremely disturbing, comparisons with other books and films that traverse similar ground and have avoided censorship suggest the possibility of additional reasons for this judgment. That is, while the film's direct approach to representing the brutal physical and sexual assault of a child certainly has much to do with it, the way in which *Bastard out of Carolina* implicates other individuals and systems in the perpetration and perpetuation of such crimes may also have played a role. For instance, Glen Waddell (Ron Eldard) is not represented as an anomalous evil duly punished for his crimes. Although he is attacked by Bone's uncles, he not only escapes justice, but continues to be accepted by Anney, who prioritizes his welfare over that of her own daughter. Anney is a complex character, in turns victim and perpetrator of the most grievous and willful neglect. What is more, there is a sense that pervades the film, heightened by characters' responses to Bone's abuse, that hers is not a unique situation. As such, *Bastard out of Carolina* confronts a mythical postwar era predicated on "family values" that continues to have political purchase, reminding audiences of the scope of abuse against girls and women as well as the myriad ways in which it was—and is—ignored, condoned, and even legalized.

This challenge to the Fifties as a locus of family values, of working- and middle-class prosperity and consumer plenty, is enacted with similar zeal in Philip Ridley's *The Reflecting Skin*. Like *Brooklyn*, *The Reflecting Skin* presents a vision of postwar America crafted from outside its borders. Ridley is a British multidisciplinary artist, one initially aligned with the YBAs (Young British Artists) of the 1990s. He has since garnered acclaim (and a degree of infamy) in theater with productions that challenge taboos of live performance. His plays, featuring brutal violence, torture, and sexuality, some of it aimed at children or young adults, generated criticism of the kind that plagued *Bastard out of Carolina*.[8] Ridley's response to this criticism abides by the same logic that could counter detractors of Huston's film. For instance, in response to the charges of obscenity, cruelty, and disgust leveled at *Mercury Fur* (2005) for suggesting (though not representing) the torture and murder of a young boy, Ridley reminds his critics that the reality of violence against children far outstrips the staged fiction of his plays.[9] Although a somewhat disingenuous defense, given that it forecloses consideration of *how* the violence is depicted and to what end, it nevertheless speaks to a desire to resurrect the historical realities of forms of violence repressed in the public imaginary, a point worth considering in relation to racist violence in *Them* (2021) or *Lovecraft Country* (2020).

Mercury Fur, according to Ridley, is also about a loss of cultural memory and what happens to people when their history is forcibly wrested from them in preparation for imperialist invasion, as happened in Iraq while Ridley was conceptualizing this play.[10] But the past is at issue more broadly across Ridley's theater productions, his artistic practice involving painting and collage, and *The Reflecting Skin*. In all areas of his creative production, the 1950s and 1960s loom large, informing a recurrent visual vocabulary. This has prompted critics to note his investment in nostalgia, though of a kind that suggests a nuanced and critical edge. For instance, Ken Urban argues that all of Ridley's characters are "sick with nostalgia" in a medical sense, and that the nature of Ridley's engagement with the concept "reflects larger, ongoing debates about nostalgia in British culture, from Thatcher's call for a return to Victorian values to the rise of Tony Blair's New Labour party and its championing of Cool Britannia, which looked back to 1960s Swinging London as its model."[11]

The Reflecting Skin provided Ridley with an opportunity to explore his interest in the worlds represented by postwar American regionalism, specifically Andrew Wyeth's *Winter* (1946), *Turkey Pond* (1944), *Wind from the Sea* (1947), and *Christina's World* (1948).[12] It is also a meditation on memory, for the film offers what Ridley explains as the dreamlike, fragmented, intensified, and distorted memories of childhood from the perspective of an adult trying to recall events—both mundane and traumatic—that transpired decades earlier. This adult perspective is never identified in explicit terms as it is in *Bastard out of Carolina* through voice-over narration. Instead, it is conveyed visually and aurally, through the intensity of color, emotion, dialogue, and music designed to undermine realism.[13] Explanatory back stories have been edited out while heavy-handed symbolism abounds, offered up with the frequency and subtlety of a "sledgehammer."[14] This absence of conventional narrative information coupled with an abundance of overdetermined props imbues the world with an unmitigated surreality.[15] Indeed art not only plays a key role in mediating the vast prairie landscapes and its sagging clapboard houses but also involves a range of practices from Max Ernst's bird heads to signify frustrated sexuality to pietà compositions to foreshadow death, to Vermeer's multilayered interiors.[16]

The Reflecting Skin catalogs a series of horrific events alternatively instigated by or thrust upon eight-year-old Seth Dove (Jeremy Cooper), a complex character in turns sympathetic and sociopathic, and someone evidently wounded by the religious fundamentalist community in which he exists. Seth becomes convinced that a widow, Dolphin Blue (Lindsay Duncan), is a vampire (she isn't) slowly killing his older brother Cameron (Viggo Mortensen) who has just returned from military service in the Pacific. Cameron was tasked with testing atom bombs and is now slowly succumbing to radiation poisoning. Meanwhile, Seth's parents are waging their own losing battles with mental health, ending in suicide by dramatic self-immolation in his father's case after being suspected in the death of Eben (Codie Lucas Wilbie), Seth's friend. This suspicion derives from the sheriff's knowledge that, long ago, his father was caught "in a full embrace" with another young man. However, both of Seth's friends, as well as Dolphin, are murdered by a gang of young men who mysteriously traverse the vast wheatfields in their black 1958 Cadillac El Dorado (Figure 7.2). It is unclear if this Cadillac, an overt symbol of the Fifties—and the only nod to the Populuxe culture in the entire film—is real or a figment of Seth's imagination. For Deborah Lovatt, this car signifies the atomic bomb, a harbinger of death and destruction that pervades the entire film.[17] For Ridley, it more prosaically symbolizes death itself, ostensibly summoned by Seth when he wants to kill off Dolphin in order to save his brother from her (supposed) vampirism.

The film's stunning prairie vistas are punctuated, if not pierced, by extreme horrors: an exploding frog, child murders, self-immolation, a buried fetus that becomes a doll to Seth, etc. As David Annandale puts it, the film's

Figure 7.2 The Cadillac El Dorado in *The Reflecting Skin* (1990)

"extraordinary visual beauty is coupled with events just as extraordinary in their horror."[18] During its premiere at Cannes, audience members walked out after several minutes. However, not all viewers or critics condemned its more grotesque predilections. Some celebrated Ridley's vision, suggesting it warranted immediate cult status.[19] That its cult status has increased in recent years—thanks to committed fan discourse and the film's 2005 restoration— suggests as much about the merits of the film as it does the changing legacy of the 1950s in the popular imagination, one now increasingly invested in its alignment with horror, a development exemplified by *Them* and *Lovecraft Country*. Other reviewers honor the film by characterizing it as David Lynch meets Terence Malick.[20] This is an apt description, especially given the nature of Lynch and Malick's own unconventional revisitations of the 1950s in *Blue Velvet* (1986) and *Tree of Life* (2011), respectively. These films, like Ridley's, do much to upend tropes of the postwar period by recalibrating them through surrealist and non-naturalist sensibilities. Ridley has even acknowledged Lynch as an influence, going so far as to classify his own film as "*Blue Velvet* with children," an apt characterization to be sure.[21]

With *The Reflecting Skin*, Ridley explores a vision of a mythic Midwest American Fifties—a time he neither experienced nor a place he ever visited— from outside as a construct to be critically interrogated by examining its images, ones created in the realms of both art and popular culture. With *Brooklyn*, director John Crowley also offers an outsider's perspective on postwar America, though to very different ends. Adapted by Nick Hornby from Colm Tóibín's 2009 novel of the same name, *Brooklyn* (2015) charts Eilis Lacey's (Saorise Ronan) emigration from Enniscorthy, Ireland, to America in 1951. This postwar transatlantic move, a common one to be sure among Europeans more broadly, was not Eilis's choice, but the will of her family and church, one guided by their desire to see her flourish in New York. County Wexford, a quaint rural domain, did not afford her the same opportunities for growth. With all the privileges enabled by a prearranged job and boarding house room as well as the counsel of a grandfatherly Irish Catholic priest, Eilis's struggles are limited to her social awkwardness and acute homesickness. Father Flood (Jim Broadbent) promises her that "homesickness is like most sicknesses. It'll make you feel wretched and then it'll move on to someone else." And indeed, eventually, it does. Eilis meets second-generation Italian Tony (Emory Cohen), passes her bookkeeping exams, and starts to feel more at ease in the various spaces that she moves through as part of her daily routine. However, after her sister's untimely death, Eilis returns to

Ireland, but not before marrying Tony. Unexpectedly she begins to see the potential for a more fulfilling life in small town Enniscorthy than previously imagined. There is the prospect of a decent job as a bookkeeper and of a decent husband in Jim (Domhnall Gleeson). But when Miss Kelly, the grocer and Eilis's former employer confronts her about her secret marital status, the decision about whether to stay in Ireland or return to Brooklyn is wrested from her. The film ends with Eilis's return voyage in 1952, this time a seasoned traveler dispensing advice to the next lot of immigrants.

For John Crowley, the aim was to avoid any hint of irony in his recreation of early 1950s Enniscorthy and Brooklyn, to always be "very directly emotional, but not sentimental."[22] He wanted the drama and world inhabited by its characters to "feel completely authentic and real." To this end, he aimed for a limited color palette that expands subtly and slightly as Eilis develops a sense of agency and control over her life. Likewise, he asked director of photography Yves Bélanger to shift from a gentle handheld quality that does not draw attention to itself to a more classical and elegant style of filming later in the film. Crowley also "never wanted [*Brooklyn*] to tip its hand toward Technicolor in any way."[23] In other words, he did not want his 1950s aligned with 1950s Technicolor film or its myriad retromediations harnessed to celebratory, nostalgic, or critical ends. That is, he wanted *Brooklyn* to stand outside of and apart from Fifties nostalgia as both a mood and a mode to return to Paul Grainge's distinction. And indeed, visually, it does. The most colorful sequence in the film, shot on location at Coney Island, is muted by haze and a range of pastels that recall postcards of the attraction more so than cinema. Eilis's costumes, carefully plotted along with her hair and make-up, also register her maturation in subtle ways, moving from soft green wool sweaters and subdued fine cotton prints to sweater sets and A-lined skirts and, finally, a yellow shirtwaist dress. While her yellow dress is bright and full-skirted, it does not approach the same chromatic vibrancy or design excess that defined the New Look. Thus, as with much about the visual dimensions of the film, it suggests a temporal state not quite yet fully into the 1950s and a spatial one not quite yet detached from Ireland.

Brooklyn's refusal to subscribe, in visual terms, to a now well-worn Technicolor aesthetic has prompted reviewers to revel in its "anachronistic grace" or "old fashioned" nature, a quality also rooted in its pace, style of filmmaking, and simplicity of focus on the emotional growth of a protagonist in ways aligned with the Woman's Film of the 1930s and 1940s.[24] For others, the film's "grace" is found in the way it feels like a "memory play" or "an old photograph without a frame, an implied flashback." That is, according to Glenn Kenny, "nothing in the film takes place in the present, but everything in it is carried on an invisible current of imaginative retrospection."[25] With this characterization, Kenny, like Crowley, seems intent on avoiding the word nostalgia, highlighting instead emotion and authenticity, as if to steer discourse about the film away from cinematic expectations about films set during the 1950s, especially those American (or, rather, Hollywood) in origin.[26] But *Brooklyn* does trade in nostalgia, specifically through heritage tropes, another factor most positive reviews seem at pains to avoid. What is more, because of the film's structure, it transposes these tropes into an American context. That is to say, *Brooklyn* imports Irish (and more generalized British) visions of the postwar period through cinematically well-entrenched images, sites, and practices.[27] While this might complicate what the Fifties looks like for a transnational audience or, more specifically, (North) American viewership accustomed to certain visions of 1950s New York, it does little to expand the ideological implications of the images it both trades in and seeks to counter.

The "heritage film" is an expansive and deeply politicized term, one that has evolved beyond its origins to describe late-twentieth century debates about preservation, national identity, taste, history, and class. It was first used by Andrew Higson to account for period dramas of the Merchant-Ivory variety, ones derived from literary sources that generate visually sumptuous pasts often at odds with narratives invested in social critique. "Post-heritage," was then coined by Claire Monk to account for more complex and self-conscious engagements with the British past that directly confronted issues of gender and sexuality, as in Sally Potter's *Orlando* (1992) and Jane Campion's *The Piano* (1993). More recently, scholars have sought to systematize Monk's "post-heritage" designation into a methodology for identifying such impulses in screen fiction, for instance, Will Stanford Abbiss's proposal of five "guiding elements," including "interrogation, subversion, subjectivity, self-consciousness, and ambiguity."[28] Likewise, the term has been adopted and adapted beyond Britain's borders to account for tendences in other European and World cinemas.[29] There are ways in which debates around heritage and its expansion finds alignment with cinematic representations of the 1950s, to the point that critical purchase may be found by applying some of the terms of debate around history and the politics of heritage, postheritage, and counterheritage to American examples. Although beyond the scope of this chapter, I do hope the introduction of the term here is suggestive for thinking through what it might offer engagements with American case studies of the 1950s.[30]

For Ruth Barton, *Brooklyn* represents a "thoughtful reworking of the heritage film and of the emigrant narrative," explaining that its production design generates the kind of visual pleasures that have defined the conventional costume drama while its protagonist embodies the strength of characters that populated "the 1950s cycle of women's films without their punitive moralising."[31] As Crowley explains, Eilis decides to engage in premarital sex, but it is never punished, nor is she subject to that requisite Catholic guilt. What is more, Eilis's experience of emigration as emotionally difficult but not traumatic, sets *Brooklyn* apart from other Irish historical films that foreground the lifelong negative effects of such journeys.[32] And yet, as Barton rightly points out, *Brooklyn* nevertheless belongs to a "shift in film culture that has witnessed the erasure of the politically engaged, formally innovative cinema of the earlier generation of Irish filmmakers by proponents of conventional storytelling and, particularly, the language of melodrama."[33] This political disengagement seems to happen on several levels, though primarily with respect to immigration and gender, erasures that have a ripple effect on how its heritage film tropes and tendencies then frame its American 1950s setting.

While *Brooklyn* may depart from other tales of Irish emigration, the "memory play" or recollective feel of the film makes ignoring the present as a framework a rather challenging endeavor. As such, it is particularly difficult to hold in abeyance the persistent stream of migrant tragedies from the last decade that have befallen those attempting to travel by sea to Europe. Indeed, for this reason Gareth Millington characterizes the film as little more than "an exercise in nostalgia," and one that "lacks any critical resonance."[34] The contrast it generates between "the migrant urban experience of the mid-twentieth century" and the plight of those arriving on "English shores today" is exceptionally stark.[35] Indeed there is nothing in the film that speaks to the migrant experience outside of the very individual and personal challenges faced by Eilis: the sadness on the faces of the family she leaves behind, the rough seas, the seasickness, the cramped sleeping quarters, and shared washrooms. When she arrives at Ellis Island and successfully makes her way through customs, a bright light shines from behind the door to America without even a hint of irony.

This lack of "critical resonance" can also be applied to the film's treatment of gender, despite the critical celebration of Saorise Ronan's nuanced performance, one suggestive of her development of personal agency.[36] Indeed, in this respect, the film presents something of a paradox or perhaps, more accurately, an alibi. On the one hand, for a film that replicates much about earlier Woman's films, Eilis's growth exceeds the constraints placed on her at the time. While her choices remain limited and ultimately come down to an Irish or Italian-American husband, the assuredness and assertiveness with which she makes her choices convince us that they are indeed (mostly) hers to make. And yet there is so much of the gendered experience of immigration and the gendered experience of living in a city, one often traversed in the dark, that is completely side-stepped, as if the film's laser focus on Eilis's emotional journey through homesickness is a form of misdirection away from other realities. Indeed, the film sets up so many spaces where gendered violence or various forms of harassment typically occurs that it starts to become obvious that it *isn't* happening: on the ship crossing the Atlantic, walking the streets at night, attending dances, meeting young men she knows nothing about. Even Crowley admits the film upends expectation with respect to Tony, leading viewers to wonder if he is not who he seems.[37] And yet these threats, implicit to gendered experiences of the city and of immigration, never materialize.

There is also a marked lack of criticality with respect to the Catholic church, especially in regard to the context in which *Brooklyn* was released. Of course, the film is not about the abuses perpetrated by Catholic priests nor can it be, given the ways in which such figures are positioned in the film: as benevolent sponsor and kindly counselor in the case of Father Flood, or leading mass and a wedding ceremony in a small Irish town. But *Brooklyn*'s release in 2015, after *Doubt* (2008) and a spate of other films, just before *Spotlight* (2017), and during a period of sustained international press in Europe and North America documenting the long and extensive history of child sex abuse in the Catholic church, makes it difficult not to see priest characters informed by these crimes. For Ruth Barton, such films (as well as various popular television series) did much to create "associated links between the Irish Catholic Church and child abuse."[38] More than that, one of the two determining tropes of twenty-first-century Irish film was the "loss of Church authority" in the wake of these—and other—revelations.[39] This was eroded further through other films that tackled such subjects, including ones with transnational success, including *The Magdalene Sisters* (2002), set in the early 1960s and released during "an ongoing two year media frenzy that pursued revelations of clerical child sexual abuse across every Catholic diocese in the United States."[40]

Brooklyn is also an anomaly in the context of Irish film, released at a time when "concerns about the past were a thing of the past" and Irish filmmakers—though not necessarily British filmmakers—turned away from Irish history and period films more generally.[41] It harkens back to an earlier period of Irish heritage film of the 1990s, when such offerings were "structurally and thematically conservative" rather than postheritage films that self-consciously interrogated their own historicity or character constructions.[42] It does so through its disavowal of twenty-first-century concerns that inflect its reception, but also through an appeal to a set of heritage film tropes aligned with Ireland and the United Kingdom more broadly that are effectively imported to America through a series of doublings. These tropes, I want to suggest, are of a certain kind and mobilized in specifically conservative ways. As such they bear little resemblance to the kind assessed by Belén Vidal in her analysis of how a mannerist aesthetic helps frame the critical potential of period film tropes like the house, tableau, or letter to complicate the feminine in relation to history.[43]

For instance, the dance hall, a site of postwar working-class socialization, appears across a range of 1950s-set British and Irish films.[44] Typically modest and a bit dreary, the space nevertheless becomes infused with the possibility of romance, sociality, and escape. In *Brooklyn*, the dance hall of Enniscorthy is mirrored by the church basement dance hall in Brooklyn (Figure 7.3). Both are rather unremarkable and unadorned and in stark contrast to what might be a more decidedly American equivalent, the high school dance. Whereas a deliberate slowness pervades the dance hall, echoed through slower tempo music and slower ballroom dancing, a far greater range of musical and dance styles mark the experience of dancing in often well-lit and highly decorated American gyms. In *Brooklyn*, the live music in one dance hall–set sequence evolves from a traditional Irish ballad to an American one, "Yellow Rose of Texas," (originally a racist minstrel song), to a soft jazz number as if to chart a physical journey across the Atlantic, and a temporal one from an Irish past to the film's American present, but all of it utterly subdued in terms of sound, color, and movement. As a church-sponsored dance in Brooklyn patrolled by Father Flood, this event is also one governed by the strictures of chaste heterosexual courtship, with patriarchal gender dynamics firmly and unquestioningly entrenched.

Figure 7.3 Church basement dance in *Brooklyn* (2015)

Another site of importance is the dinner table in both private (homes) and public (restaurants) places. What begins for Eilis as a women-only affair, first in the form of dinners with her mother and sister in Enniscorthy and later with the other lodgers in the Brooklyn boarding house, evolves into a patriarchal affair, suggestive of future familial dynamics and hierarchies through family or romantic dinners with Eilis's two suitors.[45] The various private settings all share an appeal to tradition through set design that harkens to historical periods well before the early 1950s (Figure 7.4). This is in stark contrast to the midcentury modern or "newness" often used to describe domestic interiors in American films and television. That is, instead of sleek spindly legged furniture and atom clocks, we see William Morris–style wallpaper, dark wooden furniture, and lacework. These old-fashioned spaces—both in Enniscorthy and Brooklyn—are spaces of communality and mostly comfort, without a hint of the toxic patriarchy well-entrenched cinematically through the likes of other 1950s-set British and Irish period films, most famously the violent outbursts of a tyrannical father in Terence Davies's *Distant Voices, Still Lives* (1988). In other words, *Brooklyn* imports a sanitized vision of working-class familial relations into America, eschewing the more critical visions that have populated period films from the British Isles.

There are a number of other pairings too, ones designed to show both contrast and similarity between the two locations and Eilis's two possible futures, but I want to select two that have implications for visions of the American Fifties. True to heritage form, *Brooklyn* offers scenes of Ireland showcasing

Figure 7.4 Dinner at the boarding house in *Brooklyn* (2015)

the expansive and lush green countryside. Although in recent years, this image has shifted from its association with childhood, innocence, and the Irish past/history to one with the potential for horror (as is also the case, as noted, for American long-form television), *Brooklyn* subscribes to the former by foregrounding the serenity of nature and the beauty of such spaces long entrenched in the Irish imaginary.[46] A similar view is offered of America in a scene that, at first glance, could be Ireland. Tony has taken Eilis to an empty green field on Long Island and asks her to imagine herself living there, in one of many soon-to-be-built houses that will constitute a future community. This space is thus presented as a somewhat liminal one at this moment in the film, between Ireland and America and thus also between the past and the present or, more accurately, future. When Eilis agrees to Tony's proposition, we are prompted to see in this space, as A.O. Scott argues, a neighborhood materialize before our eyes.[47]

However, transplanting this Irish (and more broadly British) heritage trope into this particular American setting in a way that engenders both a historical consciousness and a look forward in time engages the historical realities attached to this particular geographical space. For one thing, despite centuries of visual cultural production that have framed American landscapes as vast empty resources to be settled, explored, extracted or variously aligned with God, the picturesque, or the sublime, such ideological images were generated in an effort to eradicate in visual terms the presence of North America's Indigenous peoples. For another, Long Island was also the site of the first Levittown community that, as detailed in Chapter 3, is now as much a shorthand for suburbia as it is suburban segregation practices, racist violence, and civil rights struggles involving the Housing Act more generally. In fact, Long Island continues to be one of the most segregated boroughs in New York.[48] In other words, it is difficult not to imagine Eilis and Tony's future house as part of such a development, despite the fact that the film fails to open up space for any criticality with respect to what it meant to be a white Irish settler in Long Island in the early 1950s. The various histories this positionality brings in its wake percolate through, unintentionally perhaps, because of the "historicalness" written into the landscape trope imported from the heritage film.

By the time Tony shows Eilis that vast Long Island tract of empty green countryside, the viewer has already been given ample opportunities to consider a series of perplexingly inaccurate representations of postwar racialized experiences. Like many films set in the 1950s that privilege white coming-of-age narratives, Black characters are inserted as extras to signal the existence of diversity in the world represented, but without sharing anything of their lived experiences. Early on in the film, several Black women have been positioned conspicuously in the foreground of the scene documenting Eilis's first pedestrian commute to her new job. This scene is later repeated to suggest that the same group of individuals travels together on foot every day to work. Likewise, Black families are also placed in the foreground of the beach scenes at Coney Island and Black women appear as extras in Bartocci's department store as shoppers. As much historical research has shown, these public spaces were subject to various forms of official and unofficial segregation and discrimination during the 1950s. Certain sites within Coney Island (and other large amusement venues) were segregated while those spaces not subject to Jim Crow laws were often areas in which Black patrons experienced racist harassment by white perpetrators.[49] Likewise, while department stores may not have banned Black consumers outright, various strategies and the unabashed racism of white sales staff made many feel unwelcome. What is more, these stores maintained discriminatory hiring practices well past the 1950s.[50]

The beach, the street traversed for work, and the store as Eilis's place of employment also find equivalents set in Ireland. The Irish manifestations of these sites are comparatively empty, quaint, and small, in order to highlight the vibrancy and possibility of life in America. But some of these sites, as tropes found in heritage films and thus images discursively shaped not just by their cinematic, but also their academic and popular historiographical contexts, carry with them ways of seeing their counterparts in *Brooklyn*'s American 1950s. Furthermore, their mobilizations in this film, one whose minor engagements with a young woman's agency belies an otherwise notable lack of criticality and erasure of both past and present circumstances around race and the Church in particular, may expand the visual purview of what the Fifties looks like, but seems to reintroduce ideologically the conservatism that other films have sought to undo. That is, *Brooklyn* imports some of the less critical tendencies of heritage films while gesturing in empty ways toward a postheritage concern with gender. It is particularly less critical than some of the other 1950s-set British heritage offerings that offer a wealth of possibility with re-evaluating the past. In this instance, the transnational importation of a certain approach to the past—the 1950s—underscores the conservatism inherent in the history of this period's representation and mobilization.

Directed by Denzel Washington, *Fences* (2016) is a close cinematic translation of August Wilson's play of the same name, written in 1983, first performed in 1987, and revived in 2010. It is one of Wilson's "twentieth-century cycle" plays, and thus one of many scripts, each devoted to a different decade of the past century. The majority of the theatrical cast reprised their roles for the film with Washington as the protagonist Troy, Viola Davis as his wife Rose, Russell Hornsby as the elder son Lyons, Mykelti Williamson as Troy's brother Gabriel, and Stephen McKinley Henderson as Mr. Bono, Troy's best friend. *Fences* constitutes Wilson's engagement with the 1950s and represents a Black working-class experience in Pittsburgh's Hill District by centering its focus on Troy Maxson and his strained relationships with his family (and himself). As the title suggests, the film is overtly concerned with borders: psychological and physical, but also boundaries between classes, racialized communities, and art forms.

Troy is a complex character shaped by the imbrication of intergenerational and racist traumas. His wife and sons suffer as a result, as does he. Troy's past is shaped by rejections, both familial and institutional. In fact, institutions figure prominently in *Fences*, suggesting, as Matthew Roudané argues, the experience of entrapment: Troy and his elder son both spend time in prison; Cory enlists in the Marines after Troy forbids him to accept recruitment by a college football team and thus potentially succeed where his father failed; Gabriel, who suffered severe brain damage during World War II, is eventually hospitalized; and the "institution" of Major League Baseball never invited Troy, despite his talents that, as he claims, exceeded those of Jackie Robinson. For Wilson, even Rose becomes progressively drawn to the church after she learns that Troy has fathered a child with another woman. Alberta, Troy's mistress, tragically dies in childbirth leaving Rose to raise the child, Raynell (Saniyya Sidney), as her own. Indeed, for Rose, Lyons, and Cory, the institution of the family becomes increasingly suffocating and limiting because of the patriarchal power Troy seeks to exercise at every turn. This power—wielded out of spite, love, fear, jealousy, and sometimes simply convention—wanes as the narrative progresses, with its various iterations reminding audiences of both the personal and social struggles that entwine throughout the film.

Although the narrative unfolds over a series of several weeks in 1957, it ends with an epilogue of sorts, set in 1965, as Rose and her children, including the young Raynell, gather in preparation for Troy's funeral. Troy's battles with Death, the subject of some of his tall tales throughout the film, renders this conclusion expected. As does the foreshadowing provided by his brother, (the archangel?) Gabriel, who warns Troy: "Saint Peter got your name in the book. I seen it. It say . . . Troy Maxson." For Wooden, it is this "pull of death" that motivates Troy's drive to "live and create art (manifested in storytelling)."[51] Troy's stories feature prominently in *Fences* and serve multiple functions. They situate Troy's experiences within a broader 1950s social and political world. While certain elements are clearly conjured, they nevertheless expose the historical realities of lived everyday experience for Black Americans during the 1950s. For instance, Troy's tale of his battle with pneumonia is an indictment of disparities in healthcare. They are reminders of the power of fiction to engage truths and for the deeply personal to be revelatory of the broader social forces that variously constrain and enable. This slippage between truth and fiction manifests visually at the very end, when Gabriel blows his trumpet to signal to Saint Peter to open the gates for Troy. At first, no sound emanates from Gabriel's instrument. Finally, on the third try, the raspy hollow contours of a faint note transform into a pure sustained sound, as the clouds part and sun streams down on the Maxson family (Figure 7.5). This moment of cinematic fantasy is short-lived, but enough to underscore the tenet that fiction—like Troy's apocryphal stories—have power.

Troy's stories also do much to imbue the film with an indomitable theatricality. That is, along with the limited settings, mostly unobtrusive camera work, restricted color palette, and abundance of dialogue delivered with significant emotional charge, Troy's long stories feel invariably more aligned

Figure 7.5 The clouds part for the Maxsons in *Fences* (2016)

with the stage than the screen. They are delivered with a self-conscious performativity that exceeds any sense that Troy is simply presenting for Rose, Mr. Bono, or Cory, ostensibly acknowledging an audience beyond the proscenium. What is more, the method of reply that, as Ina Archer points out, has characters repeat phrases of their interlocuters, imbues the dialogue with a musical structure.[52] As such, the delivery of words does not read as "cinematic," but suggests another performative way of speaking. Some reviewers found a degree of fault with this, including Richard Alleva, who observed that "dialogue that is colloquial enough on stage tends to sound like rhetoric when uttered on screen."[53] However, for Wilson, language was a critical component of his plays and his approach to dialogue evolved as he realized the significance of celebrating African American Vernacular English (AAVE), rather than taking pains to obscure it.[54] Indeed, the *theatrical* delivery of lines—a kind of sonic aesthetics aligned with the stage—does much to foreground and exalt language itself.

There is a tension between the cinematic and the theatrical that persists throughout *Fences*, an oscillation between moments that foreground its "filmness" and ones that signal the stage. This was a point of contention among reviewers who thought *Fences* felt too much like a play. However, frequent shifts between these two related modalities were purposefully built into the film at aesthetic, technological, and narrative levels. For instance, David Ehrlich captures a fairly common sentiment when he writes: "Washington's inability or unwillingness to use the camera as more than a recording device does a disservice to a story that's so concerned with the interplay between daily life and the dreams that we measure it against. Rather than adding to the material, the film just makes you feel like you're watching *Fences* through a screen."[55] However, I think this charge fails to account for the subtle yet poignant ways in which the camera is mobilized—quite literally in some instances—to underscore something of the phenomenological and representational shifts between theater and film that are an important part of how *Fences* complicates the representational legacy of the 1950s.

As cinematographer Charlotte Bruus Christensen recounts: "The movie had to look real, but still maintain the feel of the play. That was a very fine balance, to not escape the play or throw it away, but keep it."[56] This was, in part, accomplished through the use of 35mm film which, perhaps paradoxically, helped underscore both moments of theatricality and the production's celluloid substrate. Because "close-ups were very, very important," Christensen and Washington felt 35mm would better service their intent to generate a sense of intimacy.[57] Washington also insisted on using anamorphic lenses, what he called an "actor's lens." As Christensen explains, "If you're focused on the foreground, the background will be slightly distorted, and when you shift focus it pulls you to the face."[58] Indeed this isolation of and focus on the face is effective at suggesting interiority and creating highly charged interplays of looks. It is also through such close-ups, ones that recall the photomontages of artist Romare Bearden—a significant influence on Wilson's play and the film version—that the film engages with Black masculinity, as will be discussed shortly.

Washington's use of 35mm also supported *Fences*' "realist" aims by generating a rather precise period setting. This process began before filming in a lab at Technicolor, where Joshua Pines, ASC associate, collaborated with imaging researchers to "develop a vintage-film emulation LUT [look-up table] specifically for *Fences*."[59] In other words, the feel—generated by color, texture, and grain—was meant to evoke an older representational practice in the spirit of deliberate archaism. And, like *Bastard out of Carolina*, *Good Night, and Good Luck*, or *Carol*, this aesthetic was found outside the vibrant, saturated world of postwar Technicolor processes. It was predicated more on a nondescript pastness that, through a muted and limited color palette of browns, blues, and grays, did much to suggest the constraints experienced by the characters. Yet, despite the overarching commitment to realism, the possibilities of film were also harnessed to dramatic and "magical realist" effect. While the most "magical" moment involves Gabe parting the clouds, as described above, other more subtle strategies also deserve mention. Following the final physical and verbal altercation between Troy and Cory—which almost ends in tragedy—Cory leaves for good. Troy is shaken by this encounter, primarily because he failed to control his son. After Cory departs, the camera focuses on Troy. While his face and expression of anguish are clearly visible, the edges of the frame are highly blurred. The details of the space that surround him are wholly obscured by this cinematographic strategy meant to foreground Troy's interior state. This reads as a clichéd gesture in distinct opposition to the type of camera work used throughout *Fences* and, as such, it signals not just a cinematic convention, but cinema itself. It snaps audiences out of the theatrical milieu conjured by the scene that preceded this moment and, in doing so, serves as a reminder of *Fences'* ontological status.

These shifts between cinema and theater in ways that foreground the conventions of each with respect to space, sound, performativity, language, and historical convention are a reminder of the various powers and possibilities inherent in different representational practices. Whereas sound and space intertwine and inflect each other in specific ways in the theater to generate affective charges for the audience, other possibilities for sounds to describe space are possible within—and harnessed by—the cinematic version of *Fences*. For instance, as Alleva observes, the space of the street is activated by natural sunlight (an impossibility in any stage production of *Fences*) and layered sounds like children playing, car engines revving, and chickens clucking.[60] Indeed the chickens were a conscious addition to the "noise" of the film as a way to point to the historical reality of postwar Black—and working-class—neighborhoods in Pittsburgh, where chickens were indeed a common part of the soundtrack of everyday life.[61] For Alleva, this cinematic realism "works against the true nature of the story," for while *Fences* is "historically specific," it is a work of theatrical tragedy not well served by the "inherent naturalism of most movies."[62] I would argue, however, that the tensions generated between theatrical and cinematic conventions here, between naturalism and artifice, stage space and diegetic space as activated by various forms of light and sound are productive in challenging viewers to consider the ways in which each mode of representation engages both its specific subject (e.g., Black working-class experience in 1950s Pittsburgh) and more general intervention into representations of 1950s America. This tension, moreover, reminds viewers that what has been subject to cinematic exclusion—or misrepresentation (e.g., *The Help* [2011])—has had a vibrant existence in another art form: theater.

This tension between cinema and theater is further complicated and reinforced with a critical thrust by the stars of the film (and 2010 theater revival): Denzel Washington and Viola Davis. While Washington and Davis' star power would have certainly informed the spectatorial experience of the theater production, their star power also inflects how we read their characters in the film, especially given the heightened performativity of the delivery of their lines which prompts audiences to see them as actors and, as actors with specific on- and off-screen histories. In Washington's case, this means a certain construct of Black masculinity that enters into dialogue with Troy Maxson and, in the process, brings a construct of 1990s Black masculinity into negotiation with a 1950s one.[63] There are moments when Washington's star persona, developed through his depiction of confident, ethical, and intelligent men—both fictional and historical—makes itself felt in ways that generate empathy with Maxson and intertwine with the volatility of an individual shaped by postwar hardships. It also helps underscore the complexity of Troy, whose own sense of self is deeply fraught, weighted down by both patriarchal history and expectation but also elevated by his perceptiveness and drive.

In Davis's case there are two trajectories that converge: her roles in other period dramas like *The Help* and *Far from Heaven* (2002) and her off-screen activism in response to precisely these Hollywood casting practices. As she stated in a BFI interview, her role as Abilene prompted her to decide: "After *The Help*, I was done with aprons," accepting only parts that enabled her agency, "humanity and sexuality."[64] As such, embodied by Davis is a Hollywood history of roles for Black women that are deeply problematic for their erasure of agency, racist stereotyping, and relegation to the margins of white experience as well as a challenge to that legacy. In other words, through Davis, the institution of Hollywood—and the systemic racism according to which it has long operated—are invoked through her star persona and a performance that foregrounds its own performativity.

The experience of Black working-class families in 1950s Pittsburgh is ostensibly the key focus of *Fences*, and thus criticism of the film tends to privilege the way it engages the social realities presented therein. However, the film's force and significance cannot be reduced to its political investments or, more accurately, cannot be cleaved from its aesthetic engagement with theater and, as will be discussed, other art forms. To put it as Michael Boyce Gillespie does in *Film Blackness*, the Black lifeworld ought not determine the "sole line of inquiry."[65] Boyce Gillespie is not advocating for a "deracialized or postracial notion of black film," but instead for an approach that acknowledges how it "operates as a visual negotiation, if not tension, between film as art and race as constitutive, cultural fiction."[66] In other words, he is opening up a space, as Darby English does with respect to Black art, for a "critical dialogism of cinema as an enactment of black visual and expressive culture."[67] While *Fences*' mobilization of theater, as described above, enables precisely this kind of critical attention to be paid to the imbrication of form and politics, there are further ways in which the film reaches through past forms of Black art.

For August Wilson, the work of multidisciplinary artist and art historian Romare Bearden was particularly important.[68] Wilson found in Bearden an "artistic mentor" and aimed to replicate through theater what determined the force of Bearden's canvasses. Wilson explained that what he saw in Bearden's work "was black life presented on its own terms, on a grand and epic scale, with all its richness and fullness, in a language that was vibrant and which, made attendant to everyday life, ennobled it, affirmed its value, and exulted its presence. It was the art of a large and generous spirit that defined not only the character of black American life, but also its conscience."[69] The planes achieved by the collage effect of Bearden's work informed not only the set design of Wilson's play but also the production design of the film, which did much to replicate—with certain exceptions—the spatial dynamics of the stage. Archer explains in broad terms how "layered surfaces, hue and textures of peeling paint, brick walls, leaves and brush, and crisscrossed lines of hanging laundry" evoke Bearden's collage aesthetic.[70] But beyond the construction of diegetic spaces, there are other ways in which Bearden's photomontages align with *Fences*' aesthetic and concern with Black masculinity.

According to Kimberly Lamm, "no visual artist has paid more attention to the act of visualizing the face as a screen representation malleable and open to remaking than Romare Bearden," and more specifically in a way "that can register moments of destabilizing fluidity, subversion, and innovation as black masculinity makes and remakes itself."[71] Citing filmmaker Isaac Julien, she is interested how Bearden's work makes manifest the "fluid continuum of blackness made and remade."[72] In works such as *The Dove* and *Pittsburgh Memories* (1964), the "shifting planes and dimensions, together with the variegated photographic textures and tones" that describe both faces in close-up and the space and architecture that surrounds them speaks to the "constructed aspects of these faces" and thus to the "representation of race that is continually under construction."[73] The expressions detectable in the fragments of found images that constitute these faces are varied too. They are "puzzled, thoughtful, and ambivalent," revealing both "strength and vulnerability," and thus register as emotional responses to the people and spaces that surround them.[74] It is this exchange of looks and inscription of varied and nuanced responses on the face, often in close-up, that are harnessed in *Fences* and foregrounded through Washington's choice of lens. What Troy offers through extended close-ups are precisely these nuanced registers of emotion that complicate masculinity. His shifts in expression betray myriad self-conscious performances of masculinity that are invoked for—and specific to—his relationship with different people in his life: his sons (as father), his wife (as husband), and his friends (as confidant). Whereas for Bearden, the fragmentation of the image is central to his "critique of documentary realism" that, as Kobena Mercer argues, has played a deeply problematic role in the representation of Black men and visions of Black masculinity at the heart of racist visual discourse, Washington undercuts the "realism" otherwise on offer through these registers of performativity and with the sporadic injection of artifice (e.g., the blurred ring that surrounds Troy).[75]

Another strategy adopted by both the theater and cinematic version of *Fences* is Bearden's engagement with the "dialectic between private and public selves" by situating the action on thresholds, specifically doors and stoops.[76] For the filmic version of *Fences*, this dialectic is in some ways heightened by the frequent traversal of these thresholds as the camera follows characters inside Troy and Rose's row house. Filming on location in Pittsburgh presented challenges for the camera crew as they were required to navigate the very narrow corridors that defined these spaces.[77] However, the result, as reviewers have duly noted, is the visual reinforcement of the sense of entrapment suggesting narratively, especially for Rose, one that is not mitigated by moving the action outdoors. For especially in the backyard, the ever-present work on the eponymous fence threatens to further contain both Troy and Rose, effectively becoming an impassable threshold to the broader social world, though one of Troy's own creation.

While the backyard fence functions as a barrier that restricts movement, the front stoop holds more promise and aligns with another form of Black visual cultural and expressivity oft seen in Wilson's play and Washington's film: the street photography of Charles "Teenie" Harris. As Ina Archer observes: "The extras (local residents in period costumes) that populate the street scenes could have stepped out of the home movies and pictures of Charles 'Teenie' Harris, the African-American Hill District photographer whose work comprises a rare archive of images of the social world of Pittsburgh's black communities."[78] As a photographer for the *Pittsburgh Courier* over several decades, including during the 1950s, Harris was instrumental in visually documenting the city, and thus visualizing Black life, for what was considered one of the preeminent Black newspapers. In *Fences*, this publication is Troy's source of news, as confirmed by his reference to it when speaking to his elder son Lyons. He says: "Aw hell. . . . I wasn't looking to see you today. I thought you was in jail. Got it all over the front page of the *Courier* about them raiding Seefus' place . . . where you be hanging out with all them thugs."

In several respects *Fences* quite literally animates Harris's images. Place is offered up through only a few key locations and thus those sites become privileged indicators of the social reality at issue. Although such sites are containers for the human drama, they nevertheless become entrenched, familiar, and scrutinizable because of the long stretches of time they occupy on screen (Figure 7.6). That is, they enable a kind of contemplative viewing normally reserved for still photographic images. We can read the details, examine the relationships between the things, objects, and people that populate these sites. While *Fences* seems to mobilize Harris-inspired images, and in a way that signals their social realist thrust or documentary function of capturing Pittsburgh's Black experience, the film also signals photography itself. Such instances are most perceptible when the camera offers establishing shots of the Hill District, wide shots that capture children playing, cars parked, and row houses flanking the vibrant and busy street. In doing so, it generates an intermedial space that prompts consideration of the cinematic image as one here entwined with another representational art form. Thus, to return to Boyce Gillespie, the formal elements of Harris's images are invoked

Figure 7.6 The Maxson home and backyard in *Fences* (2016)

in *Fences*, to help generate that negotiation between the aesthetic and the political, between *Fences*' relay of a history of Black visual and expressive culture and a history of Black social experience.

I want to conclude this discussion of *Fences* by considering the contexts in which it was written, staged, filmed, and released, for its history of circulation and performance places it in a key position within certain discursive terrains invested in the legacy and meaning of the 1950s. As previously noted, Wilson wrote the play in 1983. It was first staged in 1985 at the Yale Repertory Theater and then in 1987 on Broadway. It has enjoyed many revivals, most notably in 2010 with Washington and Davis. Thus, its realization and first performances spanned the mid-1980s and placed it in a context of the Reaganite 1950s nostalgia boom when, politically, the 1950s were mobilized in political terms designed to appeal to white conservative voters. In political rhetoric, the 1950s were signaled to challenge the progressive inroads made by the social movements of the 1960s and 1970s, something Daniel Marcus attends to in his study of the Reagan era.[79] Likewise, Michael Dwyer's comprehensive account of 1980s cinematic returns to the postwar period (e.g., *Back to the Future*) demonstrates how late twentieth-century visual culture made use of the Fifties to multiple and sometimes competing (political) ends.[80] The 2010 Broadway return was midway through Obama's presidency and while, at that point, for some reviewers, optimism may have put some distance between the plays' and audiences' presents, a few years later that changed.

The December 2016 release of the film came just over a month after Donald Trump's election and, thus, after a lengthy campaign during which, as discussed in the introduction, the 1950s were invoked politically and socially to conservative and cautionary ends. In fact, many reviews of the film discussed it in precisely this context. "August Wilson's *Fences*: Is America about to Return to the 1950s?" by Mariah Feria offers a review of the film in advance of its UK premiere, but does so through the lens of Trump's impending inauguration and what that means for Black Americans.[81] Likewise, Steven Zeitchik, writing in the *Los Angeles Times*, offers a commentary on several releases titled "In the Wake of Donald Trump's Victory, Some Movies Don't Feel Like They Were Intended To." Zeitchik quotes Troy's signature line: "Some people build fences to keep people out, and other people build fences to keep people in." He observes that while before Trump's victory, such a line might have been perceived as "the stuff of period drama," now it evokes "Muslim registries and Mexican deportations" as well as, of course, that infamous wall, a point oft made by the film's commentators. For

Zeitchik, "Trump's election has, like a kind of in-multiplex time machine, suddenly made the past present."[82] Other reviewers make explicit precisely what this means. For Kareem Abdul Jabbar, in his prelude to an interview with Washington and Davis, he anticipates an inevitable "melancholy in the audience when they realize that the racial conditions and conflicts that so profoundly affect the Maxson family during the 1950s still exist today." What is more, Abdul Jabbar laments that the "recent election of Donald Trump seems like an endorsement of the racism, misogyny, homophobia and xenophobia that made the 1950s such a symbol of *Happy Days* nostalgia for whites and of humiliating repression for blacks and other marginalized people."[83]

In their attempts to cross international and class borders and venture beyond the boundaries of cinema into other art forms, the films considered here intersect with one another through a series of shared concerns, chief among them representations that admit experiences often overlooked in 1950s set films: white rural poverty and trauma, Black urban working-class labor and leisure, and women's immigration. Canonical Fifties signifiers and Technicolor palettes are absent or heavily modified here, a visual rejection of the cinematic language often tasked with producing postwar America. As such, the "otherness" of the content, to return to Harrington's (insufficient) term, as well as the "otherness" of these films' aesthetics, both do much to complicate and expand visions of the Fifties. Most of these films look beyond cinema for their approach, to photography, collage, painting, and theater, and find in these practices creative possibilities for criticality and affect, analysis and insight.

Notes

1. Michael Harrington, *The Other America* (New York: Simon and Shuster, 2012), loc. 476.
2. Ibid., loc. 468.
3. Ibid., loc. 481.
4. In the years since its publication, Harrington's approach has been subject to various degrees of criticism for its idealism and also deployment of the term "culture of poverty," a phrase later appropriated by the right and used to the detriment of those he originally hoped to help.
5. Leigh Gilmore, *The Limits of Autobiography: Trauma and Testimony* (Ithaca, NY: Cornell University Press, 2001), 55–56.

6. For a more detailed discussion of how Glen's negotiation of class and abuse of Bone has to do with his own middle-/working-class status, see Lori Watkins Fulton, "Challenging White Trash Stereotypes: The Question of Class in *Bastard out of Carolina*," in *Blue Collar Pop Culture: From NASCAR to Jersey Shore*, ed. M. Keith Booker (Santa Barbara: Praeger, 2012). Watkins Fulton argues that both the novel and film align the gravest evil with Glen, suggesting his class status entitles him to feel he can abuse Bone because he thinks she is "inferior" to him (76).
7. Ibid., 69.
8. Ridley is considered a pioneer of "in-yer-face theatre," a genre of sorts that, much like his films, is experiencing a revival. For a full account of this development, see Ondřej Pilný, *The Grotesque in Contemporary Anglophone Drama* (London: Palgrave Macmillan, 2016), 30.
9. For instance, Ridley stated: "I'm being told by my editor that I've gone too far because of this play [*Mercury* Fur] and there's the Beslan siege on television. So I'm watching children getting blown up by terrorists, while being told by my publisher that I have written an unacceptable play about cruelty to children!" Philip Ridley in conversation with Aleks Sierz, "Putting a New Lens on the World': The Art of Theatrical Alchemy," *New Theatre Quarterly* 25.2 (May 2009): 114.
10. Ibid.
11. Ken Urban, "Ghosts from an Imperfect Place: Philip Ridley's Nostalgia," *Modern Drama* 50.3 (2007): 328, 326.
12. The film also extends Ridley's interest in mid-twentieth-century American realist painting. In response, Ridley produced collages in which "all the women looked like Marilyn Monroe and all the men, James Dean or Elvis Presley." Philip Ridley, "Director's Commentary," *The Reflecting Skin*, DVD, directed by Philip Ridley (BBC Films, et al., 1990).
13. The film does not contain intense colors in a Technicolor sense, but intense hues within a limited range of yellows, browns, and greens. For instance, Ridley felt the wheat field wasn't yellow enough, so he spray-painted it Cadmium Yellow. Ridley, "Director's Commentary."
14. Ibid.
15. Ridley explains that he purposefully composed clusters of objects, each charged with meaning and the capacity to tell their own stories. Ibid.
16. Ibid.
17. Lovatt argues that "the elite power represented by the Bomb is duplicated in the film by a gleaming black Cadillac, a symbol of corporate power which, like the Bomb, functioned as 'a sublimated symbol' of American exceptionality." Deborah Lovatt, "A Terrible Beauty: The Nuclear Sublime in Philip Ridley's *The Reflecting Skin* (1991)," *European Journal of American Culture* 20.3 (November 2002): 133. For Lovatt, this engagement with the atomic weaves through the film in several ways, including by acknowledging the aestheticization inherent in discourses and images of atomic tests published during the 1950s. She writes: "*The Reflecting Skin* confronts this impulse to aestheticize, and the way this establishes a dialectic between terror and beauty, pleasure and horror. The way in which the frog and the shell's magnificent beauty

ignites the boys' destructive desires symbolically enacts this convergence of terror and beauty inherent within a nuclear aesthetic, the way in which pleasure is, paradoxically, enhanced by the annihilation of natural and living things" (137).
18. David Annadale, "Hiding in the Plain's Sight: Prairie Secrets, Prairie Horror, and the Undermining of Prairie Nostalgia in Philip Ridley's *The Reflecting Skin*," *English Quarterly* 40.1/2 (2008): 10.
19. See Matt Hills, "The Question of Genre in Cult Film and Fandom: Between Contract and Discourse," in *Sage Handbook of Film Studies*, ed. James Donald and Michael Renov (Los Angeles: Sage, 2008): 436–51.
20. Philip Kemp, "The Reflecting Skin," *Sight and Sound* 26.2 (February 2016): 100.
21. Peter Travers, "The Reflecting Skin," *Rolling Stone*, September 9, 1990. https://www.rollingstone.com/movies/movie-reviews/the-reflecting-skin-94486/.
22. Ridley, "Director's Commentary."
23. Ibid.
24. See Mark Kermode, "*Brooklyn* Review—This Fairytale of New York Casts a Spell," *The Guardian*, November 8, 2015. https://www.theguardian.com/film/2015/nov/08/brooklyn-observer-film-review-saoirse-ronan.
25. Glen Kenny, "Brooklyn," *Rogerebert.com*, November 4, 2015. https://www.rogerebert.com/reviews/brooklyn-2015.
26. A. O. Scott is prone to this tendency too. See A.O. Scott, "Resettling the Meaning of Home in *Brooklyn*," *New York Times*, November 4, 2015. https://www.nytimes.com/2015/11/04/movies/review-resettling-the-meaning-of-home-in-brooklyn-with-saoirse-ronan.html.
27. In some ways I side-step the complicated and overlapping terminology that positions Ireland as part of the British Isles but not part of Great Britain. I will use "British period film" and "British heritage" to speak about *Brooklyn*, since these genres apply in aesthetic and theoretical terms to this film. That is, debates and insights regarding "British heritage" are applicable to *Brooklyn*, for there are many points of alignment between Irish period films and those considered more definitely British.
28. See Will Stanford Abbiss, "Proposing a Post-Heritage Critical Framework: *The Crown*, Ambiguity, and Media Self-Consciousness," *Television and New Media* 21.8 (August 2020): 825–41.
29. See, for example, Paul Cooke and Rob Stone, eds., *Screening European Heritage: Creating and Consuming History on Film* (London: Palgrave Macmillan, 2016); and Sally Faulkner, ed., *Middlebrow Cinema* (London: Routledge, 2016).
30. It may also provide an opportunity to think about other 1950s set films that adopt heritage or postheritage strategies, for instance *The Deep Blue Sea* (2011), *The Dressmaker* (2015), *Phantom Thread* (2017), *Breathe* (2017), *Ladies in Black* (2018), and *Tell It to the Bees* (2018). Television series including *Call the Midwife* (2012–) may also be included here. These titles are primarily British and Australian in origin.
31. Ruth Barton, *Irish Cinema in the Twenty-First Century* (Manchester: Manchester University Press, 2019), 172.
32. Ibid.
33. Ibid.

34. Millington also notes its heritage impetus achieved visually through the film's "elegant and becalmed" feel, one extended to "the sidewalks, brownstones and stoops of downtown Brooklyn that are so judiciously depicted." Gareth Millington, *Urbanization and the Migrant in British Cinema: Spectres of the City* (London: Palgrave Macmillan, 2016), 139. While the film may look like Brooklyn, it was actually shot in Montreal.
35. Ibid., 138.
36. Nearly all of the other women in the film are reduced to one-dimensional stereotypes, caricatures that ultimately work against Crowley's stated desire for "realism" and "authenticity." They are also the source of comedy in the film in ways that the men—of any age—never are.
37. However, his insistence that Eilis marry him before leaving for Ireland is suggestive of controlling behavior. That she gives in to this demand, despite her misgivings, also suggests a future marital dynamic that, while historically accurate for many postwar heterosexual couples, undercuts the agency she seems in the process of acquiring.
38. Barton, *Irish Cinema*, 155.
39. Ibid., 15.
40. James Smith in Barton, *Irish Cinema*, 156.
41. Ibid., 27.
42. Ibid., 152.
43. See Belén Vidal, *Figuring the Past: Period Film and the Mannerist Aesthetic* (Amsterdam: University of Amsterdam Press, 2012).
44. From the Irish film *Ballroom of Romance* (1986) to Dennis Potter's Welsh-set television plays and Terence Davies's Liverpudlian worlds, dance halls populate a range of period productions across British screen media.
45. Paired courtship dinners with these two potential husbands also showcase public sites.
46. Barton, *Irish Cinema*, 28.
47. Scott writes: "Standing on a windswept patch of grass out on Long Island, Tony spins a vision of a nice house and a thriving family plumbing business: a quiet, prosperous life beyond the cramped confines of the city. Sitting in the theater, the 21st-century viewer can fill in the blanks, conjuring a time-lapse picture of the growth of the suburbs and the unfolding of a long marriage. Tony and Eilis grow old before our eyes, and the world changes around them." Scott, "Resettling the Meaning."
48. Bruce Lambert, "Study Calls L.I. Most Segregated Suburb," *New York Times*, June 5, 2002. https://www.nytimes.com/2002/06/05/nyregion/study-calls-li-most-segregated-suburb.html. A recent analysis of census data by ERASE Racism has found that since 2000, segregation has only increased. For reflection on this report, see Maya Brown, "Growing Up 'Divided,' I Always Saw Segregation on Long Island," *The Statesman*, December 1, 2019. https://www.sbstatesman.com/2019/12/01/growing-up-divided-i-always-saw-segregation-on-long-island/.
49. Cincinnati's Coney Island location's history is now defined by civil rights activist Marian Spencer's campaign to desegregate the park, which, prior to 1955, did not admit Black patrons onto its grounds.
50. See Traci Parker, *Department Stores and the Black Freedom Movement: Workers, Consumers, and Civil Rights from the 1930s to the 1980s* (Chapel Hill: University of North Carolina Press, 2019).
51. Isiah Matthew Wooden, "*Fences*," *Theatre Journal* 63.1 (March 2011): 125.

52. Ina Archer, "Giving Us Life," *Film Comment* 53.1 (January/February 2017): 36
53. Richard Alleva, "Character Studies," *Commonweal* 144.3 (February 10, 2017): 21–22. https://www.commonwealmagazine.org/manchester-sea-fences.
54. August Wilson interviewed by Bonnie Lyons and George Plimpton, "August Wilson, The Art of Theater," *Paris Review* 153 (Winter 1999): n.pag. https://www.theparisreview.org/interviews/839/the-art-of-theater-no-14-august-wilson.
55. David Ehrlich, "Fences," *Indiewire*, November 22, 2016. https://www.indiewire.com/2016/11/fences-review-denzel-washington-viola-davis-august-wilson-movie-1201748842/.
56. John Calhoun, "A Family's Passion," *American Cinematographer* 98.1 (January 2017): n.pag. https://theasc.com/ac_magazine/January2017/Fences/page1.html.
57. Ibid.
58. Ibid.
59. Ibid.
60. Alleva, "Character Studies."
61. Tim Gray, "Denzel Washington Praises the Team That Helped Him Build *Fences*," *Variety*, January 4, 2017. https://variety.com/2017/artisans/production/actor-director-denzel-washington-fences-1201951732/.
62. Alleva, "Character Studies."
63. For Melvin Donaldson, in the 1990s, "Washington's cinematic roles revised the depiction of black men and liberated black male images from the shackles of ghettocentricity and neominstrelsy that were historically associated with black masculinity" (66). "Denzel Washington: A Revisionist Black Masculinity," in *Pretty People*, ed. Anna Everett (New Brunswick, NJ: Rutgers University Press, 2012), 65–84.
64. Viola Davis, "*Fences* Star Viola Davis: 'After *The Help* I was done with aprons,'" *British Film Institute Player*, January 19, 2017. https://www.youtube.com/watch?v=YQv2BQ1qTOs. Davis also felt like the role was a betrayal for its historical inaccuracies and reliance on a "white saviour" narrative to appeal to white audiences. It was a film "created in the filter and the cesspool of systemic racism." Viola Davis, "I Betrayed Myself and My People in *The Help*," *BBC*, July 15, 2020. https://www.bbc.com/news/newsbeat-53416196.
65. Michael Boyce Gillespie, *Film Blackness: American Cinema and the Idea of Black Film* (Durham, NC: Duke University Press, 2016), 2. Boyce Gillespie argues that "black film in a manner that does not adhere alone to a focus on how cinema must oblige, portend, or emblemize social truth requires attention to cinema as an art practice with attendant and consequential questions of form and politics. The belief in black film's indexical tie to the black lifeworld foregoes a focus on nuance and occults the complexity of black film to interpret, render, incite and speculate" (2).
66. Ibid., 2.
67. Ibid., 6.
68. Though based primarily in New York, Bearden spent some time in the late 1920s in Pittsburgh as well.
69. Wilson quoted in Sandra Garrett Shannon, "August Wilson: *Ma Rainey's Black Bottom* (1982), *Fences* (1987), *Joe Turner's Come and Gone* (1984)," in *Modern American Drama: Playwriting in the 1980s*, ed. Sandra Garrett Shannon (London: Bloomsbury, 2019), 131.

70. Archer, "Giving Us Life," 34.
71. Kimberly Lamm, "Visuality and Black Masculinity in Ralph Ellison's *Invisible Man* and Romare Bearden's Photomontages," *Callaloo* 26.3 (Summer, 2003): 815 and 832.
72. Isaac Julien quoted in Lamm, "Visuality and Black Masculinity," 832.
73. Ibid., 821–22.
74. Ibid., 822.
75. Kobena Mercer quoted in Lamm, "Visuality and Black Masculinity," 822. According to Shannon, Wilson adopted Bearden's collage approach in another way. She writes: "His collages, while carefully and intricately designed, appear improvisational, akin to Jazz. Wilson reimaged Bearden's technique for the stage. As well as finding direct inspiration in the work." According to Shannon, some of Wilson's plays found their origin in Bearden's canvases. *Modern American Drama*, 132.
76. Lamm, "Visuality and Black Masculinity," 822.
77. Calhoun, "A Family's Passion."
78. Archer, "Giving Us Life," 34.
79. See Daniel Marcus, *Happy Days and Wonder Years: The Fifties and Sixties in Contemporary Cultural Politics* (New Brunswick, NJ: Rutgers University Press, 2004).
80. See Michael Dwyer, *Back to the Fifties: Nostalgia, Hollywood Film, and Popular Music of the Seventies and Eighties* (New York: Oxford University Press, 2015).
81. Mariah Feria, "August Wilson's *Fences*: Is America about to Return to the 1950s?" *Shout Out UK*, January 10, 2017. https://www.shoutoutuk.org/2017/01/10/august-wilsons-fences-is-america-about-to-return-to-the-1950s/.
82. Steven Zeitchik, "In the Wake of Donald Trump's Victory, Some Movies Don't Feel Like They Were Intended To," *LA Times*, November 22, 2016. https://www.latimes.com/entertainment/movies/la-ca-mn-trump-movies-perspective-20161116-story.html.
83. Kareen Abdul Jabbar, "Race, Family and Fences in the Trump Era," *Hollywood Reporter*, December 9, 2016. https://www.hollywoodreporter.com/video/kareem-abdul-jabbar-interviews-denzel-washington-viola-davis-race-family-fences-trump-era-9513/.

Conclusion

This project, now perhaps too long in the making, was supposed to be completed in 2020. It felt like the surge of political nostalgia for the Fifties that informed rhetoric around the 2016 US presidential election, followed by a range of critical responses to this troubling resuscitation, might initiate a final, irreversible waning of the significatory power and cultural purchase of the Fifties. As such, I felt some urgency to account for how cinema figured and fractured visions of postwar America during the first decades of the twenty-first century before the Fifties all but lost its significance as a productive means through which to interrogate specific histories and historiography, cultural memory and nostalgia, mediation and representation. However, this project was delayed—like many others—by the pandemic. In scholarly terms, this limited access to resources and stalled the completion of films I desperately hoped to see. But it also made it possible to add a number of new case studies (all the while fine-tuning my homeschooling skills, of which, apparently, I have none). In fact, the flurry of new productions invested in the Fifties *since 2020* has been remarkable, far exceeding my expectations and leading me to think we might see a waxing rather than a waning in the coming years. Titles available in theaters or through North American streaming services at the very start of 2022 include: *The Marvelous Mrs. Maisel* (2017–), *The Vast of Night* (2020), *Adrift in Soho* (2020), *Lovecraft Country* (2020), *Sylvie's Love* (2020), *Alice Fades Away* (2021), *Angel Mountain* (2021), *Being the Ricardos* (2021), *Hal King* (2021), *Them* (2021), *The Club* (2021), *West Side Story* (2021), *Living* (2022), and *Women of the Movement* (2022). Series since 2020 with individual episodes involving the Fifties include: *Chronofilm* (2020), *The Queen's Gambit* (2020), and *WandaVision* (2021).

Although I touch on some of these in the preceding chapters, as a group, I think they point to two important trajectories for future research. In keeping with a metamodern vein, a good number are invested in historicity, in excavating the relationship between past and present in ways that highlight historical processes, and in exposing in genuine and nuanced terms why the history or, rather, histories, of the 1950s matter. As such, while scholarship on the history film has tended to shy away from 1950s-set titles in the past, save for those directly invested in specific events, the debates that have engaged scholars in this subfield would enlighten analyses of—and also benefit from—many of these twenty-first-century releases.[1] In other words, as recent releases invested in the Fifties expand their purview, accounting for the experiences of marginalized constituencies and events hitherto neglected, I think much about our understanding of the cinematic evolution of representations of the postwar era can be advanced by considering Hayden White's foundational concept of "historiophoty," Natalie Zemon Davis's treatment of cinema as a "thought experiment about the past or description of 'microhistories' on screen," Robert Rosenstone's sense of "revisioning" history and ongoing advocacy for the historical "truths" revealed by cinematic representation, Robert Burgoyne's "metahistorical film," Alison Landsberg's "prosthetic memory" and "affective" historical engagement, Alan Munslow's "history genres" and "experimental historying," and Mia Treacy's arguments around "screened history."[2] Likewise, some of these Fifties releases may also productively challenge the limits of these terms, arguments, and explanatory models, revealing gaps or shortcomings in their analytical capacity through the creative ways in which history itself is figured in visual and narrative terms.[3]

What is more, a global perspective is called for here, and one that also ought to account for the often complicated collaborations between regions, nations, and nation-states in terms of production and transnational distribution. While this study highlights a specifically American Fifties in order to focus analyses in ways that account for the dynamics of a particularly American history and constructions of gendered and racialized subjectivities, confluences of media practices, and sets of political imbrications, the over 100 releases of titles set during the 1950s since 2015 include a plethora of films about experiences beyond the United States. Again, a listing provides a cursory snapshot: *Chehere: A Modern Day Classic* (India, 2015), *Le divan de Staline* (France/Portugal/Russia, 2016), *A Melody to Remember* (Korea, 2016), *Grand Hotel* (Egypt, 2016), *Los Adioses* (Mexico, 2017), *Cold War* (Poland, 2018), *Unidad XV* (Argentina, 2018), *Sew the Winter to My Skin* (South Africa, 2018), *Wie ich lernte, bei mir selbst Kind zu sein* (Austria, 2019), *A Gschicht über d'Lieb* (Germany, 2019), *Herec* (Czech, 2020), *L'ultimo paradiso* (Italy, 2021), and *The Club* (Turkey, 2021).

The second trajectory for future research privileges "long form" television investments in the 1950s, the source, recently, of creative and critical explorations of the Fifties.[4] The specific modes of production, distribution, and consumption of long form television would offer an instructive foundation for thinking through how particular historical interventions into the Fifties are enabled by such structures and practices. It might show how this format, one with a demonstrated receptiveness to aesthetic and narrative experimentation, can produce new representational approaches to history and the Fifties specifically. In fact, it has already shown how experiments with temporality enabled by a long form structure opens up new possibilities for engaging historical events by generating space for the nuances of more protracted historical processes. The same can be said of historical incidents shaped by intricate legal proceedings, multifaceted political maneuverings, or the vicissitudes of individual and collective experiences. This, in turn, productively complicates periodization itself by enabling the myriad alliances and entanglements between the social, economic, cultural, and political forces that necessarily swirl around any event. *Lovecraft Country*, for example, offers a particularly creative approach to activating these entanglements, filtering them through generic lenses that highlight their circulation in diverse cultural forms, and laying bare the connections between broader social forces and historical events (e.g., the Korean War and civil rights). In this way, long form televisual investments in the 1950s have much to contribute to thinking about representations of history, more broadly.[5]

In other words, the Fifties will continue to fracture and evolve, shaped and reshaped by the discourses and representational practices to which it is subjected and the myriad contexts—political, cultural, and media—through which it circulates. As it does so, what constitutes "The Fifties" as well as the means and modes through which it is envisioned, will necessarily evolve too, as it has for the past seven decades. Such recalibrations also fuel the percolations that enable different elements to rise to the surface. As I hope the preceding chapters have shown, even the initial dominant fractures or types have undergone remarkable changes: redlining, pioneering, the institutional preservation of white supremacy and racist violence have been written back into visions of suburban America from which they were sublimated or excluded since the 1970s; the Korean War has been reintroduced, but with links to the civil rights movement; "greasers" and their social spaces have been reconfigured to account for histories of toxic masculinity and queer subjectivities. Aesthetic experimentation that investigates the connections between cinema and other art forms (e.g., theater and opera) and cinema and related media (e.g., photography and documentary film), have also helped motivate the rise of once marginalized histories and experiences to the surface, all the while complicating the nature of historical representation itself. Likewise, experiments with genres aligned with the 1950s have been harnessed to critical effect and in the service of generating historiographical insights. Hopefully these case studies magnify even smaller "molecules"—to maintain the metaphor of percolation—from art forms to genres to individual cultural texts and objects. While poodle skirts, tailfin cars, and jukeboxes remain central to evocations of the Fifties, though now typically in iconoclastic ways, other signifiers are starting to circulate with greater frequency. And some of these are challenging what constitutes a canonical period object itself. For instance, quotations from key postwar voices are helping to compile a sonic registry of the past: James Baldwin's words in *Lovecraft Country* and *Bastard out of Carolina*. Others are invested in an aesthetic signature rather than object or image: Saul Leiter's photographic approach to the city in *Revolutionary Road* and *Carol*. In terms of space, the department store functions as a key site in *Brooklyn* and *Lovecraft Country*.

Although the previous chapters note both instances of critical efficacy and problematic limitations in specific films' engagements with the Fifties, taken as a whole, the titles considered here offer a multifaceted and fractured vision of postwar America. Despite the many well-documented problems with classificatory schemes, I hope my suggestion to think about individual titles through the rubrics provided by the Leave It to Beaver Fifties, the Jukebox Fifties, the Cold War Fifties, the Retromediated Fifties, and a kind of "Other" Fifties, offers something of an organizing principle and framework for making sense of the analytical potential locatable in certain films. And, however much the Futuristic Fifties is an outlier here—a strange inclusion for a project focused on historical representation—I wish it to serve as a reminder of how expansive our visual envelop is when it comes to the Fifties and of the complexity of visual culture in all its circulations and percolations.

As such, I hope that however limited in scope these examples are (for there are well over 500 Fifties-focused films I did not even mention in the preceding pages), they nevertheless help point to cinema's role in periodizing the past, in continually reshaping the contours and content of that past, inflecting how historiographical concerns and history itself might be engaged. Although the Fifties nostalgia economy has enjoyed a complex set of alignments with postmodernism, effectively growing up together, the former now survives the latter (though with certain strains of the latter surviving within former). And, while particular metamodern sensibilities that account for shifts in approaches to history do have some explanatory potential for making sense of twenty-first-century interventions into postwar America, I suspect the Fifties will evolve beyond its metamodern inclinations too. That is, once metamodern strategies have done the conceptual work of filling the gaps in postmodernisms' modes of representing the past, new forces, contexts, fears, desires, realities, and media practices will recalibrate the Fifties once again, sustaining the process of percolation and enabling the 1950s to adapt for its myriad futures. This process is not unique to the Fifties. As such, I hope this study contributes to the necessarily multiple ways in which we ought to approach cinema's role in shaping the past and our access to it.

Notes

1. This is not to suggest that scholarship on the history film ignores the 1950s, but instead that it tends to privilege other periods or events. It is the nature of the cinematic approach to the 1950s, often framed through concepts of artifice and intertextuality and invested in aesthetics, that has rendered it a less desirable (and ostensibly reliable?) candidate for analysis through a rubric invested in questions of historicity. Anthologies that do include Fifties-focused films tend to include terms like "cultural memory," "popular memory," "nostalgia," "media," and "retro" in their titles and subtitles. "History on Film" studies and edited collections continue to privilege wars, singular events, battles, revolutions, and, on occasion, movements, but typically through a biographical approach.
2. See Hayden White, "Historiography and Historiophoty," *American Historical Review* 93.5 (December 1988): 1193–99; Natalie Zemon Davis, *Slaves on Screen* (Cambridge, MA: Harvard University Press, 2000); Robert Rosenstone, ed., *Revisioning History: Film and the Construction of a New Past* (Princeton: Princeton University Press, 1995); Robert Rosentone, *Visions of the Past: The Challenge of Film to Our Idea of History* (Cambridge, MA: Harvard University Press, 1995); Robert Burgoyne, *The Hollywood Historical Film* (Oxford: Blackwell, 2008); Alison Landsberg, *Prosthetic Memory The Transformation of American Remembrance in the Age of Mass Culture* (New York: Columbia University Press, 2004) and *Engaging the Past: Mass Culture and the Production of Historical Knowledge* (New York: Columbia University Press, 2015); Alun Munslow, "Genre and History/Historying," *Rethinking History* 19.2 (2015): 158–76. https://doi.org/10.1080/13642529.2014.973711, and Mia Treacey, *Reframing the Past: History, Film, and Television* (London: Routledge, 2016).
3. Specifically, while some of these terms are designed to account for postmodern filmic interventions into history and historiographical debates, they may need a degree of adaptation to interrogate films and television series inflected by metamodern tendencies. For instance, while the aesthetic experimentation signaled by "metahistorical" or "revisioning" may be extremely useful for considering *Lovecraft Country* as "historical,"

the series' structure of feeling and specific mobilizations of generic intertextuality may show how such terms themselves can be expanded and updated in light of its long form and aesthetic approach.
4. Although the term itself has been subject to some debate, I use it to refer to miniseries, anthologies, and "quality" television series. See Jason Mittell, *Complex TV: The Poetics of Contemporary Television Storytelling* (New York: New York University Press, 2015).
5. See Kathryn Pallister, ed., *Netflix Nostalgia: Streaming the Past on Demand* (Lanham: Rowman and Littlefield, 2019).

Works Cited

"*Fences* Star Viola Davis: 'After *The Help* I Was Done with Aprons.'" *British Film Institute Player*, January 19, 2017. https://www.youtube.com/watch?v=YQv2BQ1qTOs.

"National Board Attacks State Censored Action." *National Board of Review Magazine* 5, no. 4 (April 1930). https://nationalboardofreview.org/award-years/1930/.

"*Sylvie's Love* Q&A With Tessa Thompson & More." SCAD Film Fest 2020, *Entertainment Weekly*, November 2, 2020. https://www.youtube.com/watch?v=AKE3xAprLQg.

"Viola Davis: I Betrayed Myself and My People in *The Help*." Newsbeat. *BBC News*, July 15, 2020. https://www.bbc.com/news/newsbeat-53416196.

Abbiss, Will Stanford. "Proposing a Post-Heritage Critical Framework: *The Crown*, Ambiguity, and Media Self-Consciousness." *Television and New Media* 21, no. 8 (August 2020): 825–41. https://doi.org/10.1177/1527476419866427.

Abdul-Jabbar, Kareem. "Denzel Washington and Viola Davis Interviewed by Kareem Abdul-Jabbar: Race, Family and *Fences* in the Trump Era." Movie Features. *Hollywood Reporter*, November 30, 2016. https://www.hollywoodreporter.com/movies/movie-features/denzel-washington-viola-davis-interviewed-by-kareem-abdul-jabbar-race-family-fences-trump-era-951145.

Allen, Frederick Lewis. *Only Yesterday: An Informal History of the Nineteen-Twenties*. New York: Blue Ribbon Books, 1931.

Alleva, Richard. "*Manchester by the Sea* & *Fences*." Character Studies. *Commonweal*, January 27, 2017. https://www.commonwealmagazine.org/manchester-sea-fences.

Anderson, Kristin. "Behind the Scenes of *Hail, Caesar!* Perming Josh Brolin and Making Scarlett Johansson a Modern-Day Esther Williams." Designers. *Vogue*, February 8, 2016. https://www.vogue.com/article/hail-caesar-mary-zophres-costume-designer-coen-brothers.

Annandale, David. "Hiding in the Plain's Sight: Prairie Secrets, Prairie Horror, and the Undermining of Prairie Nostalgia in Philip Ridley's *The Reflecting Skin*." *English Quarterly* 40, no. 1/2 (2008): 10–13.

Archer, Ina. "Giving Us Life." *Film Comment* 53, no. 1 (January–February 2017): 32–36. http://www.jstor.org/stable/44991004.

Baker, Robert S. "History and Periodization," *Clio* 26, no. 2 (Winter 1997): 135+. https://link.gale.com/apps/doc/A19791101/AONE?u=anon~870353a7&sid=googleScholar&xid=6cf722df.

Bal, Mieke, and Norman Bryson. "Semiotics and Art History." *Art Bulletin* 73 (June 1991): 174–208. https://doi.org/10.2307/3045790.

Barker, Jennifer. "Sparks Fly: Mediated Gesture, Affect, and Mise-en-Scene in *Carol*." *Mediaesthetics: Journal of Poetics of Audiovisual Images* 2 (2017): n.p. http://dx.doi.org/10.17169/mae.2017.66.

Barton, Ruth. *Irish Cinema in the Twenty-First Century*. Manchester: Manchester University Press, 2019.

Bastién, Angelica Jade. "*Them* Is Pure Degradation Porn." *Vulture*, April 14, 2021. https://www.vulture.com/article/review-them-amazon-series.html.

Blake, David Haven. *Liking Ike: Eisenhower, Advertising, and the Rise of Celebrity Politics*. New York: Oxford University Press, 2016.

Bloom, Esther. "When America Was 'Great,' Taxes Were High, Unions Were Strong and Government Was Big." Business. *The Atlantic*, September 28, 2015. https://www.theatlantic.com/business/archive/2015/09/when-america-was-great-taxes-were-high-unions-were-strong-and-government-was-big/407284.

Borgstrom, Michael. "Suburban Queer: Reading *Grease*." *Journal of Homosexuality* 58, no. 2 (2011): 149–163. https://doi.org/10.1080/00918369.2011.539473.

Botti, David. "Why Trump Voters Wished They Lived in the 1950s." US & Canada. *BBC News*, August 24, 2016. http://www.bbc.com/news/av/world-us-canada-37161449/why-trump-voters-wished-they-lived-in-the-1950s.

Bradford, K. "Grease Cowboy Fever; or, the Making of Johnny T." *Journal of Homosexuality* 43, no. 3–4 (2003): 15–30. https://doi.org/10.1300/J082v43n03_02.

Braxton, Greg. "Does Amazon Prime's *Them* Take Its Racist Violence Too Far?" *LA Times*, April 9, 2021. https://www.latimes.com/entertainment-arts/tv/story/2021-04-09/amazon-them-covenant-little-marvin-lena-waithe-violence.

Breen, Margaret Sönser. "The Locations of Politics: Highsmith's *The Price of Salt*, Haynes' *Carol*, and American Post-War and Contemporary Cultural Landscapes." *Gramma: Journal of Theory and Criticism* 25 (2018): 9–29. https://doi.org/10.26262/gramma.v25i0.6588.

Brewer, Roy. "The Use of Habanera Rhythm in Rockabilly Music." *American Music* 17, no. 3 (Autumn 1999). 300–317. https://doi.org/10.2307/3052665.

Brickman, Barbara Jane. *"Grease": Gender, Nostalgia, and Youth Consumption in the Blockbuster Era*. New York: Routledge, 2017.

Brody, Richard. "Review: *Sylvie's Love* Revives the Art of the Classic Hollywood Romance." *New Yorker*, December 22, 2020. https://www.newyorker.com/culture/the-front-row/review-sylvies-love-revives-the-art-of-the-classic-hollywood-romance.

Brown, D'Shonda. "*Them* Covenant Creator Little Marvin Talks Dismantling the American Dream." *Essence*, April 7, 2021. https://www.essence.com/entertainment/little-marvin-them/.

Brown, Marshall. "The Din of Dawn." In *On Periodization: Selected Essays from the English Institute*, edited by Victoria Jackson, para. 18–52. Ann Arbor: University of Michigan Publishing, 2010. https://quod.lib.umich.edu/cgi/t/text/text-idx?c=acls;idno=heb90047.

Brown, Maya. "Growing up 'Divided,' I Always Saw Segregation on Long Island." *The Statesman*, December 1, 2019 https://www.sbstatesman.com/2019/12/01/growing-up-divided-i-always-saw-segregation-on-long-island/.

Bryan, Bishop. "How the Coen Brothers Used New-School Effects to Create Old-School Hollywood in *Hail, Caesar!*" *Verge*, February 8, 2016. https://www.theverge.com/2016/2/8/10926066/hail-caesar-coen-brothers-special-effects-dan-schrecker-interview.

Buck-Morss, Susan. "The Cinema Screen as Prosthesis of Perception: A Historical Account." In *The Senses Still: Perception and Memory as Material Culture in Modernity*, edited by Nadia Seremetakis, 45–62. Boulder, CO: Westview Press, 1994.

Burgin, Victor. *The Remembered Film*. London: Reaktion, 2004.

Burgoyne, Robert. *The Hollywood Historical Film*. Oxford: Blackwell, 2008.

Bussard, Katherine A. *Unfamiliar Streets*. New Haven: Yale University Press, 2014.

Calhoun, John. "A Family's Passion." *American Cinematographer* 98, no. 1 (January 2017): 82–88. https://theasc.com/ac_magazine/January2017/Fences/page1.html.

Cantoral, Mary. "Rising Up from the Sunken Place: Representation as Resistance in *Get Out*." *Medium*, February 18, 2021. https://medium.com/@marycantoral/rising-up-from-the-sunken-place-cd0ce57bfdc7.

Caputi, Mary. *A Kinder, Gentler America: Melancholia and the Mythical 1950s.* Minneapolis: University of Minnesota Press, 2005.

Champlin, Charles. "'50s as Seen through *Grease*." *Los Angeles Times*, June 16, 1978.

Clark, Kevin L. "Creators Little Marvin and Lena Waithe Get Us Right with *Them*." *Ebony*, April 5, 2021. https://www.ebony.com/entertainment/creators-little-marvin-and-lena-waithe-get-us-right-with-them/.

Clark, Lesley. "Happy Days? The 1950s for Trump Supporters." Elections. *McClatchy*, October 25, 2016. http://www.mcclatchydc.com/news/polsitics-government/election/article110293997.html.

Clooney, George, and Grant Heslov. "Director's Commentary." *Suburbicon*. Black Bear Pictures et al., 2017. DVD.

Considine, Austin. "In *Them*, A Black Family Is Haunted by Real-Life Monsters." *New York Times*, April 8, 2021. https://www.nytimes.com/2021/04/08/arts/television/them-amazon-series.html.

Cooke, Paul, and Rob Stone, eds. *Screening European Heritage: Creating and Consuming History on Film*. London: Palgrave Macmillan, 2016.

Corfield, Penelope. *Time and the Shape of History*. New Haven: Yale University Press, 2007.

Cox, Michael. "Good Night and Good Luck." *Millennium: Journal of International Studies* 35, no. 2 (2007): 435–437. https://doi.org/10.1177/03058298070350020501.

Crary, Jonathan. *Techniques of the Observer: On Vision and Modernity in the Nineteenth Century*. Cambridge, MA: MIT Press, 1992.

Daigle, Allain. "Of Love and Longing: Queer Nostalgia in *Carol*." *Queer Studies in Media & Popular Culture* 2, no. 2 (June 2017): 199–211. https://link.gale.com/apps/doc/A496450965/AONE?u=anon~ab299f2a&sid=googleScholar&xid=8d898880.

Dargis, Manohla. "Glib Laughs and Race Hate in *Suburbicon*." *New York Times*, October 26, 2017. https://www.nytimes.com/2017/10/26/movies/suburbicon-review-george-clooney-matt-damon-julianne-moore.html.

Davis, Fred. "Decade Labeling: The Play of Collective Memory and Narrative Plot." *Symbolic Interaction* 7, no. 1 (1984): 15–24.

Davis, Nick. "The Object of Desire: Todd Haynes Discusses *Carol* and the Satisfactions of Telling Women's Stories." *Film Comment* 51, no. 6 (Novembe–December 2015): 30–35. http://www.jstor.org/stable/43746001.

Davis, Viola. "*Fences* Star Viola Davis: 'After The Help I Was Done with Aprons.'" Produced by British Film Institute, January 19, 2007. Video, 19:29. https://www.youtube.com/watch?v=YQv2BQ1qTOs.

Dika, Vera. *Recycled Culture in Contemporary Art and Film*. Cambridge: Cambridge University Press, 2003.

Dilley, Whitney Crothers. *The Cinema of Wes Anderson: Bringing Nostalgia to Life*. New York: Wallflower Press, 2017.

Donaldson, Melvin. "Denzel Washington: A Revisionist Black Masculinity." In *Pretty People: Movie Stars of the 1990s*, edited by Anna Everett, 65–84. New Brunswick, NJ: Rutgers University Press, 2012.

Dudziak, Mary L. *Cold War Civil Rights: Race and the Image of American Democracy.* Princeton: Princeton University Press, 2011.

Dwyer, Michael. *Back to the Fifties: Nostalgia, Hollywood Film, and Popular Music of the Seventies and Eighties.* New York: Oxford University Press, 2015.

Edwards, Paul M. *A Guide to Films on The Korean War.* Westport: Greenwood, 1997.

Edwards-Levy, Ariel. "Half of Americans Want to Take the Country Back to the 1950s." Politics. *Huffington Post,* October 25, 2016. http://www.huffingtonpost.ca/entry/americans-1950s-poll_us_580fcf0be4b08582f88c9575.

Ehrlich, David. "*Fences* Review: Viola Davis and Denzel Washington Are Sensational in a Solid August Wilson Adaptation without Any Curveballs." *IndieWire,* November 22, 2016. https://www.indiewire.com/2016/11/fences-review-denzel-washington-viola-davis-august-wilson-movie-1201748842.

Ellis, Jackson. "Interview: Chet Weise of Immortal Lee County Killers." Features/Interviews. *Verbicide,* March 4, 2005. https://www.verbicidemagazine.com/2005/03/04/interview-chet-weise-of-immortal-lee-county-killers.

Ellis, Jacqualine. "Revolutionary Spaces: Photographs of Working-Class Women by Esther Bubley 1940–1943." *Feminist Review* 53 (Summer 1996): 74–94. https://doi.org/10.2307/1395662.

Espinosa, Julio García. "For an Imperfect Cinema." *Afterimage* 3 (Summer 1971): 54–68.

Faulkner, Sally, editor. *Middlebrow Cinema.* London: Routledge, 2016.

Feria, Mariah. "August Wilson's *Fences*: Is America about to Return to the 1950s?" *Shout Out UK,* January 10, 2017. https://www.shoutoutuk.org/2017/01/10/august-wilsons-fences-is-america-about-to-return-to-the-1950s.

Fernandez, Danielle. "The 1950s, American Greatness, and Trump's Brand of Nostalgia." *Public Seminar,* August 3, 2016. http://www.publicseminar.org/2016/08/the-1950s-american-greatness-and-trumps-brand-of-nostalgia/.

Fields, Barbara J., and Karen E. Fields. *Racecraft: The Soul of Inequality in American Life.* London: Verso, 2014.

Ford, Rebecca. "'The Identical' Faith-Friendly Marketing Campaign: Churches, NASCAR and the Emmys." Movie News. *Hollywood Reporter,* September 5, 2014. https://www.hollywoodreporter.com/news/identical-faith-friendly-marketing-campaign-730539.

Friedan, Betty. *The Feminine Mystique.* New York: Dell Publishing, 1963.

Fulton, Lori Watkins. "Challenging White Trash Stereotypes: The Question of Class in *Bastard Out of Carolina*." In *Blue Collar Pop Culture: From NASCAR to Jersey Shore,* edited by M. Keith Booker, 69–86. Santa Barbara: Praeger, 2012.

Furmanovsky, Michael. "American Country Music in Japan: A Lost Piece in the Popular Music History Puzzle." *Popular Music and Society* 31, no. 3 (2008): 357–372. https://doi.org/10.1080/03007769208591485.

Gambino, Lauren. "Donald Trump Stokes Racial Fears with Appeal to White Suburban Voters." *The Guardian,* July 29, 2021. https://www.theguardian.com/us-news/2020/jul/29/donald-trump-white-suburban-voters-rule-rollback.

Garrett Shannon, Sandra. "August Wilson: *Ma Rainey's Black Bottom (1982), Fences* (1987), *Joe Turner's Come and Gone* (1984)." In *Modern American Drama: Playwriting in the 1980s Voices, Documents, New Interpretations,* edited by Sandra G. Shannon, 125–144. London: Bloomsbury, 2019.

Gibbons, Alison. "Metamodern Affect." In *Metamodernism: Historicity, Affect and Depth after Postmodernism,* edited by Robin van den Akker, Allison Gibbons, and Timotheus Vermeulen, 83–86. Lanham, MD: Rowman and Littlefield, 2017.

Gillespie, Michael Boyce. *Film Blackness: American Cinema and the Idea of Black Film*. Durham, NC: Duke University Press, 2016.
Gillespie, Michael Boyce. "B.A.D. (Black Abstraction Dreaming): A Conversation with Kevin Jerome Everson." *Black Camera* 8, no. 1 (2016): 155–168. https://doi.org/10.2979/blackcamera.8.1.0155.
Gilmore, Leigh. *The Limits of Autobiography: Trauma and Testimony*. Ithaca, NY: Cornell University Press, 2001.
Gitelman, Lisa. "Ages, Epochs, Media." In *On Periodization: Selected Essays from the English Institute*, edited by Victoria Jackson, para. 162–191. Ann Arbor: University of Michigan Publishing, 2010. https://quod.lib.umich.edu/cgi/t/text/text-idx?c=acls;idno=heb90047.
Glaser, Susan B. "Trump, Putin, and the New Cold War." *Politico*. December 12, 2017. https://www.politico.eu/article/trump-putin-and-the-new-cold-war.
Gledhill, Christine. "An Ephemeral History: Women and British Cinema Culture in the Silent Era." In *Researching Women in Silent Cinema: New Findings and Perspectives*, edited by Monica Dall'Asta, Victoria Duckett, and Lucia Tralli, 131–148. Bologna: University of Bologna Press, 2013.
Goldstein, Gary. "Escape Is the Challenge in Gritty Crime Drama *Badsville*." *Los Angeles Times*, November 30, 2017. https://www.latimes.com/entertainment/movies/la-et-mn-capsule-badsville-review-20171130-story.html.
Gray, Tim. "Denzel Washington Praises the Team That Helped Him Build *Fences*." Production. *Variety*, January 4, 2017. https://variety.com/2017/artisans/production/actor-director-denzel-washington-fences-1201951732.
Greenburg, Jennifer. *The Rockabillies*. Chicago: Center for American Places, 2010.
Grieves, Victoria M. *Little Cold Warriors: American Childhood in the 1950s*. New York: Oxford University Press, 2018.
Gruner, Oliver. *Screening the Sixties: Hollywood Cinema and the Politics of Memory*. New York: Palgrave Macmillan, 2016.
Gruner, Oliver, and Peter Krämer, eds. *Grease Is the Word: Exploring a Cultural Phenomenon* London: Anthem Press, 2020.
Hall, Mourdant. "A Boisterous Fantasy." *New York Times*, December 13, 1924. https://www.nytimes.com/1924/12/13/archives/the-screen-a-boisterous-fantasy.html.
Harrington, Michael. *The Other America*. New York: Simon and Shuster, 2012.
Harris, Aisha. "Let *Sylvie's Love* Wrap You in All Its Goodness." *NPR*, December 24, 2020. https://www.npr.org/2020/12/24/949429032/let-sylvies-love-wrap-you-in-all-its-goodness.
Harris, Dianne. *Little White Houses: How the Postwar Home Constructed Race in America*. Minneapolis: University of Minnesota Press, 2013.
Hartmann, Thom. "The New GOP 'Southern Strategy': Civil War or *Leave It to Beaver*?" *Salon*, November 19, 2021. https://www.salon.com/2021/11/19/the-new-southern-strategy-civil-or-leave-it-to-beaver_partner/.
Haynes, Todd. "Todd Haynes | NYFF53 Directors Dialogue | Carol." Produced by Film at Lincoln Center, November 20, 2015. Video, 58:18. https://www.youtube.com/watch?v=Wcyp5cSvBwg.
Haynes, Todd. "'Carol' Q&A | Todd Haynes." Produced by Film at Lincoln Center, December 11, 2015. Video, 47:42. https://www.youtube.com/watch?v=tyXweg_yf1o.
Haynes, Todd. "Q & A with Cast and Filmmakers." *Carol*. 2015; Beverly Hills, CA: Anchor Bay Entertainment, 2016. DVD.

Hebdige, Dick. "Becoming Animal: Race, Terror and the American Roots." *Parallax* 13, no. 1 (January 2007): 95–118. https://doi.org/10.1080/13534640601094957.
Heer, Janet. "America's First Postmodern President." *New Republic*, July 8, 2017. https://newrepublic.com/article/143730/americas-first-postmodern-president.
Herder, Johann Gottfried. *Auch eine Philosophie der Geschichte zur Bildung der Menschheit*. Frankfurt: Suhrkamp, 1967.
Highsmith, Patricia [Claire Morgan, pseud.]. *The Price of Salt*. New York: Coward McCann, 1952.
Higson, Andrew. "The Heritage Film and British Cinema." In *Dissolving Views: New Writing on British Cinema*, edited by Andrew Higson, 232–248. London: Cassell, 1996.
Hills, Matt. "The Question of Genre in Cult Film and Fandom: Between Contract and Discourse." In *Sage Handbook of Film Studies*, edited by James Donald and Michael Renov, 436–451. Los Angeles: Sage, 2008.
Holmes, Nathan. "The Limits and Possibilities of Suburban Iconoclasm: *Suburbicon* and *99 Homes*." In *Race and the Suburbs in American Film*, edited by Merrill Schleier, 227–246. Albany: SUNY Press, 2021.
Hutcheon, Linda. *A Poetics of Postmodernism: History, Theory, Fiction*. New York: Routledge, 1988.
Jackson, Victoria. "Introduction: On Periodization and Its Discontents." In *On Periodization: Selected Essays from the English Institute*, edited by Victoria Jackson, para. 2–17. Ann Arbor: University of Michigan Publishing, 2010. https://quod.lib.umich.edu/cgi/t/text/text-idx?c=acls;idno=heb90047.
James, Jenny M. "Maternal Failures, Queer Futures: Reading *The Price of Salt* (1952) and *Carol* (2015) against Their Grain." *Gay and Lesbian Quarterly* 24, no. 2–3 (2016): 291–314. https://doi.org/10.1215/10642684-4324825.
Jameson, Frederic. *Postmodernism: Or, the Cultural Logic of Late Capitalism*. Durham, NC: Duke University Press, 1991.
Jones, John Bush. *Our Musicals, Ourselves: A Social History of the American Musical Theater*. Lebanon, NH: University Press of New England, 2003.
Jones, Robert P. *The End of White Christian America*. New York: Simon and Shuster, 2017.
Jordanova, Ludmilla. *History in Practice*. London: Bloomsbury, 2016.
Kattari, Kimberly Adele. "Psychobilly: Imagining and Realizing a 'Culture of Survival' in Mutant Rockabilly." PhD Diss. University of Texas at Austin, 2011.
Keene, Judith. "War, Cinema, Prosthetic Memory and Popular Understanding: A Case Study of the Korean War." *Journal of Multidisciplinary International Studies* 7, no. 1 (January 2010): 1–18. https://doi.org/10.5130/portal.v7i1.1434.
Kellermann, Bernhard. *Der Tunnel*. Berlin: S. Fischer, 1913.
Kemp, Philip. "*The Reflecting Skin*." *Sight and Sound* 26, no. 2 (February 2016): 100.
Kenny, Glen. "*Brooklyn*." Reviews. *Rogerebert.com*, November 4, 2015. https://www.rogerebert.com/reviews/brooklyn-2015.
Kermode, Mark. "*Brooklyn* Review—This Fairytale of New York Casts a Spell." *Guardian* November 8, 2015. https://www.theguardian.com/film/2015/nov/08/brooklyn-observer-film-review-saoirse-ronan.
Kite, Melissa. "Balham Is About as Close as You Get, in 2015, to the 1950s." Real Life. *Spectator Australia*, September 26, 2015. https://www.spectator.com.au/2015/09/balham-is-about-as-close-as-you-get-in-2015-to-the-1950s.

Kitsch, Carolyn. "'Useful Memory' in *Time Inc.* Magazines: Summary Journalism and the Popular Construction of History." *Journalism Studies* 7, no. 1 (2006): 94–110. https://doi.org/10.1080/14616700500450384.

Knapp, Raymond, Mitchel Morris, and Stacy Wolf. *The Oxford Handbook of the American Musical*. New York: Oxford University Press, 2011.

Koek, Richard. "Modern Life in High Treason: Visual and Narrative Analysis of a Near-Future Cinematic City." In *Cities in Transition: The Moving Image and the Modern Metropolis*, edited by Andrew Webber and Emma Wilson, 72–88. London: Wallflower, 2008.

Kushner, David. *Levittown: Two Families, One Tycoon, and the Fight for Civil Rights in American's Legendary Suburb*. New York: Walker and Company, 2009.

Lachman, Edward. "Edward Lachman Shares His Secrets for Shooting Todd Haynes' *Carol*." IndieWire, Dec 3, 2015. https://www.indiewire.com/2015/12/edward-lachman-shares-his-secrets-for-shooting-todd-haynes-carol-48627.

Laderman, Charlie. "Donald Trump's 1950s Self-Help Foreign Policy." Argument. *Foreign Policy*, February 10, 2017. http://foreignpolicy.com/2017/02/10/donald-trumps-1950s-self-help-foreign-policy.

Laffly, Tomris. "*Sylvie's Love*." *RogerEbert.com*, December 23, 2020. https://www.rogerebert.com/reviews/sylvies-love-movie-review-2020.

Lambert, Bruce. "Study Calls L.I. Most Segregated Suburb" *New York Times*, June 5, 2002. https://www.nytimes.com/2002/06/05/nyregion/study-calls-li-most-segregated-suburb.html.

Lamm, Kimberly. "Visuality and Black Masculinity in Ralph Ellison's *Invisible Man* and Romare Bearden's Photomontages." *Callaloo* 26, no. 3 (Summer, 2003): 813–835. https://www.doi.org/10.1353/cal.2003.0094.

Landsberg, Alison. *Engaging the Past: Mass Culture and the Production of Historical Knowledge*. New York: Columbia University Press, 2015.

Landsberg, Alison. *Prosthetic Memory: The Transformation of American Remembrance in the Age of Mass Culture*. New York: Columbia University Press, 2004.

Latour, Bruno. *We Have Never Been Modern*. Cambridge, MA: Harvard University Press, 1993.

Lentz, Robert J. *Korean War Filmography: 91 English Language Features through 2000*. Jefferson, NC: McFarland, 2008.

Le Sueur, Marc. "Theory Number Five: Anatomy of Nostalgia Films: Heritage and Methods." *Journal of Popular Film* 6, no. 2 (1977): 187–197. https://doi.org/10.1080/00472719.1977.10661834.

LeTourneau, Nancy. "Dear Trump Voters: The 1950s Aren't Coming Back." *Washington Monthly*, July 5, 2017. https://washingtonmonthly.com/2017/07/05/dear-trump-voters-the-1950s-arent-coming-back.

Loomba, Ania. "Periodization, Race, and Global Contact." *Journal of Medieval and Early Modern Studies* 37, no. 3 (2007): 595–620. https://doi.org/10.1215/10829636-2007-015.

Lovatt, Deborah. "A Terrible Beauty: The Nuclear Sublime in Philip Ridley's *The Reflecting Skin* (1991)." *European Journal of American Culture* 20, no. 3 (November 2002): 133–144. https://doi.org/10.1386/ejac.21.3.133.

Lucas, Edward. *The New Cold War: Putin's Russia and the Threat to the West*. London: Palgrave Macmillan, 2008.

Lyons, Bonnie, and George Plimpton, "August Wilson, The Art of Theater." *Paris Review* 153 (Winter 1999): n.p. https://www.theparisreview.org/interviews/839/the-art-of-theater-no-14-august-wilson.

Malone, Travis. "Utopia, Nostalgia, *Grease*: How a Film Can Create a Stage Legacy." *Theatre Annual* 63 (2010): 45–62.

Marcks, Iain. "*Hail, Caesar*: Roger Deakins, ASC, BSC, Discusses Re-creating Classical Hollywood Genres for the Coen Brothers' Latest Comedy." *American Cinematographer* 97, no. 2 (February 2016): n.p. https://theasc.com/ac_magazine/February2016/HailCaesar/page1.html.

Marcus, Daniel. *Happy Days and Wonder Years: The Fifties and Sixties in Contemporary Cultural Politics*. New Brunswick, NJ: Rutgers University Press, 2004.

Marshall, Ernest. "The Pros and Cons of Two British Talking Films." *New York Times*, August 25, 1929. https://www.nytimes.com/1929/08/25/archives/london-film-notes-the-pros-and-cons-of-two-british-talking-films.html.

McKee, Alison L. "*The Price of Salt, Carol* and Queer Narrative Desire(s)." In *Patricia Highsmith on Screen*, edited by Wieland Schwanebeck and Douglas McFarland, 139–157. London: Palgrave Macmillan, 2018.

McRobbie, Angela. "Feminism, the Family and the New 'Mediated' Maternalism." *New Formations* 80–81 (Winter 2013): 119–138. muse.jhu.edu/article/529456.

Mendes, Sam, and Justin Haythe. "Director's Commentary." *Revolutionary Road*. Glendale: Dreamworks, 2008.

Metz, Walter. "Far from Toy Trains." *Film Criticism* 40, no. 3 (2016): n.p. https://doi.org/10.3998/fc.13761232.0040.303.

Miller, Owen. "Uncovering the Hidden History of the Korean War." *Jacobin*, June 25, 2020. https://www.jacobinmag.com/2020/06/korean-war-seventieth-anniversary-north-korea-south.

Miller, Owen. "How Korea Became a Forgotten War: An Interview with Owen Miller." By Daniel Finn. *Jacobin*, February 26, 2021. https://jacobinmag.com/2021/02/korea-forgotten-war-owen-miller-north-south.

Miller, Scott. *Sex, Drugs, Rock and Roll, and Musicals*. Lebanon, NH: University Press of New England, 2011.

Millington, Gareth. *Urbanization and the Migrant in British Cinema: Spectres of the City*. London: Palgrave Macmillan, 2016.

Mittell, Jason. *Complex TV: The Poetics of Contemporary Television Storytelling*. New York: New York University Press, 2015.

Monk, Claire. "The British Heritage-Film Debate Revisited." In *British Historical Cinema*, edited by Claire Monk and Amy Sargeant, 176–198. London: Routledge, 2002.

Monk, Claire, and Amy Sargeant. "Introduction: The Past in British Cinema." In *British Historical Cinema*, edited by Claire Monk and Amy Sargeant, 1–15. London: Routledge, 2002.

Monteith, Sharon. "The Movie-Made Movement: Civil Rights of Passage." In *Memory and Popular Film*, edited by Paul Grainge, 120–143. Manchester: Manchester University Press, 2003.

Morris, Tiyi. "Unlearning Hollywood's Civil Rights Movement: A Scholar's Critique." *Journal of African American Studies* 22 (2018): 417–419. https://doi.org/10.1007/S12111-018-9410-Z.

Morris, Wesley. "George Clooney's Awkward White Guilt in *Suburbicon*." *New York Times*, November 3, 2017. https://www.nytimes.com/2017/11/03/movies/george-clooney-suburbicon-racism.html.

Muñoz, Pablo Gómez. "Displacing Conformity: Postwar US Suburbia in 2000s Cinema and Television." In *Making Sense of Popular Culture*, edited by María del Mar Ramón-Torrijos and Eduardo de Gregorio-Godeo, 73–84. Newcastle Upon Tyne: Cambridge Scholars, 2017.

Munslow, Alun. "Genre and History/Historying." *Rethinking History* 19:2 (2015): 158–176. https://doi.org/10.1080/13642529.2014.973711.

Myers, Daisy. *Sticks 'n Stones: The Myers Family in Levittown*. York: York Country Heritage Trust, 2005.

Nadel, Alan. *Demographic Angst: Cultural Narratives and American Films of the 1950s*. New Brunswick, NJ: Rutgers University Press, 2017.

Ng, Alan. "*Hal King*." Reviews. *Film Threat*, June 19, 2021. https://filmthreat.com/reviews/hal-king/2.

Nicholls, Mark. "Sam Mendes' *Revolutionary Road* and the Talent to Bemuse." *Quarterly Review of Film and Video* 29, no. 4 (2012): 329–337. https://doi.org/10.1080/10509201003667200.

Nuccitelli, Dana. "President Trump Would Make America Deplorable Again." *Guardian*, November 6, 2016. https://www.theguardian.com/environment/climate-consensus-97-per-cent/2016/nov/07/president-trump-would-make-america-deplorable-again.

O'Brien, Gabrielle. "Looking for a Way Out: Reimagining the Gaze in *Carol*." *Screen Education* 86 (September 2017): n.p. link.gale.com/apps/doc/A560314933/AONE?u=anon~3b6f093c&sid=googleScholar&xid=58fce07f.

Oler, Tammy. "Re-Imagining *Revolutionary Road*." Screen. *Bitchmedia*, December 30, 2008. https://www.bitchmedia.org/post/re-imagining-revolutionary-road.

Olson, Jenni Veitch. "'We Go Together': Nostalgia, Gender, Class, and the London Reception of *Grease*: A New '50s Rock 'n' Roll Musical." *American Music Research Center Journal* 14 (January 2004): 77–92. https://www.colorado.edu/amrc/sites/default/files/attached-files/0506-2004-014-00-000005.pdf.

Ortner, Sherry B. "Social Impact without Social Justice: Film and Politics in the Neoliberal Landscape." *American Ethnologist* 44, no. 3 (2017): 528–539. https://doi.org/10.1111/amet.12527.

Padva, Gilad. *Queer Nostalgia in Cinema and Pop Culture*. London: Palgrave, 2014.

Pallister, Kathryn, ed. *Netflix Nostalgia: Streaming the Past on Demand*. Lanham, MD: Rowman and Littlefield, 2019.

Parker, Traci. *Department Stores and the Black Freedom Movement: Workers, Consumers, and Civil Rights from the 1930s to the 1980s*. Chapel Hill: University of North Carolina Press, 2019.

Patton, Elizabeth A. "Geographies of Racism: American Suburbs as Palimpsest Spaces in *Get Out* (2017)." In *Race and the Suburbs in American Film*, edited by Merrill Schleier, 207–226. Albany: SUNY, 2021.

Pidduck, Julianne. *Contemporary Costume Film: Space, Place and the Past*. London: British Film Institute, 2007.

Pilný, Ondřej. *The Grotesque in Contemporary Anglophone Drama*. London: Palgrave Macmillan, 2016.

Pop, Doru. "Multiplexing Marx in Contemporary Cinema." In *Contemporary Cinema and Neoliberal Ideology*, edited by Ewa Mazierska and Lars Kristensen, n.p. London: Routledge, 2017.
Propp, Vladimir. *Morphology of a Folktale*. Austin: University of Texas Press 1968.
Public Religion Research Institute. "Better or Worse since the 1950s? Trump and Clinton Supporters at Odds over the Past and Future of the Country." October 25, 2016. https://www.prri.org/press-release/better-worse-since-1950s-trump-clinton-supporters-odds-past-future-country.
Ravizza, Eleonora. "The Politics of Melodrama: Nostalgia, Performance, and Gender Roles in *Revolutionary Road*." In *Poetics of Politics: Textuality and Social Relevance in Contemporary American Literature and Culture*, edited by Sebastian M. Herrmann et al., 63–80. Heidelberg: Winter, 2015.
Ravizza, Eleonora. *Revisiting and Revising the Fifties in Contemporary US Popular Culture: Self-Reflexivity, Melodrama, and Nostalgia in Film and Television*. Berlin: J.B. Metzler, 2020.
Reinhard, Wolfgang. "The Idea of Early Modern History." In *Companion to Historiography*, edited by Michael Bentley, 281–292. London: Routledge, 2003.
Richards, Jeffrey. "*Things to Come* and Science Fiction in the 1930s." In *British Science Fiction Cinema*, edited by I.Q. Hunter, 16–33. London: Routledge, 1999.
Richardson, Chris. "The Empty Self in *Revolutionary Road* or: How I Learned to Stop Worrying and Love the Blonde." *European Journal of American Culture* 29, no. 1 (2010): 5–18. https://doi.org/10.1386/ejac.29.1.5/1.
Ridley, Philip. "Director's Commentary." *The Reflecting Skin*. New York: Film Movement, 2019. DVD.
Ridley, Philip, and Aleks Sierz. "'Putting a New Lens on the World': The Art of Theatrical Alchemy." *New Theatre Quarterly* 25, no. 2 (May 2009): 109–117. https://doi.org/10.1017/S0266464X09000207.
Roediger, David. *Working toward Whiteness: How America's Immigrants Became White*. New York: Basic Books, 2005.
Rohy, Valerie. "See It Now: Queer History and Archival Fantasy." *Textual Practice* 33, no. 9 (October 2019): 1635–1647. https://doi.org/10.1080/0950236X.2018.1458748.
Rosenstone, Robert. *Visions of the Past: The Challenge of Film to Our Idea of History*. Cambridge, MA: Harvard University Press, 1995.
Rosenstone, Robert, ed. *Revisioning History: Film and the Construction of a New Past*. Princeton: Princeton University Press, 1995.
Ross, Alexander G. "'We Were Just Trying to Entertain': *Grease* in Production." In *Grease Is the Word: Exploring a Cultural Phenomenon*, edited by Oliver Gruner and Peter Krämer, 41–58. London: Anthem Press, 2020.
Rowley, Stephen. "Buffeted by Culture: Urban Planners, Notional Places, and Narratives of Fakery." *Planning Theory and Practice* 19, no. 4 (2018): 633–638. https://doi.org/10.1080/14649357.2017.1393171.
Saraiya, Sonia, and Cassie da Costa. "Who Is the Racism Horror Anthology *Them* Really For?" *Vanity Fair*, April 2021. https://www.vanityfair.com/hollywood/2021/04/them-amazon-little-marvin-lena-waithe.
Sass, Ann. "Robert Frank and the Filmic Photograph." *History of Photography* 22, no. 3 (1998): 247–253.

Scott, A. O. "Resettling the Meaning of Home in *Brooklyn*." *New York Times*, November 4, 2015. https://www.nytimes.com/2015/11/04/movies/review-resettling-the-meaning-of-home-in-brooklyn-with-saoirse-ronan.html.
SEFT Manchester Discussion Group. "*Grease*: The Wobbly Hot-Dog of the Seventies." *Framework* 0, no. 9 (Spring 1979): 39. https://www.lib.uwo.ca/cgi-bin/ezpauthn.cgi?url=http://search.proquest.com/scholarly-journals/grease-wobbly-hot-dog-seventies/docview/1311775532/se-2?accountid=15115.
Segrave, Kerry. *Jukeboxes: An American Social History*. Jefferson, NC: McFarland, 2002.
Serres, Michael, with Bruno Latour. *Conversations on Science, Culture, and Time*. Translated by Roxanne Lapidus. Ann Arbor: University of Michigan Press, 1995.
Shapiro, Meyer, H. W. Janson, and E. H. Gombrich. "Criteria of Periodization in the History of European Art." *New Literary History* 1, no. 2 (Winter 1970): 113–125. https://doi.org/10.2307/468623.
Shute, Nerina. "Ungentle Women of 1950." *Film Weekly*, June 3, 1929.
Sierz, Aleks. "'Putting a New Lens on the World': The Art of Theatrical Alchemy." *New Theatre Quarterly* 25:2 (May 2009): 109–117.
Siskind, Lawrence J. "The Two Houses of the Marvelous Mrs. Maisel." The Blogs. *Times of Israel*, January 7, 2019. https://blogs.timesofisrael.com/the-two-houses-of-the-marvelous-mrs-maisel.
Sklar, Robert, and John N. Hart. "*Revolutionary Road*." *Cinéaste* 34, no. 2 (Spring 2009): 73–75. http://www.jstor.org/stable/41690770.
Slade, Andrew. "'You Are the Most Beautiful Creature': The Ethics of Masculinity in *Revolutionary Road*." *Quarterly Review of Film and Video* 34, no. 7 (2017): 664–677.
Slocum, David. *Hollywood and War: The Film Reader*. New York: Routledge, 2006.
Smith, Jason Scott. "The Strange History of the Decade: Modernity, Nostalgia and the Perils of Periodization." *Journal of Social History* 32, no. 2 (1998): 263–285. http://www.jstor.org/stable/3789661.
Smith, Victoria L. "The Heterotopias of Todd Haynes: Creating Space for Same Sex Desire in *Carol*." *Film Criticism* 42, no.1 (2018): n.p. http://dx.doi.org/10.3998/fc.13761232.0042.102.
Soister, John T., and Henry Nicolella. *Down from the Attic: Rare Thrillers of the Silent Era through the 1950s*. Jefferson, NC: McFarland, 2016.
Sprengler, Christine. "Modern Art and Mediated Histories: *Pleasantville, Mona Lisa Smile* and *Far from Heaven*." In *The Past in Visual Culture: Essays on Memory, Nostalgia and Media*, edited by Jilly Boyce Kay, Cat Mahoney, and Caitlin Shaw, 12–31. Jefferson, NC: McFarland, 2016.
Sprengler, Christine. *Screening Nostalgia: Populuxe Props and Technicolor Aesthetics in Contemporary American Film*. Oxford: Berghahn Books, 2009.
Stasukevich, Iain. "A Mid-Century Affair." *American Cinematographer* 96, no. 12 (2015): 52–63. https://theasc.com/ac_magazine/December2015/Carol/page1.html.
Street, Sarah. *Transatlantic Crossings: British Feature Films in the United States*. London: Continuum, 2002.
Sun, Kristen. "'Breaking the Dam to Reunify Our Country': Alternate Histories of the Korean War in Contemporary South." *International Journal of Korean History* 20 no. 2 (August 2015): 85–120. https://doi.org/10.22372/ijkh.2015.20.2.85.
Swain, John, D. "The Last Man on Earth." *Munsey Magazine* 80, no. 2 (November 1923): 193–208.

Symmons, Tom. *The New Hollywood Historical Film, 1967–78*. London: Palgrave Macmillan, 2016.

Trachtenberg, Alan. "Seeing What You See: Photographs by Helen Levitt." *Raritan* 31, no. 4 (2012): 1–18. https://www.researchgate.net/publication/294539438_Seeing_What_You_See_Photographs_by_Helen_Levitt.

Travers Peter. "*The Reflecting Skin.*" Movie Reviews. *Rolling Stone*, September 9, 1990. https://www.rollingstone.com/movies/movie-reviews/the-reflecting-skin-94486.

Treacey, Mia. *Reframing the Past: History, Film, and Television*. London: Routledge, 2016.

Urban, Ken. "Ghosts from an Imperfect Place: Philip Ridley's Nostalgia." *Modern Drama* 50, no. 3 (2007): 325–345. https://doi.org/10.3138/md.50.3.325.

Vermeulen, Timotheus, and Robin van den Akker. "Notes on Metamodernism." *Journal of Aesthetics and Culture* 2, no. 1 (2010): 1–14. https://doi.org/10.3402/jac.v2i0.5677.

Vesentini, Andrea. "Sheltering Time: The Containment of Everyday Life in Nuclear-Shelter Film Narratives." *Material Culture* 47, no. 2 (Fall 2015): 41–58.

Vidal, Belén. *Figuring the Past: Period Film and the Mannerist Aesthetic*. Amsterdam: University of Amsterdam Press, 2012.

Wallace, Steve, and Myron Davis. "Hal Analysis Episode II w/ Director Myron Davis." Premiered September 13, 2021. Video, 28:58. https://www.youtube.com/watch?v=9zX-z16cLX8.

Wallace, Steve, and Larob K. Rafael. "Hal Analysis Episode III with Larob K. Rafael." Premiered September 27, 2021. Video, 29:21. https://www.youtube.com/watch?v=cDlmIxF-bhU.

Wallace, Steve, and Sharaé Moultrie. "Hal Analysis IV w/ Sharaé Moultrie." Premiered October 11, 2021. Video, 29:15. https://www.youtube.com/watch?v=6acmHp8RTik.

Wallace, Steve. "A New Opera for a New Generation." *Hal King . . . the Movie*. Accessed January 24, 2022. https://www.halkingthemovie.com/about.

Warfield, Scott. "From Chicago to Broadway: The Origins of *Grease*." In *Grease Is the Word: Exploring a Cultural Phenomenon*, edited by Oliver Gruner and Peter Krämer, 23–40. London: Anthem Press, 2020.

Weissman, Terri. *The Realisms of Berenice Abbott: Documentary Photography and Political Action*. Los Angeles: University of California Press, 2011.

Wells, Liz. *Photography: A Critical Introduction*. London: Routledge, 2015.

Wesling, Donald. "Michel Serres, Bruno Latour, and the Edges of Historical Periods." *Clio* 26, no. 2 (Winter 1997): 189. https://www.lib.uwo.ca/cgibin/ezpauthn.cgi?url=http://search.proquest.com/scholarly-journals/michel-serres-bruno-latour-edges-historical/docview/1300309358/se-2?accountid=15115.

Westerbeck, Colin, and Joel Meyerowitz. *Bystander: A History of Street Photography*. London: Lawrence King, 1994.

White, Hayden. "Historiography and Historiophoty." *American Historical Review* 93, no. 5 (December 1988): 1193–1199.

White, Patricia. "Sketchy Lesbians: *Carol* as History and Fantasy." *Film Quarterly* 69, no. 2 (2015): 8–18. https://doi.org/10.1525/fq.2015.69.2.8.

Williams, Raymond. *Culture and Society: 1780–1950*. New York: Columbia University Press, 1983.

Wilson, Sloan. *The Man in the Gray Flannel Suit*. New York: Arbor, 1983.

Woodard, Bronte. *Grease*. Shooting Script, June 9, 1977.

Wooden, Isiah Matthew. "Fences." *Theatre Journal* 63, no. 1 (March 2011): 123–125.

Wyatt, Justin. *High Concept: Movies and Marketing in Hollywood*. Austin: University of Texas Press, 1994.
Yates, Richard. *Revolutionary Road*. New York: Little, Brown and Co., 1961.
Zeitchik, Steven. "In the Wake of Donald Trump's Victory, Some Movies Don't Feel Like They Were Intended To." *Los Angeles Times*, November 22, 2016. https://www.latimes.com/entertainment/movies/la-ca-mn-trump-movies-perspective-20161116-story.html.
Zemon Davis, Natalie. *Slaves on Screen*. Cambridge, MA: Harvard University Press, 2000.
Zerubavel, Eviatar. *Time Maps: Collective Memory and the Social Shape of the Past*. Chicago: University of Chicago Press, 2004.

Index

For the benefit of digital users, indexed terms that span two pages (e.g., 52–53) may, on occasion, appear on only one of those pages.

Figures are indicated by *f* following the page number

Abbiss, Will Stanford, 196–97
Abbott, Berenice, 181
Abdul Jabbar, Kareem, 212–13
Abrams, J. J., 140
Allen, Frederick Lewis, 34–35, 62
Alleva, Richard, 204–5, 207
All That Heaven Allows, 176–77
All the Young Men, 128
"alternative facts," 5–6
American Graffiti, 102
Americanization, 2
Anderson, Wes, 4, 5
Annandale, David, 193–94
Archer, Ina, 204–5, 209, 210–11
archival footage, in *Good Night, and Good Luck,* 144–47, 157n.35
Arden, Eve, 103–4
art direction
    in *Brooklyn,* 197, 200
    in *Carol,* 184n.19
    future and past through, 63–64
    in *Hal King,* 133–34
    in *High Treason,* 53–54
    in *La La Land,* 166
    in *The Last Man on Earth,* 56–57
    in *Revolutionary Road,* 76–77
    in *Suburbicon,* 84–85
Ashe, Eugene, 167
Astaire, Fred, 106
The Atlantic, 11–12
Atomic Fifties, 16–17, 127
    cinema of, 147–48
    civil rights movement and, 148
    Hidden Figures and, 148–54
    home and, 151–53
    The Reflecting Skin's imagery and, 214–15n.17

Auch eine Philosophie der Geschichte zur Bildung der Menschheit (One More Philosophy of History for the Edification of Mankind) (Herder), 27
Avalon, Frankie, 110, 113
Ayla, 2, 16, 130

Back to the Future, 47n.24
Badlands, 114
Badsville, 15–16, 116*f*
    costumes in, 116–17
    Fifties characterizations in, 115–16
    greasers in, 115, 117–18
    music in, 117
    1970s nostalgia for 1950s and, 116–17
    parents in, 117
    setting and premise of, 115
Baker, Robert S., 28
Baldwin, James, 189, 221–22
Barker, Jennifer, 176–77
Barton, Ruth, 197, 198–99
Bastard Out of Carolina, 17–18, 190*f*
    aesthetics of, 189
    censorship challenges of, 190–91
    class boundaries and, 188, 189–90
    costumes in, 189–90
Bastién, Angelica Jade, 93
Bearden, Romare, 206, 209–10
"Beauty School Dropout," 110, 113
Becker, Judy, 184n.19
Being the Ricardos, 161–62
Bélanger, Yves, 195
Benjamin, Walter, 48n.44
Bezos, Jeff, 153–54
Big Jim McClain, 156n.27
biopics, 18
Birch, Patricia, 110

Black Lives Matter, 18
Blackmail, 52–53
Black Power, *Hal King* and, 131–32, 137–39, 138f
Blake, David Haven, 37
Blast from the Past, 16–17, 71, 148
Bloom, Ester, 11–12
Blue Velvet, 193–94
Blystone, John G., 54–55
B-movie creature features, 18–19
Boatwright, Ruth Anne "Bone," 188–89
Boffin, Tessa, 179–80, 181
Borgstrom, Michael, 118
Boyce Gillespie, Michael, 208–9, 211–12, 217n.65
bradford, k., 118
Brando, Marlon, 100–1, 114
Branson, Richard, 153–54
Breen, Margaret Sönser, 185n.36, 186n.56
Brewer, Roy, 125n.38
Brickman, Barbara Jane, 106–7, 110
Brief Encounter, 185n.36
British cinema, period films in, 41, 42–43
British heritage film, 215n.27
Brody, Richard, 168–69
Brooklyn, 17–18, 38, 200f, 201f
   art direction in, 197, 200
   Catholic church and, 198–99
   class boundaries and, 200–1
   color in, 195
   costumes in, 195
   gender in, 197–98, 202–3
   hair and makeup in, 195
   Irish heritage films and, 199–202
   music in, 199
   nostalgia and, 195–97
   premise of, 194–95
   race in, 202
   realism and, 195
   suburban domesticity and, 201–2
Brown, D'Shonda, 95
Brown, Marshal, 47n.16
Bubley, Esther, 173, 176, 180
Buck-Morss, Susan, 39–41, 48n.44
Bush, George, H. W., 9–10
Bush, George, W., 5–6
Bussard, Katherine A., 179–80
Butler, Judith, 96n.16

The Butler, 38

Campion, Jane, 196–97
Caputi, Mary, 36–37
Carlos, John, 138
Carmen: A Hip Hopera, 132–33
Carmen Jones, 132–33
Carol, 17, 38, 162, 174f, 177f
   art direction in, 184n.19
   awareness of looking in, 176
   color use in, 171–75
   costumes in, 173–74, 184n.19
   critical praise of, 169
   deliberate archaism and, 170–71, 176–77
   Far From Heaven's aesthetic look compared to, 170, 171–72
   gender roles and, 178–79
   race and, 186n.56
   realism and, 170
   Retromediated Fifties and, 169–82
   sexuality and, 169, 181–82
   space in, 179
   street photography and, 169–73, 176–77, 178–80
   Super 16mm film use in, 170–71
   "surface realism" and, 184n.19
   suspension of time in, 176–78
   truth and, 181–82
Catholic church, *Brooklyn* and, 198–99
Champlin, Charles, 102
change, constancy and, 46n.13
Channing, Stockard, 106–7
Charlottesville Unite the Right rally, 97n.27
Chazelle, Damien, 165
child sex abuse, Catholic church and, 198–99
Christensen, Charlotte Bruus, 206
cinema. *See also* heritage films; period films
   of Atomic Fifties, 147–48
   Cold War categories with, 127
   the crowd, cities and, 39, 48n.44
   Fences' shifts between theater and, 204–6, 207–8, 210
   future research on Fifties and, 219–20
   future visions through, 63–64

global perspective for Fifties and, 220
"imperfect," 133–34
Korean War Fifties representation in, 128
McCarthyism and, 147
1950s defined and fractured by, 1–2
periodization of Fifties and, 37–44
politics utilizing, 40
of Retromediated Fifties, 161–62
cities, cinema and, 39, 48n.44
Citizen Cohn, 16
civil rights movement, 16–17. *See also* race
acts of resistance in, 149–50
Atomic Fifties and, 148
Hal King and, 131–32, 137–38
Hidden Figures and, 148–51
Korean War Fifties and, 140–41
Levittown and, 70, 85–86, 88–89
in *Lovecraft Country,* 153–54
McCarthyism and, 150–51
Trumbo and, 143–44
class boundaries, 188, 189–90, 200–1, 213
classificatory schemes, 13–14
Clinton, Bill, 9–10
Clooney, George, 80–82, 84–85, 90, 143–44
Coen, Ethan, 80–81, 90, 162–63
Coen, Joel, 80–81, 90, 162–63
Colbert, Stephen, 5–6
Cold War, 127. *See also* Atomic Fifties; Korean War Fifties; McCarthyite Fifties
colonialism, periodization and, 46n.6
conservatism, 1950s and, 9
constancy, change and, 46n.13
continuity
periodization and, 61–62
The Tunnel and, 61
Conway, Kellyanne, 5–6
Corfield, Penelope, 29–30, 46n.13, 57
costumes
in *Badsville,* 116–17
in *Bastard Out of Carolina,* 189–90
in *Brooklyn,* 195
in *Carol,* 173–74, 184n.19
in *Hal King,* 134–36
in *High Treason,* 50
in *The Last Man on Earth,* 55–56

Courbet, Gustave, 60–61
Cox, Michael, 156n.30
Crary, Jonathan, 46n.6
Crisis in Levittown, 84, 86–87
the crowd, cinema and, 39, 48n.44
Crowley, John, 194–95, 197–98
Cry Baby, 114
culture
in *The Last Man on Earth,* 56
in *The Tunnel,* 61

Daigle, Allain, 182
Damon, Matt, 84–85
Dargis, Manohla, 82
Davies, Myron, 131–32, 137
Davies, Terence, 200
Davis, Fred, 33–34, 61–62
Davis, Myron, 131–32
Davis, Viola, 207–8, 212, 217n.64
Deakins, Roger, 77, 78, 163
Dean, James, 100–1, 104, 106, 114
Dean, Tacita, 4
decade periodization, 34–36, 61–62
Dee, Sandra, 105
deliberate archaism, 17, 20n.1, 23n.29
Carol and, 170–71, 176–77
Hail, Caesar! and, 163
retromediation compared to, 161
Sylvie's Love and, 167
desegregation
Hidden Figures and, 149–50
Levittown and, 88
Dika, Vera, 102–3
Dilley, Whitney Crothers, 5
discontinuity, periodization and, 61–62
Distant Voices, Still Lives, 200
Dodson, Dan W., 86–87
domestic utopias, of suburbia, 71
Donaldson, Melvin, 217n.63
The Donna Reed Show, 70
Doubt, 198–99
The Dove, 209–10
drag king identities, *Grease* and, 118
Dutton, Lucie, 53
Dwyer, Michael, 36, 47n.24, 212

Earhart, Amelia, 56–57
Edison, Thomas Alva, 102

Ehrlich, David, 205–6
Eisenhower, Dwight D., 37, 171–72
Elevated Train Platform with Gum Machines, New York City, c.1951, 173
Eliasson, Olafur, 4
Ellis, Jacqueline, 180
Elvey, Maurice, 50–53, 58
The End of White Christian America (Jones), 21n.8
English, Darby, 208–9
Espinosa, Julio García, 133
The Exorcist, 95

fallout shelters, 71
Falone, Greg, 125n.42
fantasy, in period films, 41
Far From Heaven, 38, 72, 161–62
　Carol's aesthetic look compared to, 170, 171–72
Father Knows Best, 38, 70
female gaze, street photography and, 170
The Feminine Mystique (Friedan), 73–74
feminism, *Revolutionary Road* and, 78–80
Fences, 17–18, 205f, 211f
　cinema and theater shifts in, 204–6, 207–8, 210
　color in, 206–7
　entrapment experiences in, 203–4, 210–11
　language in, 204–5
　locations in, 210–12
　performativity of, 207–8, 209–10
　premise of, 203–4
　race and gender in, 207–10
　realism and, 207
　street photography and, 210–12
　35mm film use in, 206–7
　Trump's election and, 212–13
　truth and, 204
Feria, Mariah, 212–13
Fernandez, Danielle, 11–12
Fifties. *See also* Atomic Fifties; Hollywood Fifties; Korean War Fifties; McCarthyite Fifties; 1950s
　Badsville characterizations of, 115–16
　cinema and periodization of, 37–44
　evolving concept of, 221–22
　future research on cinema and, 219–20

　future research on television and, 220–21
　global perspective for cinema and, 220
　of *Grease,* 102–3, 122–23
　greasers as icons of, 113–14
　media conceptions of, 43–44
　metamodernism and, 222–23
　1950s compared to, 14, 36–37
　nostalgia and, 43–44
　objects of, 32–33, 40
　"otherness" and, 187–88
　period films of, 41–42
　postmodernism and, 222–23
　reframed, 17–18
　Retromediated, 17
Figuring the Past (Vidal), 23n.30
Film Blackness (Boyce Gillespie), 208–9
Fire and Fury (Wolff), 12
First Man, 148
Floyd, George, 94
Foreign Policy, 12
Forrest Gump, 38
For the Boys, 130
Foucault, Michel, 27
foundational fractures, 15
fractures, definition of, 22n.25
Franks, Robert, 178
Fraser, Jean, 179–80, 181
Friedan, Betty, 73–74
The Front, 16

Gallardo, AJ, 117
Garland, Judy, 141–42
gender, 18
　in *Brooklyn,* 197–98, 202–3
　Carol and roles of, 178–79
　in *Fences,* 207–10
　Grease and performativity of, 106–7
　in *Hidden Figures,* 151–52
　in *High Treason,* 53
　The Last Man on Earth and, 54–56
　in *Revolutionary Road,* 74, 78–80
　suburban domesticity and disappointment with roles of, 74
　Suburbicon and, 87–88
geography, of periodization, 28–29
Get Out, 91–92, 98n.53
Gibb, Barry, 108

INDEX   243

Gibbons, Alison, 170
Gilmore, Leigh, 188–89
Gitelman, Lisa, 43–44
Gledhill, Christine, 53
Glee, 101
Goldstein, Gary, 115
Gondry, Michel, 4
Good Night, and Good Luck, 3–4, 16, 127
   archival footage in, 144–47, 157n.35
   McCarthyite Fifties and, 143–47, 144*f*
   premise of, 143–44
   sexuality in, 146–47
   Trumbo's aesthetics of the past
      compared to, 145
Grainge, Paul, 195
Grease, 15–16
   age of cast in, 106–7
   Dean reference in, 104
   drag king identities and, 118
   fans of, 101
   Fifties of, 102–3, 122–23
   greasers in, 113–14
   intertextuality of, 110
   jukebox at center of, 110–14, 112*f*
   legacy of, 100–1, 122–23, 125n.42
   metamodernism and, 103
   multiple pasts in, 102–3
   music of, 101, 107–10
   1950s celebrities cast and referenced
      in, 103–6
   nostalgia and, 109
   performativity of gender in, 106–7
   race and, 121–22
   roller derby and, 118–19
   sexual innuendo in, 109–10
   space in, 111–13, 111*f*
   subversive nature of, 106–7
   youth in, 103
"Grease" (song), 108
"Greased Lightnin'," 110, 126n.58
Grease Live!, 101, 121–22, 126n.58
Grease: Rise of the Pink Ladies, 101
greasers, 15–16, 113–15, 117–19
Green, Misha, 140
Greenburg, Jennifer, 100–1, 119–21, 120*f*
Greene, Dennis, 121–22
Grieves, Victoria M., 123n.2
Griffith, D. W., 39

Gruner, Oliver, 35, 102–3
Guilty by Suspicion, 16

Hail, Caesar!, 17, 163*f*
   deliberate archaism and, 163
   "multiplexed Marxism" and, 164
   premise of, 162–63
   Retromediated Fifties and, 162–64
   "surface realism" and, 164
hair and makeup
   in *Brooklyn*, 195
   in *Hal King*, 134–36
Hal King, 16, 127, 136*f*
   art direction in, 133–34
   Black Power and, 131–32, 137–39, 138*f*
   choreography in, 137
   civil rights movement and, 131–32, 137–38
   costumes in, 134–36
   hair and makeup in, 134–36
   as "imperfect cinema," 133–34
   music and, 132–33
   premise of, 131–32
   temporal indeterminacy of, 134–37, 139–40
Happy Days, 102
Harrington, Michael, 187, 213n.4
Harris, Charles "Teenie," 210–12
Hatoum, Mona, 4
Haynes, Todd, 17, 38, 162, 169–71, 176, 178–79
Haythe, Justin, 75–76, 77
Hearts of the World, 39
The Heavenly Kid, 114
Hebdige, Dick, 121–22
Heer, Jeet, 5–7
The Help, 149–50, 208, 217n.64
Herder, Johann Gottfried, 27
heritage films. *See also* period films
   British, 215n.27
   Irish, 199–202
   "museum aesthetic" of, 49n.56
   terminology of, 196–97
Heron, Gil Scott, 153–54
Heslov, Grant, 80–81
Hidden Figures, 16–17, 127, 151*f*
   Atomic Fifties and, 148–54
   desegregation and, 149–50

Hidden Figures (cont.)
  gender roles in, 151–52
  home and, 151–53
  McCarthyism and, 150–51
  metamodernism and, 151–52, 153–54
  premise of, 148–49
  race, civil rights movement and, 148–51
  violence in, 149
High School Musical, 101
Highsmith, Patricia, 169, 183n.16
High Treason, 14–15, 51*f*
  art direction in, 53–54
  censorship and ban of, 52–53
  costumes in, 50
  future of 1950s in, 50–52
  gender in, 53
  Metropolis compared to, 52–53
  technological determinism and, 54
  television in, 53–54
Higson, Andrew, 49n.56, 196–97
history, nostalgia replacing, 7
Hitchcock, Alfred, 52–53
Hollywood Fifties, 17, 143, 162
Holmes, Nathan, 90–92, 93–94
homages, 18–19
home, *Hidden Figures* and, 151–53. *See also* suburban domesticity
The Hook, 128
Hopper, Edward, 77
Hornby, Nick, 194–95
horror. *See also* violence
  Get Out and, 92–93
  Lovecraft Country and, 92–93, 98–99n.55
  Them and, 93–94
The House on Carroll Street, 16
House Un-American Activities Committee (HUAC), 10–11, 16, 142–43, 171–72
Huston, Anjelica, 188–89
Hutcheon, Linda, 23n.31

The Identical, 117–18
I Dream, 132–33
I Love Lucy, 161–62
Immortal Lee County Killers, 117
"imperfect cinema," 133–34
Indignation, 130

individualism, as McCarthyism antidote, 156n.28
intertextuality, 3
  of *Grease*, 110
  WandaVision and, 161–62
"In the Sweet By and By," 86
Irish heritage films, 199–202
"It's Raining on Prom Night," 112–13
"I Wish I Was in Dixie," 86

Jameson, Fredric, 5–6, 7–8
Johnson, Katharine, 149–51, 157n.45
Jones, John Bush, 109–10
Jones, Robert P., 8, 21n.8
Jordanova, Ludmilla, 45n.4
jukeboxes. *See also Grease*
  economic logic of, 107
  in *Grease*, 110–14, 112*f*
  as iconic object, 102
  symbolism of, 113–14
Julien, Isaac, 209–10

Kattari, Kimberly Adele, 119
Keene, Judith, 130–31
Kellermann, Bernhard, 58
Kelly, Gene, 106
Kennedy, John F., 35
Kenny, Glenn, 195–96
Kite, Melissa, 44–45
Kleiser, Randal, 104
Koeck, Richard, 53–54
Korean War Fifties, 16, 127
  American cinema and, 130
  cinema grappling with, 128
  civil rights movement and, 140–41
  Hal King and, 131–40
  iconic images of, 130–31
  Lovecraft Country and, 140–42, 141*f*
  memory and, 129–31
  race and, 136–39, 140
  South Korean cinema and, 128–30
  Sunshine Policy Era and, 128
Kushner, David, 69
The K-Wals, 120*f*

Lachmann, Ed, 170–71, 175–76, 184n.19, 184n.24
LA Confidential, 161–62

Laderman, Charlie, 12
La La Land, 17, 165f
   art direction in, 166
   metamodernism and, 165, 166–67
   nostalgia in, 165–67
   Retromediated Fifties and, 165–67
Landsberg, Alison, 144–46
Lang, Fritz, 52–53
The Last Man on Earth, 1, 14–15, 51–52
   art direction in, 56–57
   costumes in, 55–56
   culture and nature in, 56
   gender and, 54–56
   periodization and, 57
Latour, Bruno, 27–28
Lean, David, 185n.36
Leave It to Beaver, 38. *See also* suburban domesticity
   suburban domesticity imagery and, 69, 70
   2020 election and, 95n.4
Lee, Christopher H. K., 129–30
Lee, John H., 128–29
Lee Daniel's The Butler, 149–50
Leiter, Saul, 77, 78, 175–77, 178–79, 184n.31, 221–22
LeSueur, Marc, 161, 164, 184n.19
Letourneau, Nancy, 8
Levitt, Helen, 172–73, 180
Levitt, William, 69–70
Levittown. *See also Suburbicon*
   civil rights movement and, 70, 85–86, 88–89
   Crisis in Levittown and, 84, 86–87
   description of, 69–70
   desegregation and, 88
   race and, 70
   suburban domesticity imagery and, 69
Life magazine, 39
Liking Ike (Blake), 37
Lippmann, Walter, 34–35, 62
Little Marvin, 92–95
Loomba, Ania, 46n.6
The Lords of Flatbush, 114
Lost Bastards, 16, 129–30
Lost Memories, 128
Lovatt, Deborah, 192–93, 214–15n.17
Lovecraft, H. P., 140

Lovecraft Country, 16, 127, 220–21
   civil rights movement and space race in, 153–54
   horror and, 92–93, 98–99n.55
   Korean War and, 140–42, 141f
"Love Is a Many Splendored Thing," 108
The Loveless, 114
Lovers and Lollipops, 172–73
Lucifer in the Sky with Diamonds, 117
Lynch, David, 193–94

MacArthur, 130
Mad Men, 11–12, 72–73
The Magdalene Sisters, 198–99
Maier, Vivian, 178
"Make America Great Again." *See also* Trump, Donald
   nostalgia and, 7–8, 11–12
   Suburbicon and, 81–82
Malick, Terence, 74–75, 193–94
Malone, Travis, 106–7, 124n.10
The Manchurian Candidate, 130–31
The Man in the Gray Flannel Suit (Wilson, S.), 73–74
Man in the High Castle, 155n.6
Marcus, Daniel, 9–10, 21n.13, 36
Marshall, Ernest, 52, 64n.4
The Marvelous Mrs. Maisel, 72–73
MASH (1970), 130
M*A*S*H (1972–83), 130, 137
Mast, Audrey Michelle, 121
Mazzei, Andrew, 53–54
McCarthyism, 10–11, 16
   cinematic, 147
   civil rights movement and, 150–51
   Hidden Figures and, 150–51
   individualism as antidote to, 156n.28
   race and, 88
McCarthyite Fifties, 16, 127
   Good Night, and Good Luck and, 143–47, 144f
   Trumbo and, 143–44, 145, 147
   waves of, 142–43
McIntyre, Diane, 131–32
McKee, Alison, 178–79
McRobbie, Angela, 78–80, 96n.16
media
   Fifties conceptions by, 43–44

media (*cont.*)
    periodization and, 33–34, 37, 43–44
    Suburbicon's use of, 84–85, 86–87
The Meekers, 117
Meet Me in St. Louis, 141–42
melodrama, in *Revolutionary Road*, 74, 78
memory. *See also* nostalgia
    Korean War Fifties and, 129–31
    The Reflecting Skin and, 192
Mendes, Sam, 73–74, 76–78
Mercer, Kobena, 209–10
Mercury Fur, 192
metamodernism
    definition of, 4
    examples of, 4
    Fifties and, 222–23
    Grease and, 103
    Hidden Figures and, 151–52, 153–54
    La La Land and, 165, 166–67
    nostalgia and, 5
    periodization and, 29–30
    Suburbicon and, 85–86, 90–91
Metropolis, 52–53
Miller, Owen, 130, 154n.3
Millington, Gareth, 197
Monk, Claire, 41–43, 196–97
Moore, Julianne, 84–85
Morris, Errol, 172–73
Morris, Tiyi M., 149–50
Morris, Wesley, 82, 97n.29
"multiplexed Marxism," *Hail, Caesar!*
    and, 164
Muñoz, Pablo Gómez, 74–75
Munsey Magazine, 54–55
Murrow, Edward R., 143–44, 146–47
"museum aesthetic," of heritage
    films, 49n.56
music
   in *Badsville*, 117
   in *Brooklyn*, 199
   of *Grease*, 101, 107–10
   Hal King and, 132–33
   in *Suburbicon*, 86
   in *Them*, 95
Myers, Daisy, 87–89, 98n.45

Nadel, Alan, 10–11, 21–22n.17
nature, in *The Last Man on Earth*, 56

Newton-John, Olivia, 105, 106–7
New Woman of 1920s, 53, 55–56
Ng, Alan, 133
Nicholls, Mark, 78–79
1920s
    New Woman of, 53, 55–56
    periodization of, 34–35
1950s. *See also* Fifties
    cinema defining and fracturing, 1–2
    contemporary culture and prevalence
       of, 2–3
    fertility rate in, 123n.1
    Fifties compared to, 14, 36–37
    Grease casting and referencing
       celebrities of, 103–6
    happiness norms of, 10–11
    High Treason and future of, 50–52
    imagining, 14–15
    McCarthyism in, 10–11
    1970s nostalgia for, 10, 116–17
    politics and nostalgia for, 5–13
    poverty in, 187–88, 213n.4
    recreating aesthetics of, 3–4
    Republicans drawn to, 9–10
    tropes of, 12–13
    white supremacy and, 9
1970s
    1950s nostalgia in, 10, 116–17
    rockabilly revival of, 114
No Name in the Street (Baldwin), 189
Norman, R. G., 110–11
North Korea, 128. *See also* Korean War
    Fifties
nostalgia
    Brooklyn and, 195–97
    Fifties and, 43–44
    Grease and, 109
    history replaced by, 7
    in *La La Land*, 165–67
    "Make American Great Again" and,
       7–8, 11–12
    metamodernism and, 5
    for 1950s in 1970s, 10, 116–17
    for 1950s in politics, 5–13
    periodization and, 35
    postmodern, 7–8, 152–53
    The Reflecting Skin and, 192
    Sylvie's Love and, 167–68

Trump's election and, 8–9, 11–12
Nuccitelli, Dana, 11–12

Obama, Barack, 9–10, 212
October Sky, 148
One More Philosophy of History for the Edification of Mankind (Auch eine Philosophie der Geschichte zur Bildung der Menschheit) (Herder), 27
Operation Chromite, 16, 128–29
Opie, Catherine, 4
Orkin, Ruth, 172–73
Orlando, 196–97
Ortner, Sherry B., 156n.29
The Osmonds, 117
"otherness," Fifties and, 187–88
The Outsiders, 114

Paris Blues, 168–69
Participant Media, 156n.29
Patton, Elizabeth A., 98n.53
Peele, Jordan, 91–92, 140
Pemberton-Billing, Noel, 52–53
Pence, Mike, 22n.22
percolation, theory of, 30–32
performativity
　of *Fences,* 207–8, 209–10
　of gender in *Grease,* 106–7
　in *Revolutionary Road,* 96n.16
period films, 14. *See also* heritage films
　in British cinema compared to American cinema, 41, 42–43
　of Fifties, 41–42
　genres in, 41–42
　heritage films and, 49n.56
　race and insufficient representations in, 89
　realism and fantasy in, 41
period identities, complexity of, 62–63
periodization, 13–14
　cinema and Fifties, 37–44
　criticism of, 27–28
　decade, 34–36, 61–62
　definition of, 27
　discontinuity and, 61–62
　geography of, 28–29
　The Last Man on Earth and, 57
　limitations of, 19–20

　media and, 33–34, 37, 43–44
　metamodernism and, 29–30
　of 1920s, 34–35
　nostalgia and, 35
　politics of, 28
　race, colonialism and, 46n.6
　television in, 37–38
　theory of percolation and, 30–32
　waning, 19
periods of time, 29–30
photography. *See* street photography
The Piano, 196–97
Pidduck, Julianne, 42–43
Pines, Joshua, 206–7
Pittsburgh Memories, 209–10
Pleasantville, 3–4, 71–72, 82, 102, 161–62
police, in *Suburbicon,* 87
politics. *See also* McCarthyism; Republicans
　cinema utilized by, 40
　nostalgia for 1950s in, 5–13
　of periodization, 28
poodle skirts, 32–33
Pop, Doru, 164, 183n.7
Porgy and Bess, 132–33
post-heritage, 196–97
postmodernism, 3–5
　Fifties and, 222–23
　nostalgia and, 7–8, 152–53
　Trump and, 5–7
　truth and, 5–6
Potter, Sally, 196–97
poverty, in 1950s, 187–88, 213n.4
Powell, Sandy, 184n.19
Presley, Elvis, 106, 114
The Price of Salt (Highsmith), 169, 183n.16
production design. *See* art direction
Public Religion Research Institute (PRRI), 8
Pudovkin, Vsevolod, 48n.44

queer sensibility. *See also* sexuality
　of *Good Night, and Good Luck,* 146–47
　of greasers, 118–19

race. *See also* civil rights movement
　in *Brooklyn,* 202
　Carol and, 186n.56
　in *Crisis in Levittown,* 86–87

race (*cont.*)
   in *Fences,* 207–10
   Get Out and, 91–92
   Grease and, 121–22
   greasers and, 115
   Hidden Figures, 148–51
   Korean War Fifties and, 136–39, 140
   Levittown and, 70
   McCarthyism and, 88
   period films and insufficient representations of, 89
   periodization and, 46n.6
   Pleasantville and, 82
   Revolutionary Road and, 75–76, 80
   rockabilly culture and, 121–22
   suburban domesticity depictions and, 74–75, 91–92
   Suburbicon and, 81–84, 87–89, 97n.33
   Sylvie's Love and, 167–69
   on television, 69–70
   Them's depictions of violence and, 92–94
   Trump and, 70
Race and the Suburbs in American Film (Schleier), 91–92
"racecraft," 98n.48
Rahenge Sadaa Gardish Mein Taare, 2
Ravizza, Eleonora, 22–23n.26, 74, 78
Reagan, Ronald, 9–10, 40
realism
   Brooklyn and, 195
   Carol and, 170
   Carol and "surface," 184n.19
   Fences and, 207
   Hail, Caesar! and "surface," 164
   in period films, 41
   street photography and, 179–81
   "surface," 164, 184n.19
Rebel without a Cause, 100–1, 114
The Reflecting Skin, 16–18, 148, 188, 193*f*
   Atomic Fifties imagery in, 214–15n.17
   legacy of, 193–94
   memory and, 192
   nostalgia and, 192
   premise of, 192–93
   violence in, 191–92
Reinhard, Wolfgang, 46n.11
Republicans
   1950s appealing to, 9–10

   rockabillies compared to, 120–21
Retreat!, 16, 130
Retromediated Fifties, 17
   Carol and, 169–82
   Hail, Caesar! and, 162–64
   La La Land and, 165–67
   suburban domesticity and, 162
   Sylvie's Love and, 167–69
   WandaVision and, 161–62
retromediation, deliberate archaism compared to, 161
Revolutionary Road, 15, 76*f*, 77*f*
   art direction in, 76–77
   critical aims of, 80
   feminism and, 78–80
   gender roles in, 74, 78–80
   house as prison in, 78
   melodrama in, 74, 78
   performativity in, 96n.16
   premise of, 73–74
   race and, 75–76, 80
   street photography inspiration for, 78, 80
   suburban domesticity and, 70–71, 73–80
   Technicolor vision of suburban domesticity in, 74–78
Richard, Jeffrey, 58–59
Richardson, C., 96n.16
Ridley, Philip, 191–94, 214n.8, 214n.9
The Right Stuff, 148
Roadracers, 114
The Rockabillies, 119–21, 120*f*
rockabilly culture. See also *Grease*
   greasers and, 15–16
   Greenburg's work on, 119–21, 120*f*
   history of, 125n.38
   1970s revival of, 114
   race and, 121–22
   Republicans compared to, 120–21
Rohy, Valerie, 145–47, 157n.35
roller derby, *Grease* and, 118–19
Ronan, Saoirse, 197–98
Roudané, Matthew, 203–4
Rowley, Stephen, 80
Ruff, Matt, 140

Sargeant, Amy, 42–43

Saturday Night Fever, 106
Schleier, Merrill, 91–92
Schrecker, Dan, 164
Scott, A. O., 200–1
Segrave, Kerry, 107
Serres, Michel, 29, 30–32, 103
71, 128–29
sexual innuendo, in *Grease,* 109–10
sexuality, 18
    Carol and, 169, 181–82
    in *Good Night, and Good Luck,* 146–47
    greasers and, 118–19
    street photography and, 179–80
    suburban domesticity depictions and, 74–75
Sha Na Na, 109, 121–22
The Shape of Water, 148
Shapiro, Meyer, 28
Shute, Nerina, 50
sincerity, *Suburbicon* and, 90
Sirk, Douglas, 38
Siskind, Lawrence J., 73, 96n.7
Sklar, Robert, 78–79, 96n.16
Skoll, Jeff, 156n.29
Slade, Andrew, 78–79
Smith, Jason Scott, 33, 34–35, 61–62
Smith, Tommie, 138
Smith, Victoria, 179
Sobchack, Vivian, 103–4
"sociomental topographies of the past," 46n.10
South Korea cinema, 128–30. *See also* Korean War Fifties
    popularity of, 155n.7
    Sunshine Policy Era and, 128
space
    in *Carol,* 179
    in *Grease,* 111–13, 111*f*
space race. See *Hidden Figures*
Spotlight, 198–99
The Stonebreakers, 60–61
street photography
    Carol and, 169–73, 176–77, 178–80
    color and, 172–73, 176
    decisive moments in, 175
    female gaze and, 170
    Fences and, 210–12
    realism and, 179–81

Revolutionary Road's inspiration from, 78, 80
    sexuality and, 179–80
    social injustice exposed through, 179–80
    suspension of time in, 176–78
    truth and, 181–82
Stubblefield, Clyde, 137
suburban domesticity. See also *Revolutionary Road*; *Suburbicon*; *Them*
    in *Blast from the Past,* 71
    Brooklyn and, 201–2
    in *Far From Heaven,* 72
    gender roles and disappointment with, 74
    imagery of, 69, 70
    in *Pleasantville,* 71–72
    as prison, 78
    race and depictions of, 74–75, 91–92
    Rebel without a Cause and, 100–1
    Retromediated Fifties and, 162
    Revolutionary Road and, 70–71, 73–80
    sexuality and depictions of, 74–75
    Technicolor vision of, 74–78, 84–85
    in television, 72–73
    underbelly of, 73–75
    white supremacy and, 89
Suburbicon, 15, 70–71, 83*f*
    art direction in, 84–85
    critical failures of, 80–82
    gender and, 87–88
    historical inaccuracies of, 87–89
    Levittown and, 80–81
    "Make America Great Again" and, 81–82
    McCarthyism and race in, 88
    media use in, 84–85, 86–87
    metamodernism and, 85–86, 90–91
    music in, 86
    police in, 87
    race and, 81–84, 87–89, 97n.33
    sincerity and, 90
    Technicolor vision of suburban domesticity in, 84–85
    violence and aesthetics of, 83–84, 87–88
    white supremacy, suburban domesticity and, 89

"Summer Nights," 109–10
A Summer Place, 108
Sun, Kristen, 128
Sunshine Policy Era, 128
Super 16mm film, *Carol* using, 170–71
"surface realism"
    Carol and, 184n.19
    Hail, Caesar! and, 164
Swain, John D., 54–55
Sylvie's Love, 17, 161–62, 168f
    color in, 183n.14
    deliberate archaism and, 167
    nostalgia and, 167–68
    race and, 167–69
    Retromediated Fifties and, 167–69
Symmons, Tom, 103–4

Tail Gunner Joe, 16
Technicolor vision of suburban domesticity, 74–78, 84–85
technological determinism, *High Treason* and, 54
teenagers, 15–16
television. *See also specific shows*
    future research on Fifties and, 220–21
    in *High Treason*, 53–54
    in periodization, 37–38
    race on, 69–70
    suburban domesticity in, 72–73
"Tell Me More," 109–10
temporal indeterminacy, of *Hal King*, 134–37, 139–40
Thatcherism, 2
theater, *Fences*' shifts between cinema and, 204–6, 207–8, 210
Them, 15, 70–71, 92f
    audience for, 93
    horror and, 93–94
    inspiration for, 94–95
    music in, 95
    premise of, 92–93
    race and violence in, 92–94
theory of percolation, 30–32
Thing to Come, 38
35mm film, *Fences* use of, 206–7
time. *See also* periodization
    metaphors explaining, 47n.16
Time and the Shape of History (Corfield), 29
Tóibín, Colm, 194–95

Townsend, Steve, 132–33
Transatlantic Tunnel. See *The Tunnel*
Travolta, John, 106–7, 118
The Tree of Life, 74–75, 193–94
Trumbo, 16
    civil rights movement and, 143–44
    Good Night, and Good Luck's aesthetics of the past compared to, 145
    McCarthyite Fifties and, 143–44, 145, 147
    premise of, 143–44
Trumbo, Dalton, 143
Trump, Donald. *See also* "Make American Great Again"
    cabinet choices of, 22n.22
    Fences and election of, 212–13
    nostalgia and election of, 8–9, 11–12
    postmodernism and, 5–7
    race and, 70
truth
    Carol and, 181–82
    Fences and, 204
    postmodernism and, 5–6
    street photography and, 181–82
"truthiness," 5–6
Tucci, Michael, 106–7
Der Tunnel (Kellermann), 58
The Tunnel (1935), 14–15, 51–52, 60f
    continuity and, 61
    culture in, 61
    setting of, 58–59
    technological futurism in, 59–61
    Der Tunnel novel compared to, 58
2020 election, *Leave It to Beaver* and, 95n.4

Urban, Ken, 192

van den Akker, Robin, 4–5, 9–10, 30, 166–67
Vermeulen, Timotheus, 4, 9–10, 30, 166–67
Vertigo, 84–85, 166
Vesentini, Andrea, 71
Vidal, Belén, 23n.30, 41, 42–43, 199
violence. *See also* horror
    in *Hidden Figures*, 149
    in *The Reflecting Skin*, 191–92
    Suburbicon's aesthetics and, 83–84, 87–88
    Them's depictions of race and, 92–94

Wagner, Richard, 132–33

Waithe, Lena, 92–93
Walker, 3–4
Wallace, Steve, 131–33, 134–35, 137
WandaVision, 140, 161–62
The Wanderers, 114
Washington, Denzel, 203, 205–8, 209–10, 212, 217n.63
Washington Journal, 8
Watkins Fulton, Lori, 214n.6
The Way We Were, 16
"The Weather Project," 4
Weissman, Terri, 181
Welch, Joseph, 147
Welcome to Dongmakgol, 128
Wesling, Donald, 45n.4
Westside Story (1961), 115
Westside Story (2021), 115
White, Patricia, 173, 182

white supremacy. *See also* race
   1950s and, 9
   suburban domesticity and, 89
"Whitey's on the Moon" (Heron), 153–54
The Wild One, 114
Williams, Raymond, 27
Wilson, August, 203, 204–5, 209, 212–13
Wilson, Janelle, 152–53
Wilson, Sloan, 73–74
Wolff, Michael, 12, 22n.22
Women of the Movement, 149–50
World War I, 39

Yates, Richard, 73–74, 75–77
"You're the One That I Want," 101, 109–10

Zeitchik, Steven, 212–13
Zerubavel, Eviatar, 46n.10

Printed in the USA/Agawam, MA
April 17, 2023

808600.024